IMAGES
of America

THE POLISH COMMUNITY OF SALEM

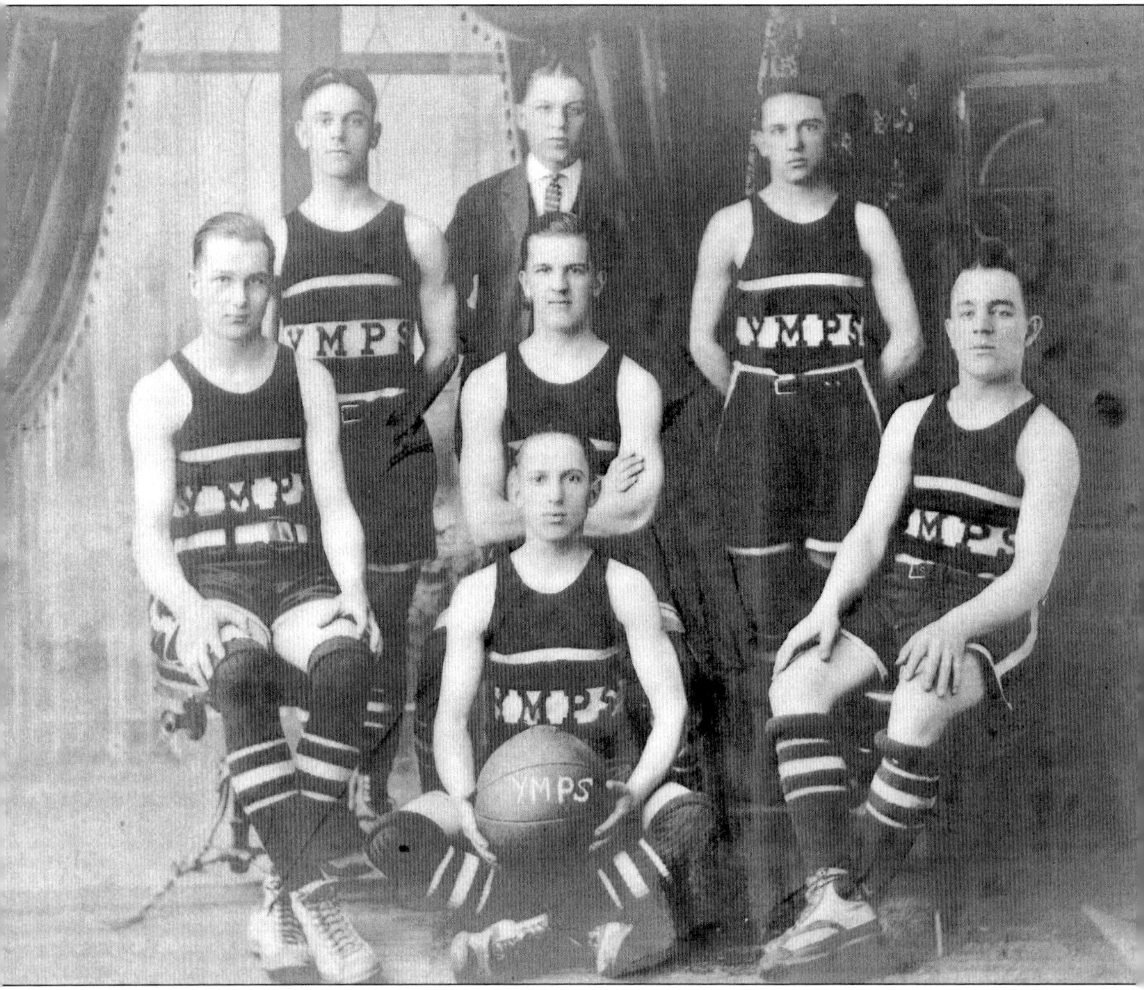

Originally founded in 1897 as a fraternal organization to provide medical and financial assistance to Polish immigrants, the St. Joseph Society of Salem, Massachusetts, evolved as a social organization in the first quarter of the 20th century. Pictured is one of the first Young Men's Polish Society basketball teams sponsored by St. Joe's in the early 1920s. (Rita Nowak Carter.)

ON THE COVER: St. John the Baptist schoolgirls in traditional Polish costumes, followed by members of the St. Joseph Society carrying Polish and American flags, marched on Hawthorne Boulevard to a service at St. John the Baptist Church in 1948. The girls are, from left to right, Mary Zielska, Helen Sobiesielska, Mary Malionek, Dorothy Hincman, Patricia Sobocinski, and Joan Jackowicz. (Dorothy Sobocinski Filip.)

IMAGES
of America

THE POLISH COMMUNITY OF SALEM

Felicia L. Wilczenski, EdD, and
Emily A. Murphy, PhD

ARCADIA
PUBLISHING

ISBN 978-0-7385-7563-6

Published by Arcadia Publishing
Charleston, South Carolina

Printed in the United States of America

Library of Congress Control Number: 2011920132

For all general information, please contact Arcadia Publishing:
Telephone 843-853-2070
Fax 843-853-0044
E-mail sales@arcadiapublishing.com
For customer service and orders:
Toll-Free 1-888-313-2665

Visit us on the Internet at www.arcadiapublishing.com

This book is dedicated to the memory of Salem's Polish immigrants.

Contents

ACKNOWLEDGMENTS

This book was possible because of the untiring work of a group of dedicated volunteers who traced their family roots to the Salem's Ward One neighborhood. Rita Nowak Carter and Linda Baldwin Moustakis, assisted by Gerry Nowak Cosgrove and Julie Kowalski Whalen, collected images and information for this photographic history of the Polish community. We extend special thanks to Lissie Cain and Laura Saylor, our editors at Arcadia, for their guidance in preparing this work for publication.

For sharing their treasured photographs and memories of Salem's Polish community, we are indebted to the following people and organizations: Christina Szybiak Bash (CSB), Thaddeus Buczko (TB), Richard Carpenter (RC), Rita Nowak Carter (RNC), Geraldine Nowak Cosgrove (GNC), Melaine Meler Czyprvna (MMC), Nelson Dionne (ND), Paul Dobbs (PD), Kathryn Nowak Estomo (KNE), Dorothy Sobocinski Filip (DSF), Chuck Graczyk (CG), Anna Kocialka Jaglowski (AKJ), John Kobuszewski (JK), Alicia Wroblewski Maguire (AWM), Paula Malionek (PM), Norma Martin (NM), Martha Meade (MM), Jane Brudzynski Moroney (JBM), Linda Baldwin Moustakis (LBM), Mary Halik Nowak (MHN), Don Olszewski (DO), Patricia Sobocinski Papa (PSP), Pauline Pelletier (PP1), Peter Plecinoga (PP), Ronald Plutnicki (RP), Polish Legion of American Veterans (PLAV), Barbara Pszenny Robinson (BPR), Salem Maritime National Historic Site (NPS), St. John the Baptist Parish (SJB), Dorothy Hincman Semenchuk (DHS), Julie Kowalski Whalen (JKW), Regina Plutnicki Wharff (RPW), Felicia Louise Wilczenski (FLW), Margaret Zdancewicz Wilkens (MZW), Stanley Wisniewski (SW), Alice Pronska Wojciechowski (APW), Alice Sobiesielska Zujewski (ASZ), Maryann Zujewski (MZ), and Frank Zdanowicz (FZ).

INTRODUCTION

In the mid- to late 1800s, refugees from a fragmented and occupied Poland began arriving in the United States to escape unimaginable poverty and political oppression. They left the "old country" with hopes of a better life and never looked back. Polish immigrants who came to Salem, Massachusetts, settled in the seaside Ward One neighborhood. This Derby Street area became "Little Poland," where everybody spoke Polish and got groceries at Witkos's food mart, furniture at Karbowniczak's store, kielbasa at Sobocinski's meat market, hats at Mary Robaczewski's millenary shop, hairdos at Regina Plutnicki's beauty studio, doughnuts at Jastremski's bakery, and coal from John Matula.

The Polish immigrants banded together to form both religious and secular associations. Founded in 1897 as a mutual aid organization, the St. Joseph Society provided economic and social assistance to families emigrating from Poland. A Roman Catholic parish, established in 1903, helped maintain Polish religious values, language, and culture through its church services and school. The Salem branch of a national society, the Falcons Nest No. 188 was launched in 1910 to attend to the fraternal and financial welfare of its members. The Polish Legion of American Veterans formed in 1930 to honor war heroes. These institutions were the bedrock of the community, serving to sustain the Polish identity and ideals in the new country as well as preserving the traditions that the immigrants brought with them from their homeland.

For Polish immigrants in the 1900s, life revolved around family, church, and community. Weddings and anniversaries were huge celebrations at the St. Joseph's or Falcons' Halls. Everyone followed holiday traditions of *wigilia* (Christmas Eve supper) and *swieconka* (blessing Easter foods). Church events and Polish clubs were opportunities to socialize. Ward One community members were either participants or audiences for theater groups, musical concerts, and sports teams. In the summer, there were Polish American Citizen Club lawn parties and picnics featuring polka bands.

By the end of the 20th century, the Polish neighborhood lost its distinctiveness. With the first generation of United States–born children, the identity of Polish immigrants began transforming to that of full-fledged citizens. Second-, third-, and fourth-generation Polish Americans acquired the educational, income, and social status to fulfill the dreams of the immigrants in coming to America. Along with their varied successes came marriages to non-Poles and moves away from the old neighborhood. Eventually, "Little Poland" became less of an enclave and more of a nostalgic memory.

This book traces the achievements and contributions of the Polish community of Salem from its humble beginnings. It is a collective effort to honor those early immigrants and to celebrate their legacy.

One

Neighborhood

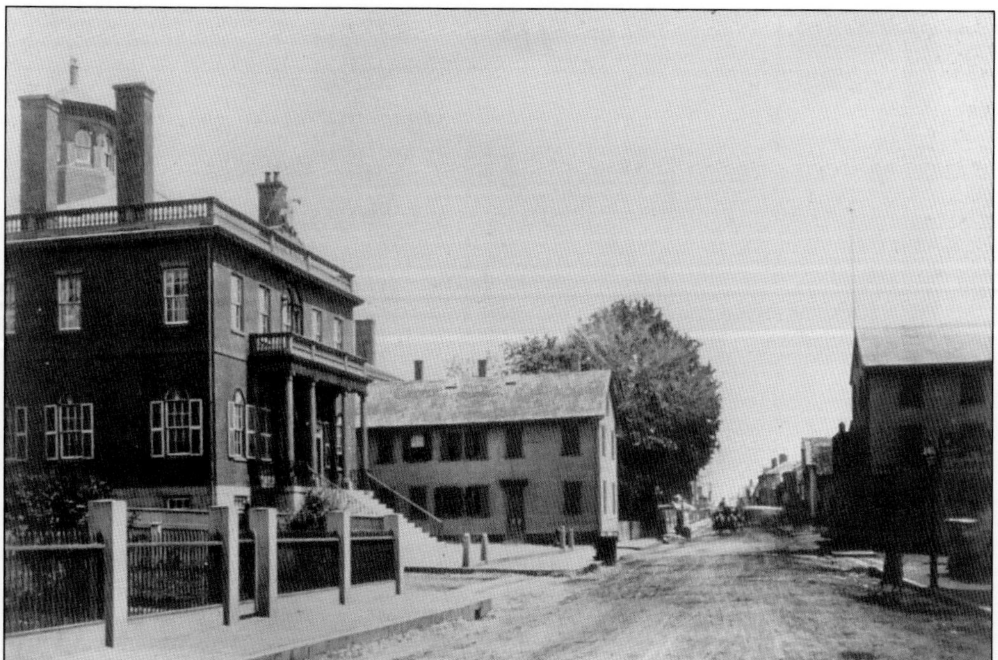

Polish people started to arrive in Salem in the late 19th century. Pictured is a view of Derby Street in Salem as it appeared to those early immigrants in the 1890s. Derby Street was a main road in Ward One that ran parallel to the ocean, connecting Salem center to Salem Willows. (NPS.)

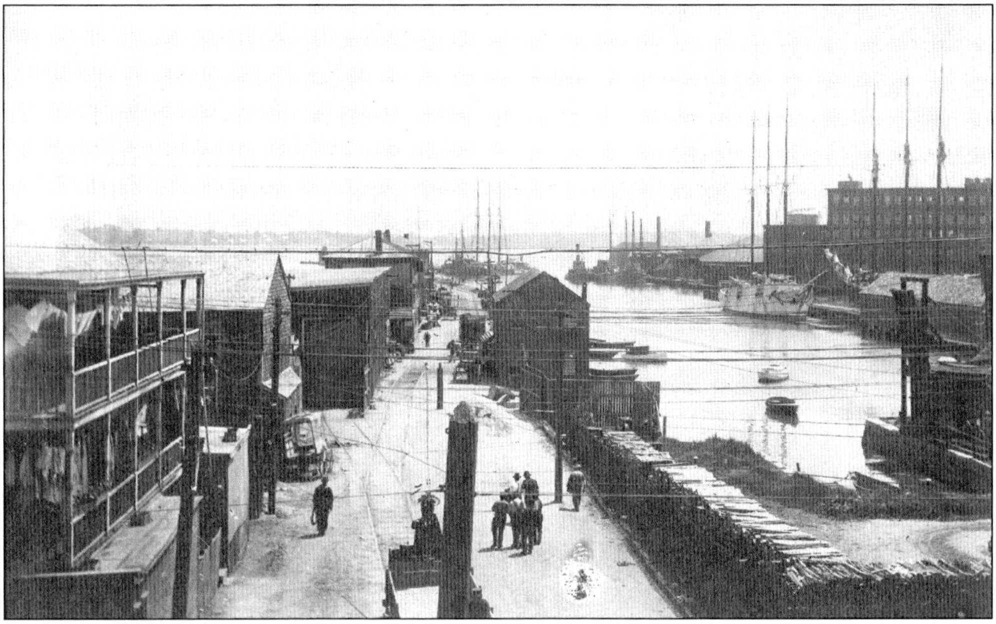

Located in Ward One, Derby Wharf, the longest of three wharves extending into Salem Harbor, was a bustling port at the turn of the 20th century. Richard Derby, a wealthy merchant, began construction in 1762 and continued developing the wharf until it reached its current half-mile length in 1806. The wharf area became part of the Salem Maritime National Historic Site in 1938. (NPS.)

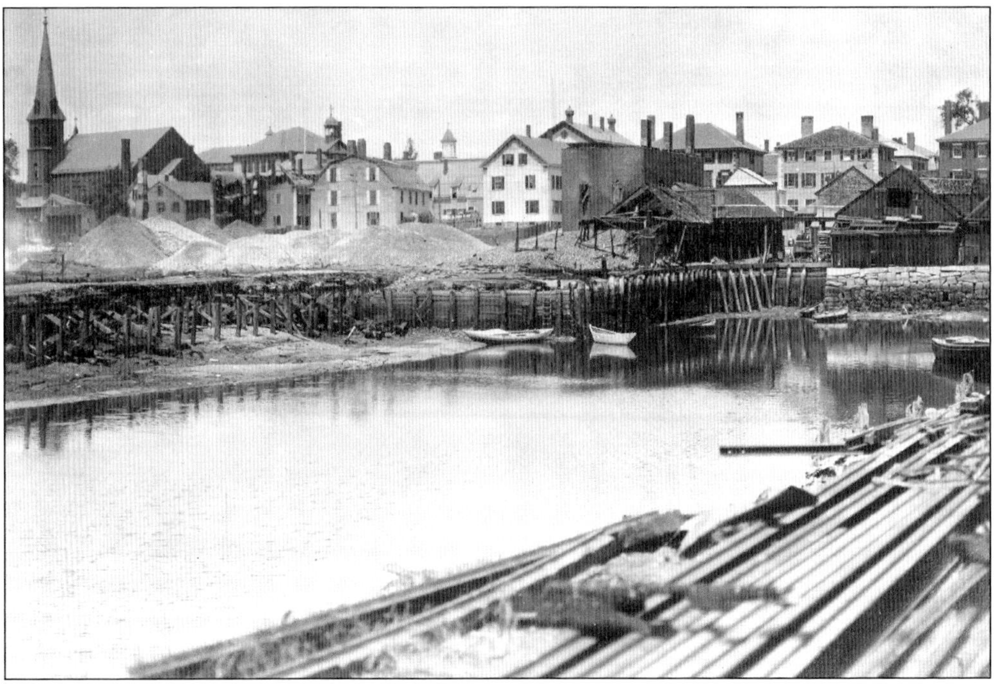

A devastating fire in 1914 destroyed a large section of Salem. This picture shows the damage to the Central Wharf taken from a Derby Wharf vantage point. The spire of St. Mary's Immaculate Conception Church on Hawthorne Boulevard can be seen to the left. (NPS.)

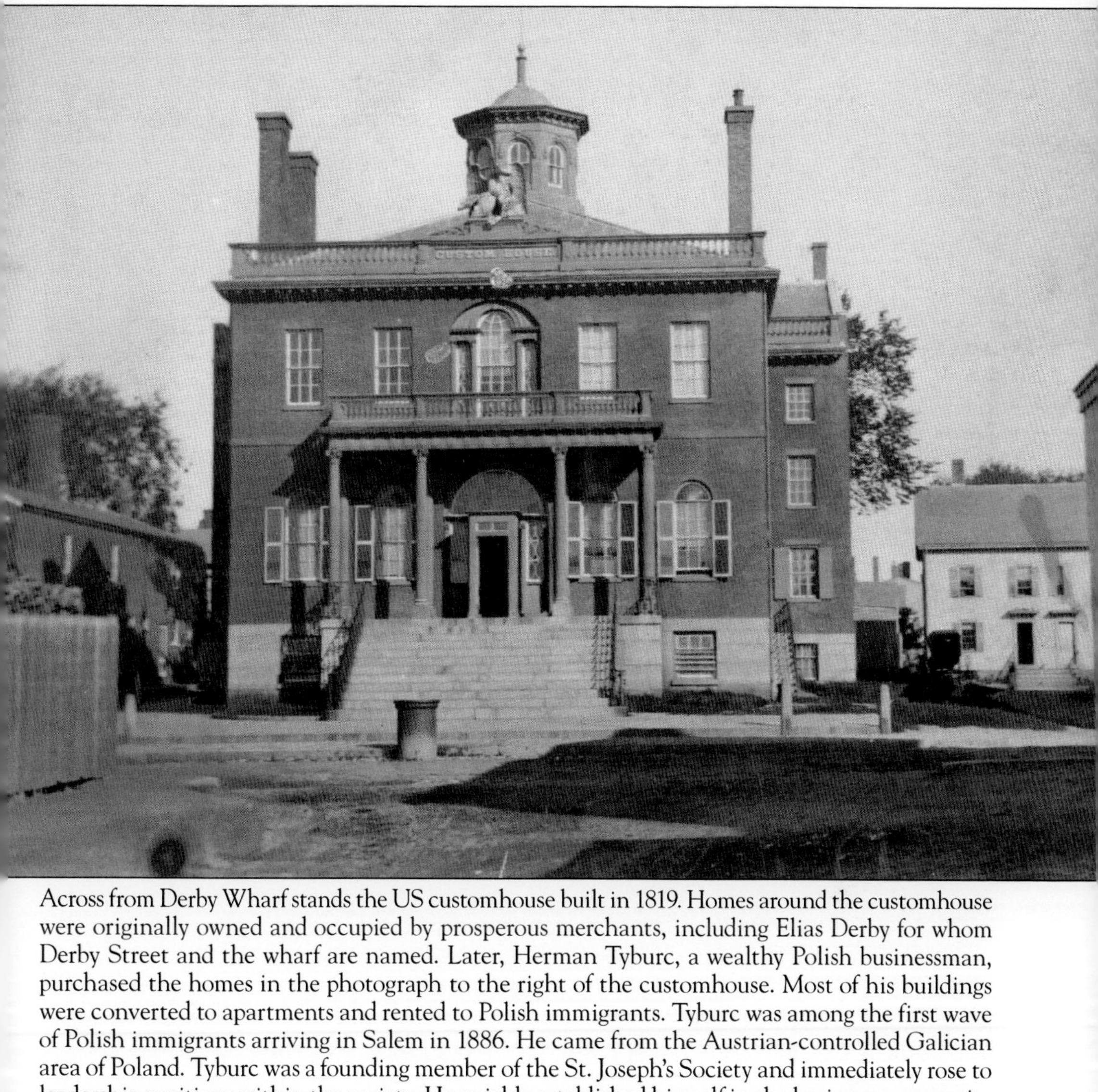

Across from Derby Wharf stands the US customhouse built in 1819. Homes around the customhouse were originally owned and occupied by prosperous merchants, including Elias Derby for whom Derby Street and the wharf are named. Later, Herman Tyburc, a wealthy Polish businessman, purchased the homes in the photograph to the right of the customhouse. Most of his buildings were converted to apartments and rented to Polish immigrants. Tyburc was among the first wave of Polish immigrants arriving in Salem in 1886. He came from the Austrian-controlled Galician area of Poland. Tyburc was a founding member of the St. Joseph's Society and immediately rose to leadership positions within the society. He quickly established himself in the business community owning two leather companies that employed Polish workers and buying considerable real estate that housed immigrant families. In Salem's Polonia, Tyburc might have been called a *szlachta*, which is someone belonging to a privileged class with landed property holdings. (NPS.)

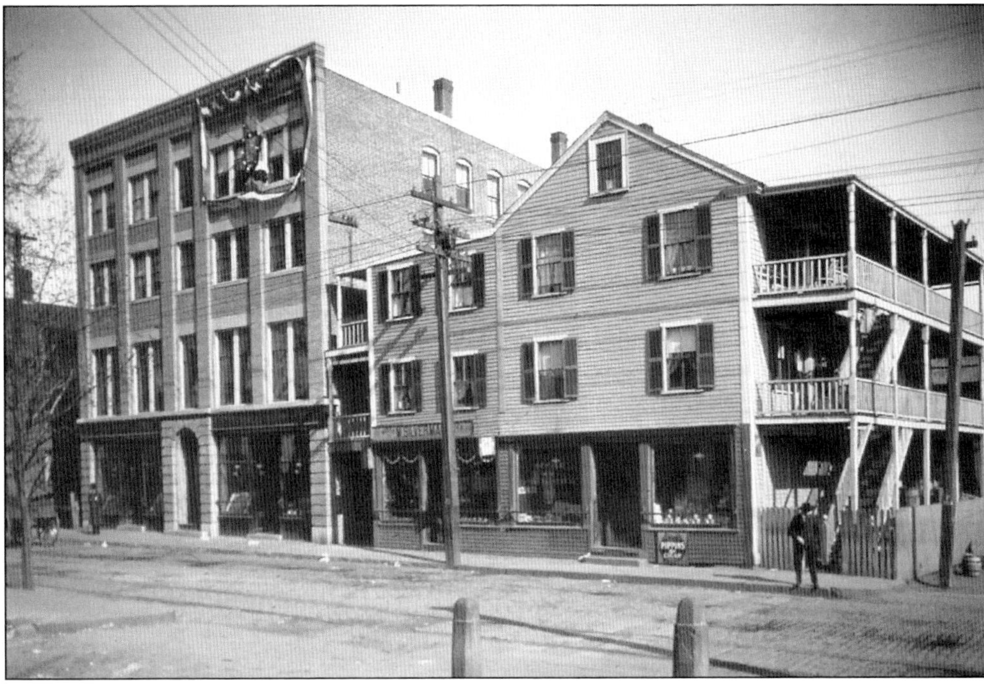

Next to the wharves and across from the Derby House, 165 Derby Street accommodated several businesses and apartments. On the left is the Kotarski Building (169 Derby Street), which served as a meeting place for the newly formed Falcons' fraternal organization. Residents of the area recalled that a pool hall was located on the first floor in the 1920s. (NPS.)

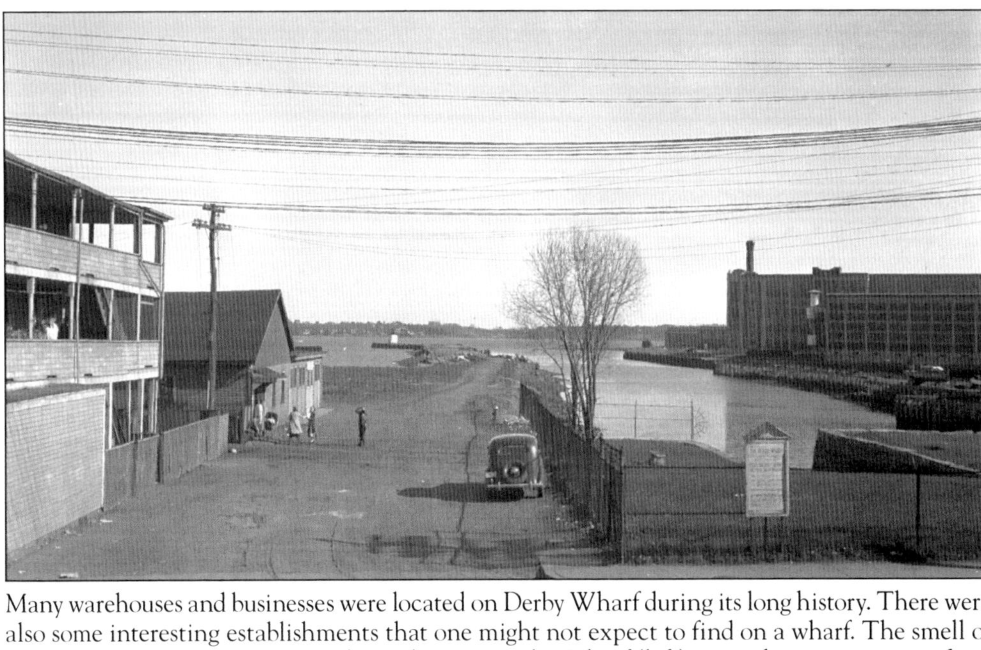

Many warehouses and businesses were located on Derby Wharf during its long history. There were also some interesting establishments that one might not expect to find on a wharf. The smell of freshly baked goods from Jastremski's Bakery on Derby Wharf (left) enticed many customers from the Polish community during the 1930s. (NPS.)

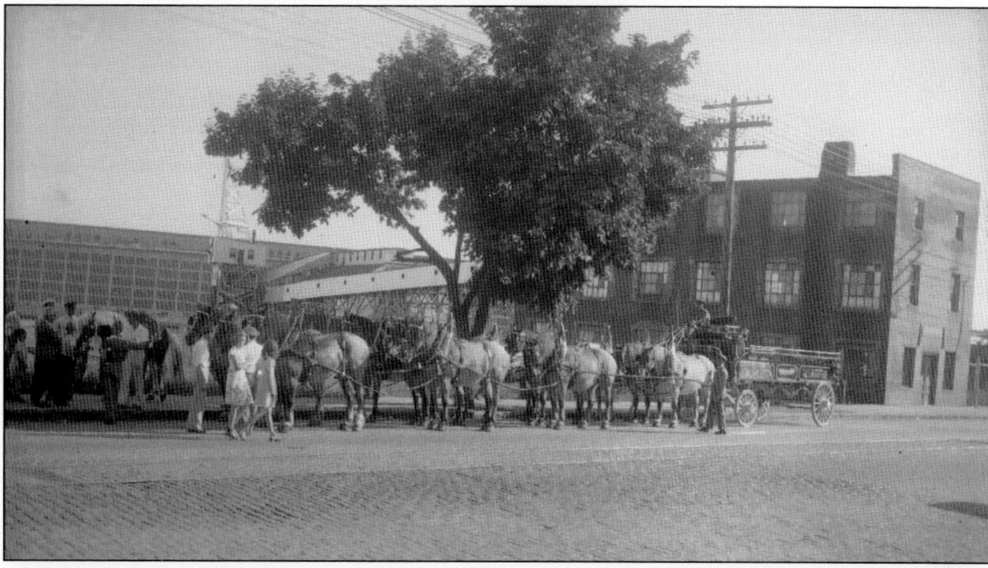

Without benefit of television for advertising, merchants had to take a direct approach to market their wares. Here, a *piwo* (beer) promotion for Genesee Twelve Horse Ale (with 12 horses) made its way down Derby Street around 1940. Forrester's Warehouse was the three-story brick building in the background. (NPS.)

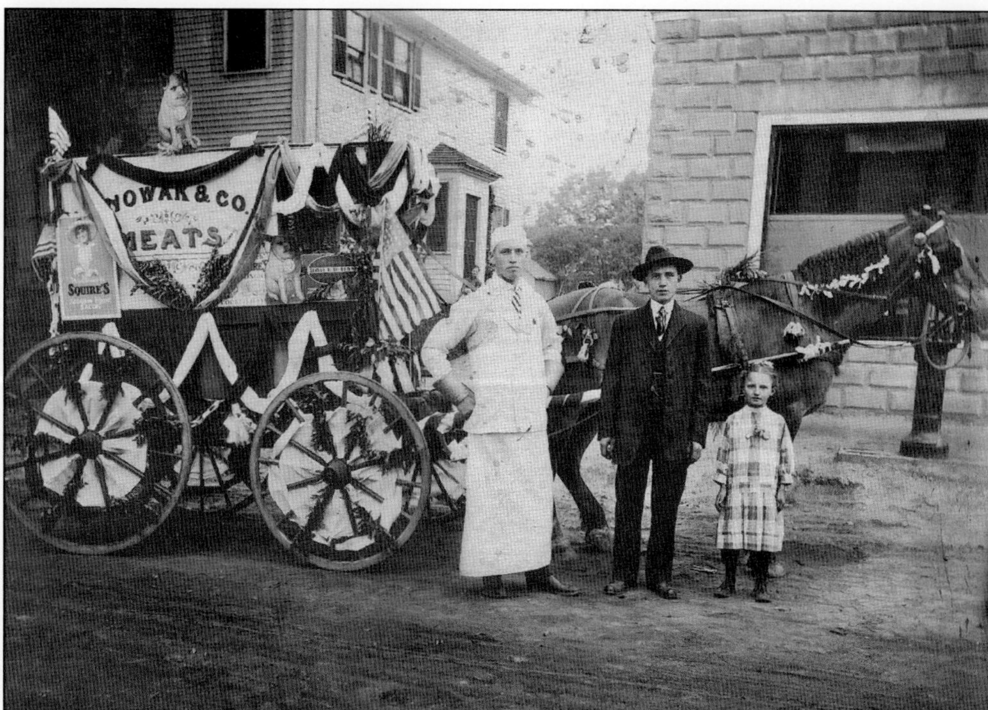

Nowak and Company advertised its meat products using a decorated wagon. This early-1930s version of a "float" might have been part of a parade to commemorate Poland's or the United States's independence day. It was a very clever way to publicize business and attract customers! (JKW.)

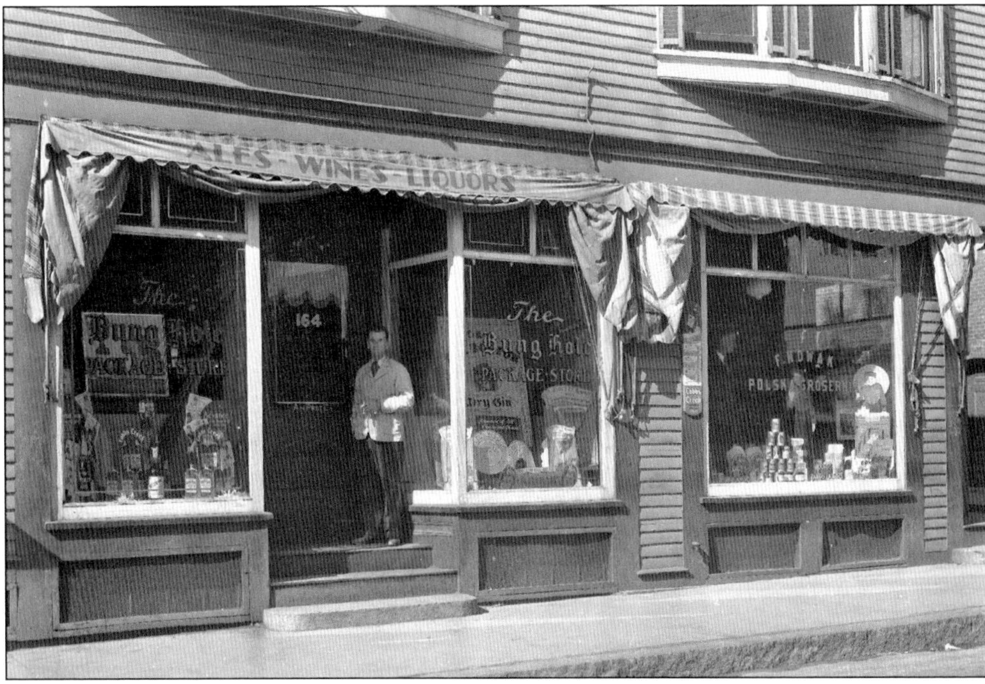

The Kohn's building on the corner of Derby Street and Palfrey Court was occupied by a package store known as the "Bunghole" and Frank Nowak's *Polska grosernia* (Polish grocery) in the 1930s. Frank made kielbasa (sausages) in his home on Palfrey Court to sell in the store. (NPS.)

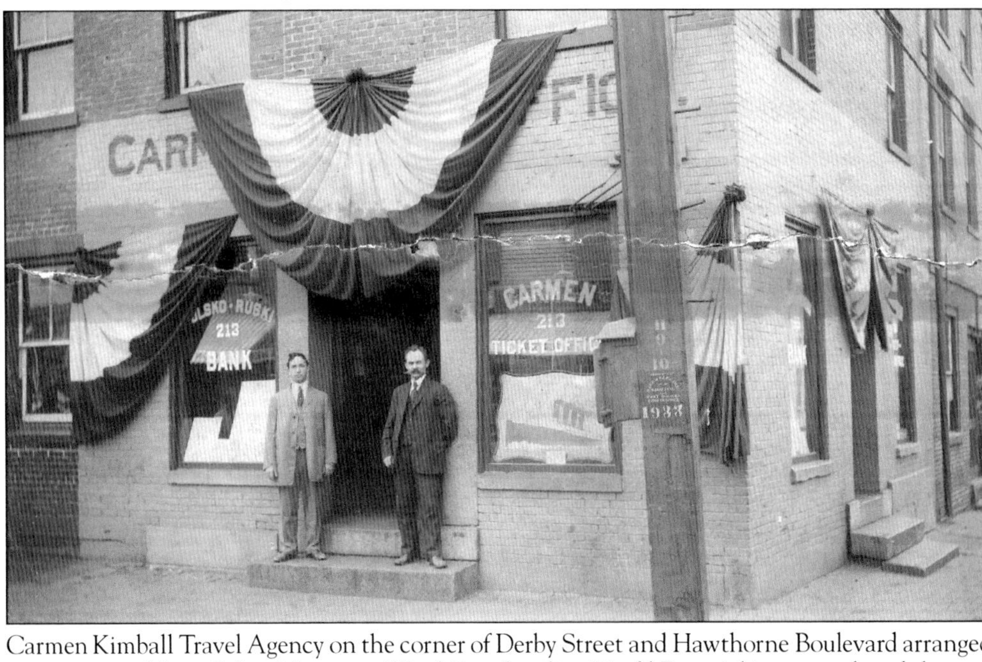

Carmen Kimball Travel Agency on the corner of Derby Street and Hawthorne Boulevard arranged passage to and from Poland for many Ward One families. Teofil Bartnicki was employed there as an interpreter and courier. The Polsko-Rubki (Industrial) Bank was located next door. Known locally as Zarembski's Bank after its president, the bank provided a financial infrastructure for the Polish community by lending money for business ventures and homes. (LBM.)

A major storm buried Salem in February 1920. The "king of the hill" is four-year-old Waldemar Wysocki, the eldest child of Zygmunt and Sophia (née Jastrzembska) Wysocki. The snow bank outside their home at 62 Forrester Street was more than twice his size! (MM.)

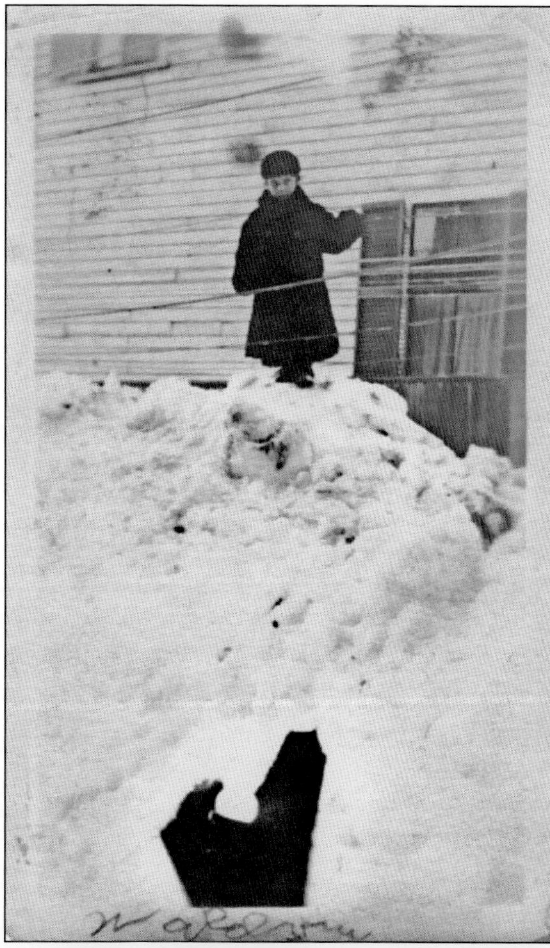

Without the benefit of snowblowers in the 1940s, the whole family pitched in to clear pathways when snow blanketed Salem. Although it may have been more fun than work for the children, a young Clarence Wojciechowski "helped" shovel snow after a blizzard in February 1940. (APW.)

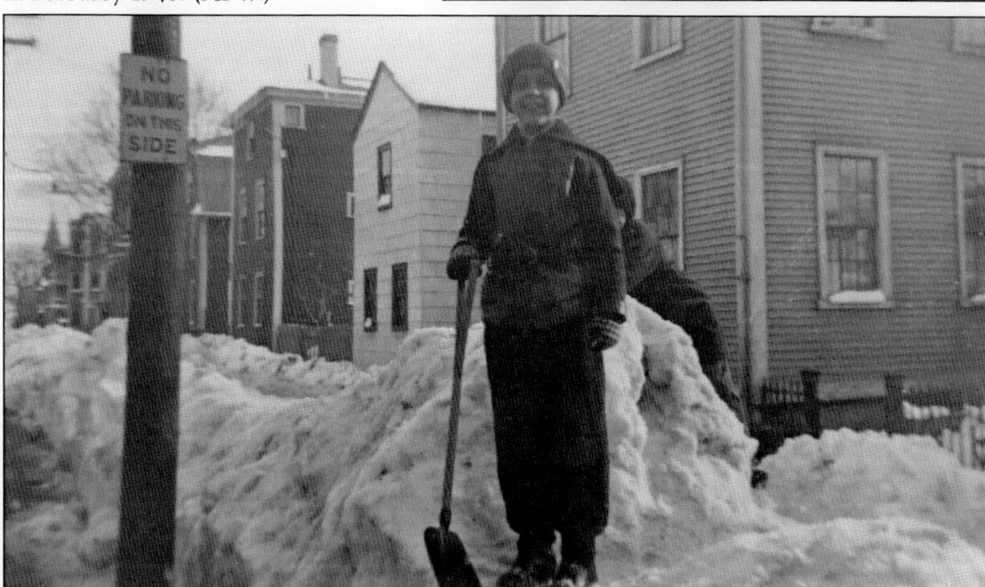

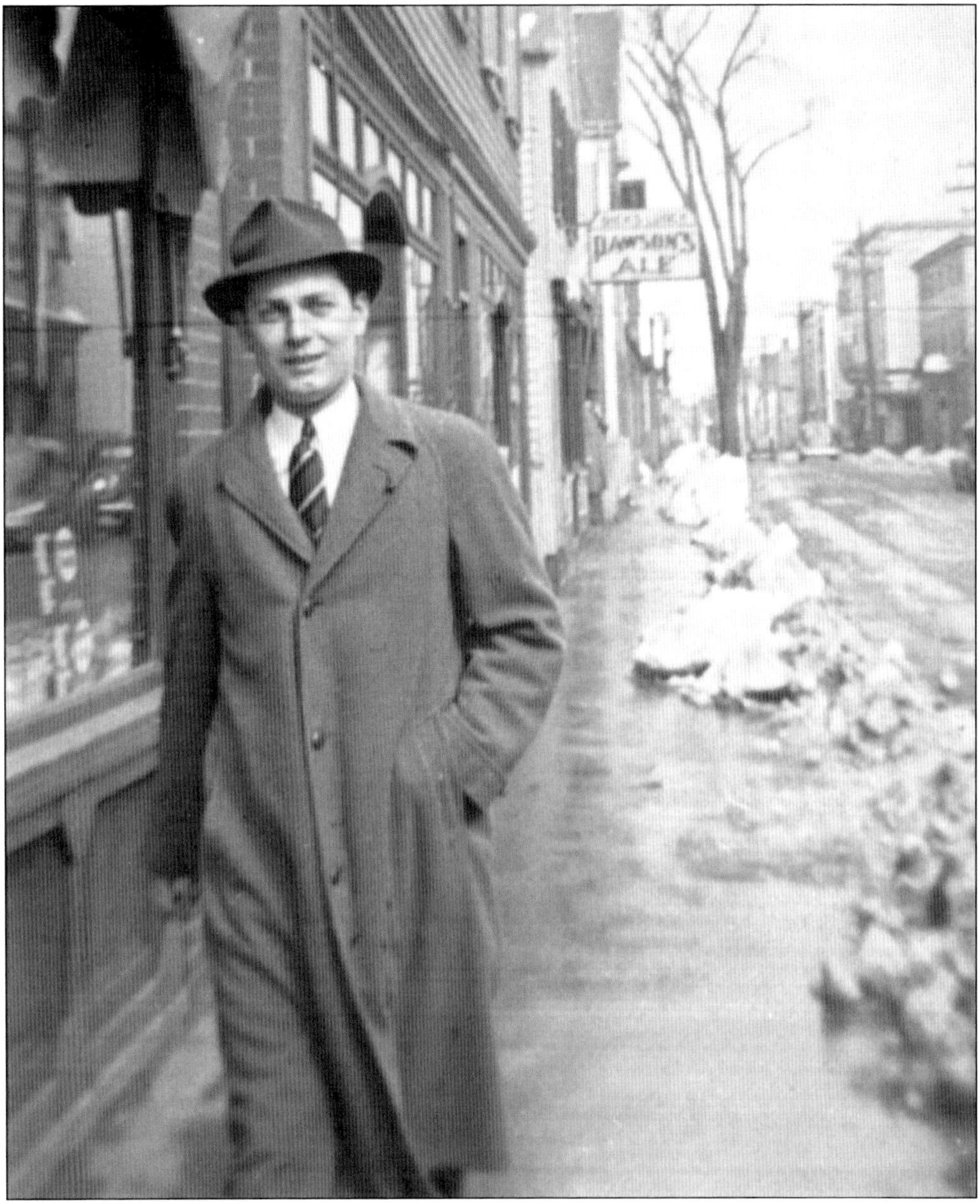

Polish Salem was a smaller community than others in Massachusetts—such as Boston, Worcester, and Chicopee—but it was a distinctive district during the first half of the 20th century. Derby Street, also known as "the Polish Main Street," was the heart of the Polish community. The street was lined with Polish markets, businesses, organizations, and family residences. Trolley cars ran to and from Salem Willows. Today, Derby Street, which runs next to Salem Harbor, has lost its identity as a Polish ethnic enclave but still retains a strong connection with the city's seafaring history. Many of the existing buildings are associated with the international trade carried on in the 1760s to the 1820s. Tourists can walk down Derby Street to visit historic waterfront sites in the area including the customhouse and House of Seven Gables. Derby Street is also the main access road to Pickering Wharf, a business, residential, and marina complex constructed in the 1970s. (NPS.)

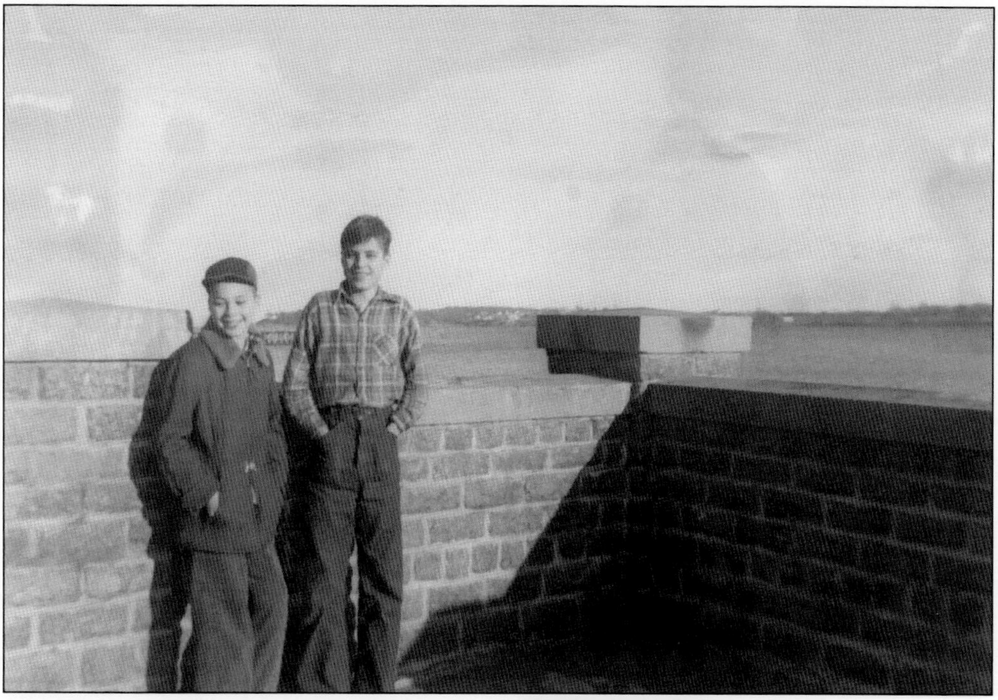

For this photograph in the early 1950s, brothers Richard (left) and Kenneth Carpenter were standing at the sea wall at the foot of Daniels Street with Salem Harbor in the background. Because of its proximity to the ocean, the Derby Street area was once considered an undesirable location. Times certainly have changed! Now the Derby waterfront district is highly valued. (RC.)

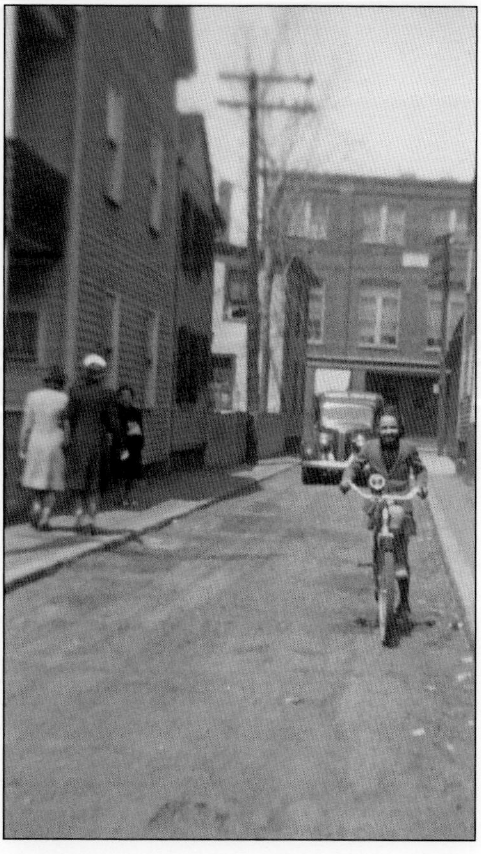

By the 1920s, the Polish community was firmly established in the area around Derby Street. The residents persuaded the city to rename Grant Street to Kosciuszko Street in honor of the famous Polish hero of the American Revolution, Tadeuz Kosciuszko. St. Joseph's Hall is in the background. (NPS.)

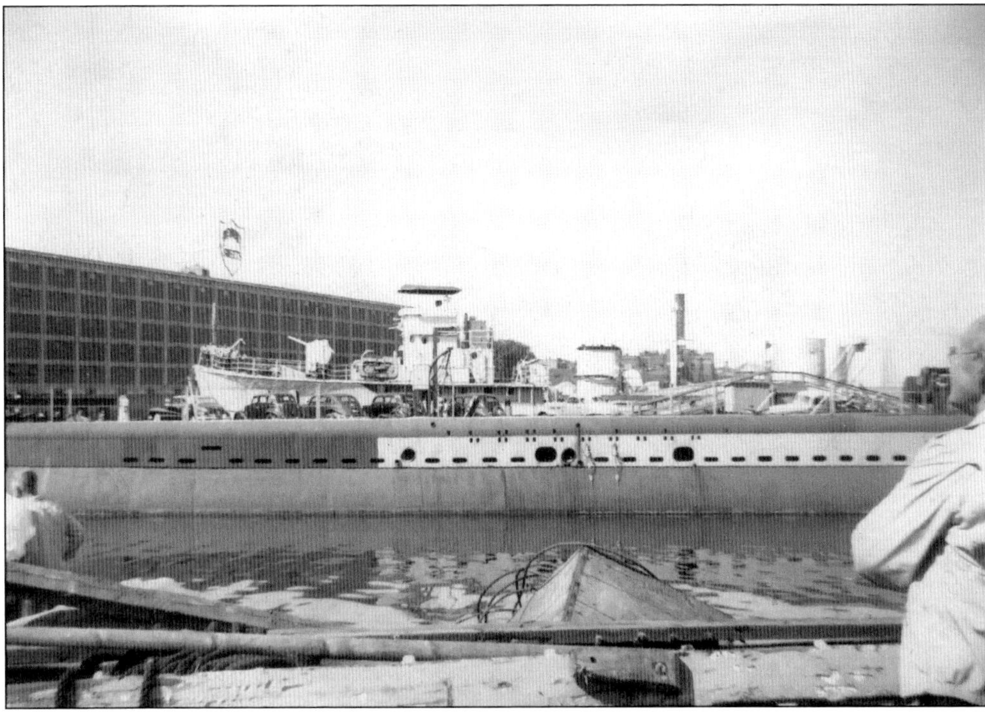

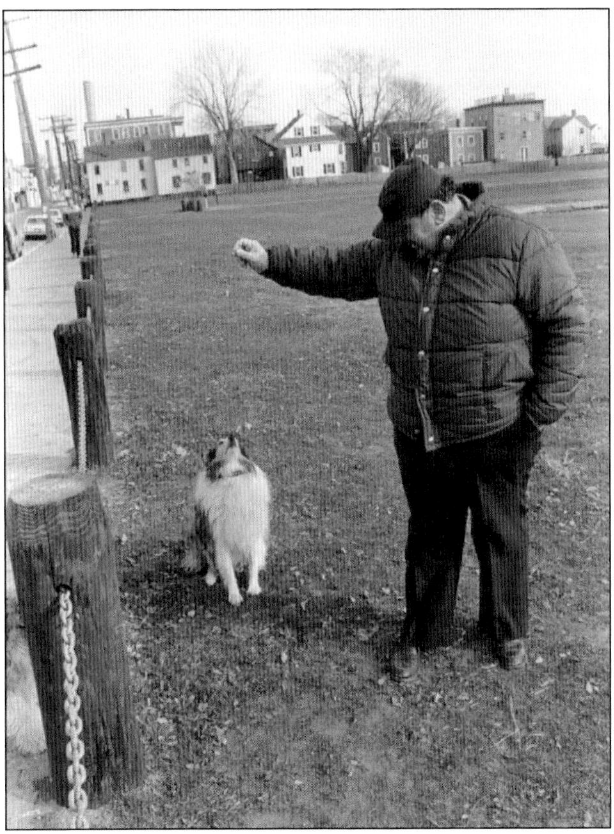

The USS *Shad*, a "Gato" class submarine, was berthed at Central Wharf from the late 1940s until 1960. The *Shad* had a distinguished history earning six battle stars in the Atlantic and Pacific theaters during World War II. After the war, a Naval Reserve Training Center was established at the current location of the Salem Maritime National Historic Site. The submarine was opened to the public on weekends in the mid-1950s. (NPS.)

Raymond Szczuka and his dog Duke were often seen out for a walk at the park on Derby Wharf in the 1970s. As a bartender at St. Joseph's Hall and other Polish Clubs, Raymond was a well-known figure in the neighborhood. A number of the old homes occupied by Polish residents were demolished to make room for the park, now a Salem Maritime National Historic Site. (RC.)

Two

KINSHIPS

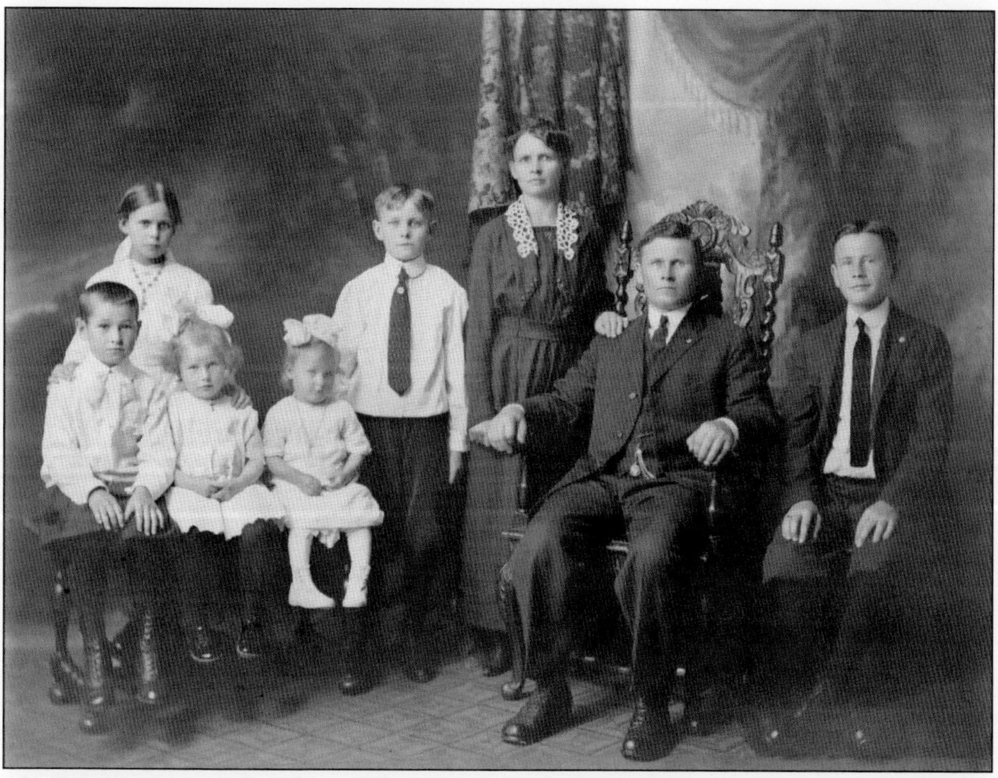

The Polish came to Salem from different partitions of their homeland. Some emigrated from the Russian East, some from the German West, and some from the Austro-Hungarian South. Although there were regional conflicts among the Poles themselves and animosity toward them from the general population, the immigrants came together as a community, forming families and friendships. The Nowak family was photographed around 1915. They are, from left to right, John, Josephine, Helen, Matilda, Anthony, Tekla, Frank, and Joseph. (RNC.)

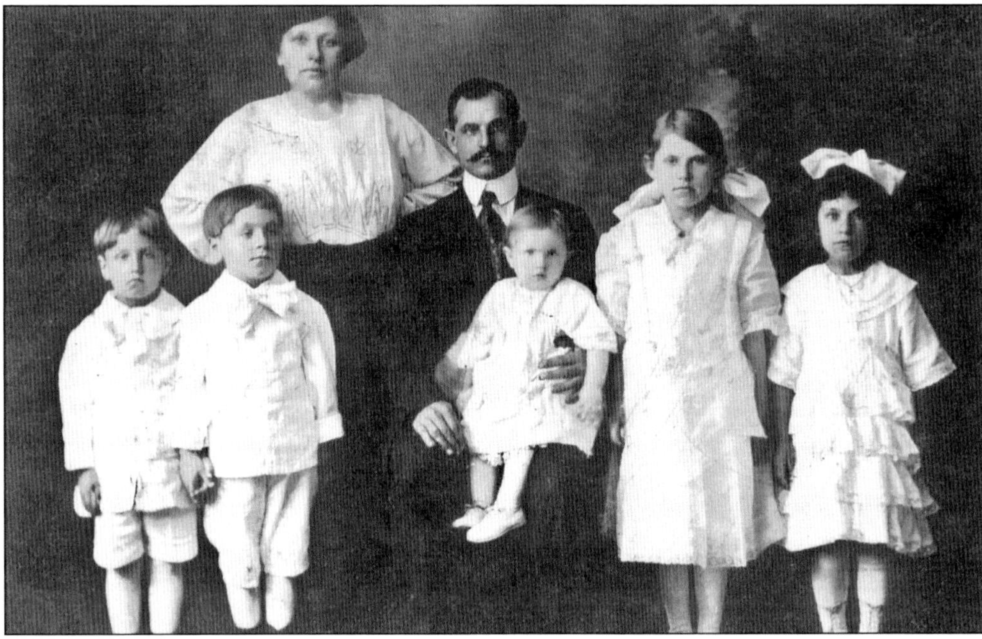

Joseph and Julianna Plutnicki came to Salem in the early 1900s to join other relatives from Poland. They were active members of St. John the Baptist Parish and the St. Joseph's Society. The Plutnickis relocated around the neighborhood whenever they found more affordable rent but raised their children in the center of Polish community life. Shown above in 1920 are, from left to right, Anthony, Matthew, Julianna, Joseph, baby Regina, Genevieve, and Mary. Twelve years later, in 1932, the five Plutnicki children were grown, and a sixth sibling was born. The family now included, from left to right, (sitting) Mary, Julianna, Joseph, Genevieve, and Frank; (standing) Anthony, Regina, and Matthew. (Both, FLW.)

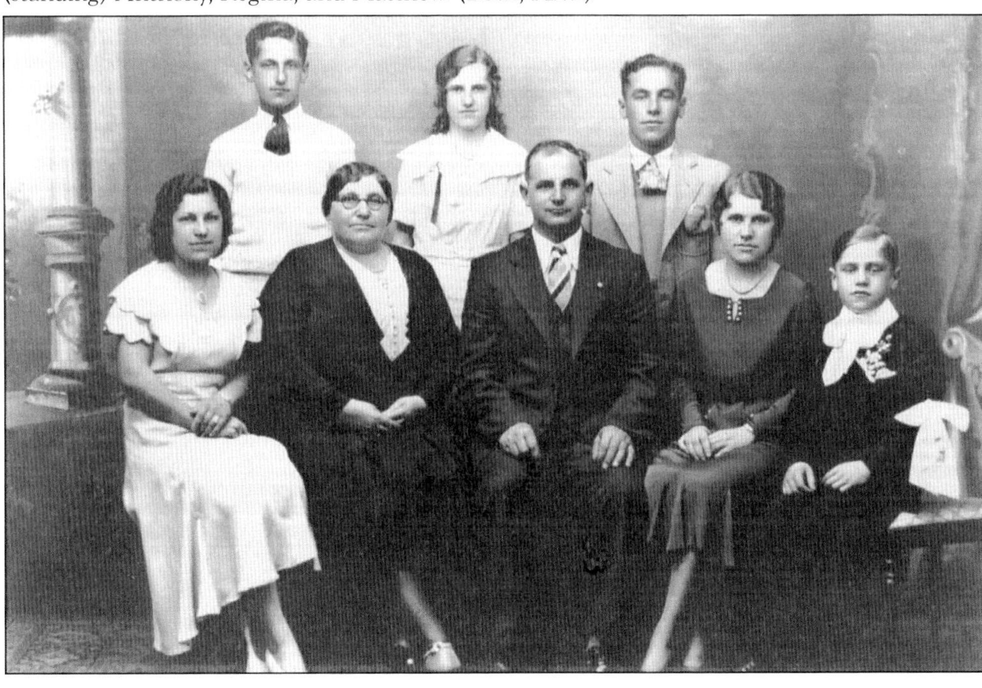

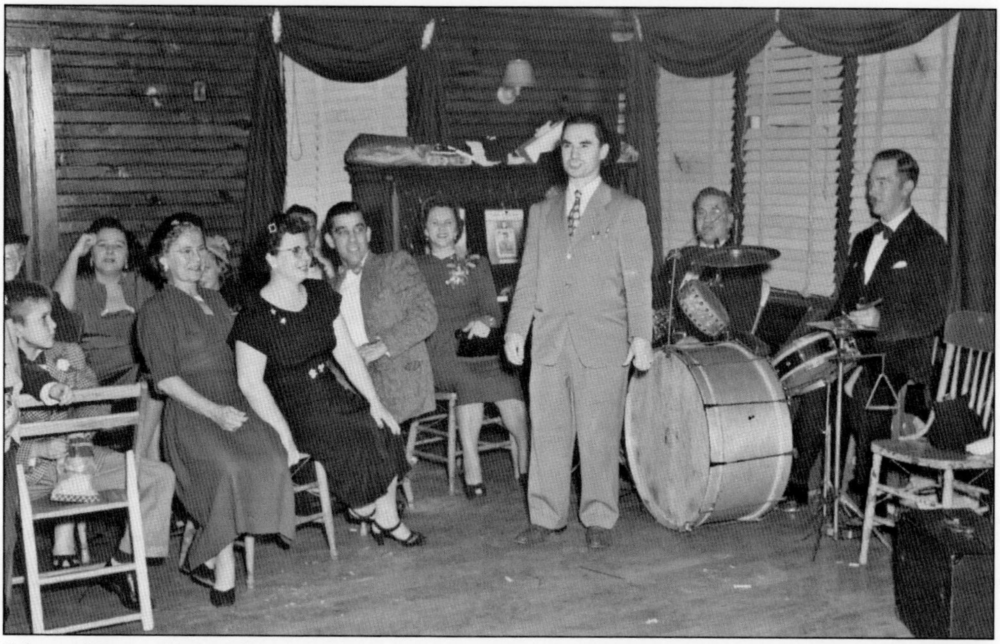

Edmund Bartnicki was known throughout the Polish community for his extraordinary voice. He was frequently called upon to sing at celebrations and religious ceremonies. In this mid-1940s photograph, Eddie is singing to the delight of family and friends gathered at Lebel's Grove, formerly a recreation area in Danvers, Massachusetts, established in the 19th century. (LBM.)

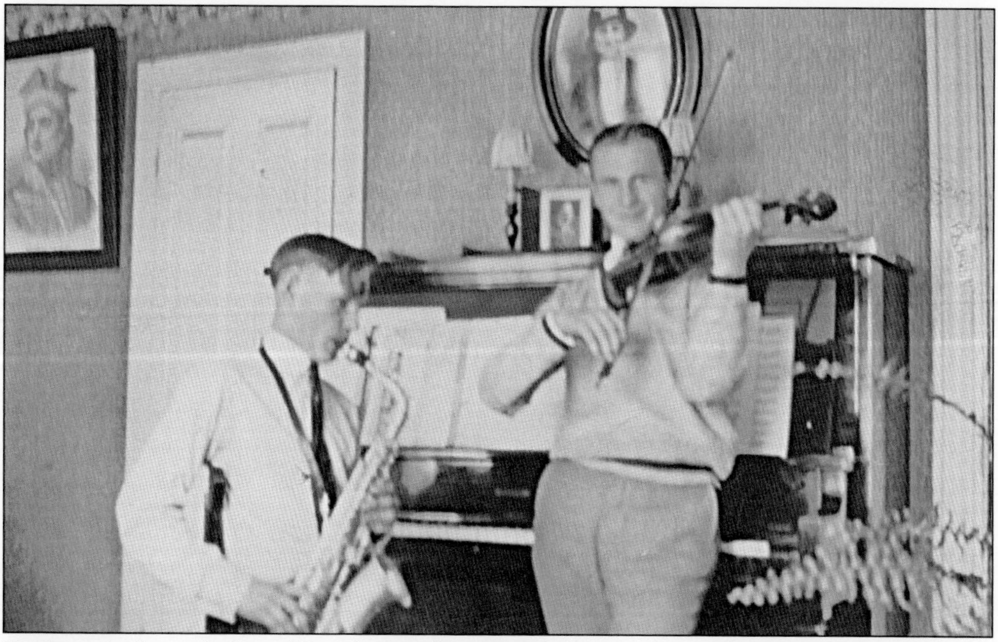

Brothers Anthony (left) and Joseph Nowak practiced the saxophone and violin in their home on Palfrey Court. They played in a musical group that entertained at neighborhood social events in the mid-1920s. Joseph continued playing the violin for enjoyment throughout his life, but Anthony stored his saxophone in the attic. Note the picture of Gen. Kazimierz Pulaski in the upper left. The Poles were proud to display their military heroes from the American Revolution. (RNC.)

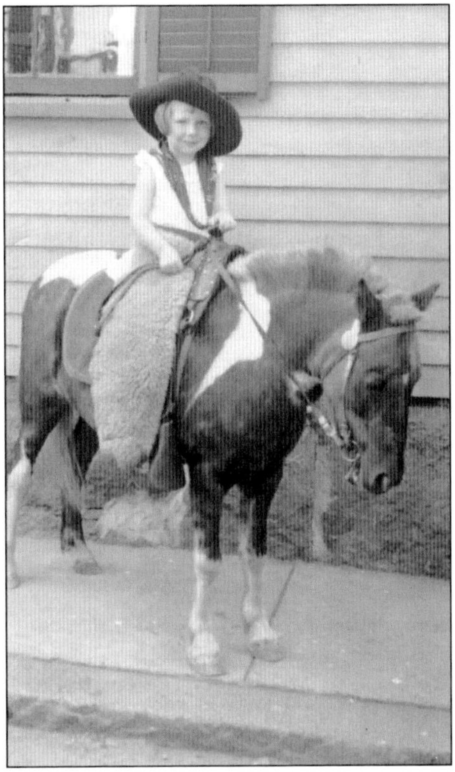

"Cowgirl" Joan Kalapinski is pictured around 1940 sitting on a pony outside her Herbert Street home. In the 1940s, enterprising Salem photographer Abdo traveled up and down the streets of the Ward One neighborhood with a pony, props, costumes, and, of course, his camera to offer families interesting photo ops! (MZW.)

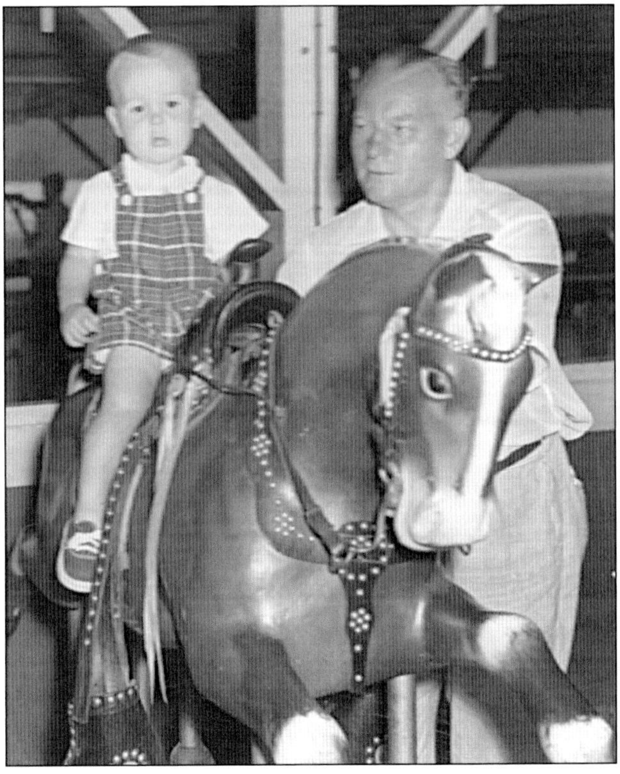

Salem Willows Waterfront Amusement Park is one of the oldest in the United States. It was named for the European white willow trees planted in 1801 to provide shaded walkways. Park visitors can still enjoy the beaches, arcade, and children's rides. Pictured here is Adam Dobrosielski giving his grandson Paul a ride on the flying horses in 1955. (PD.)

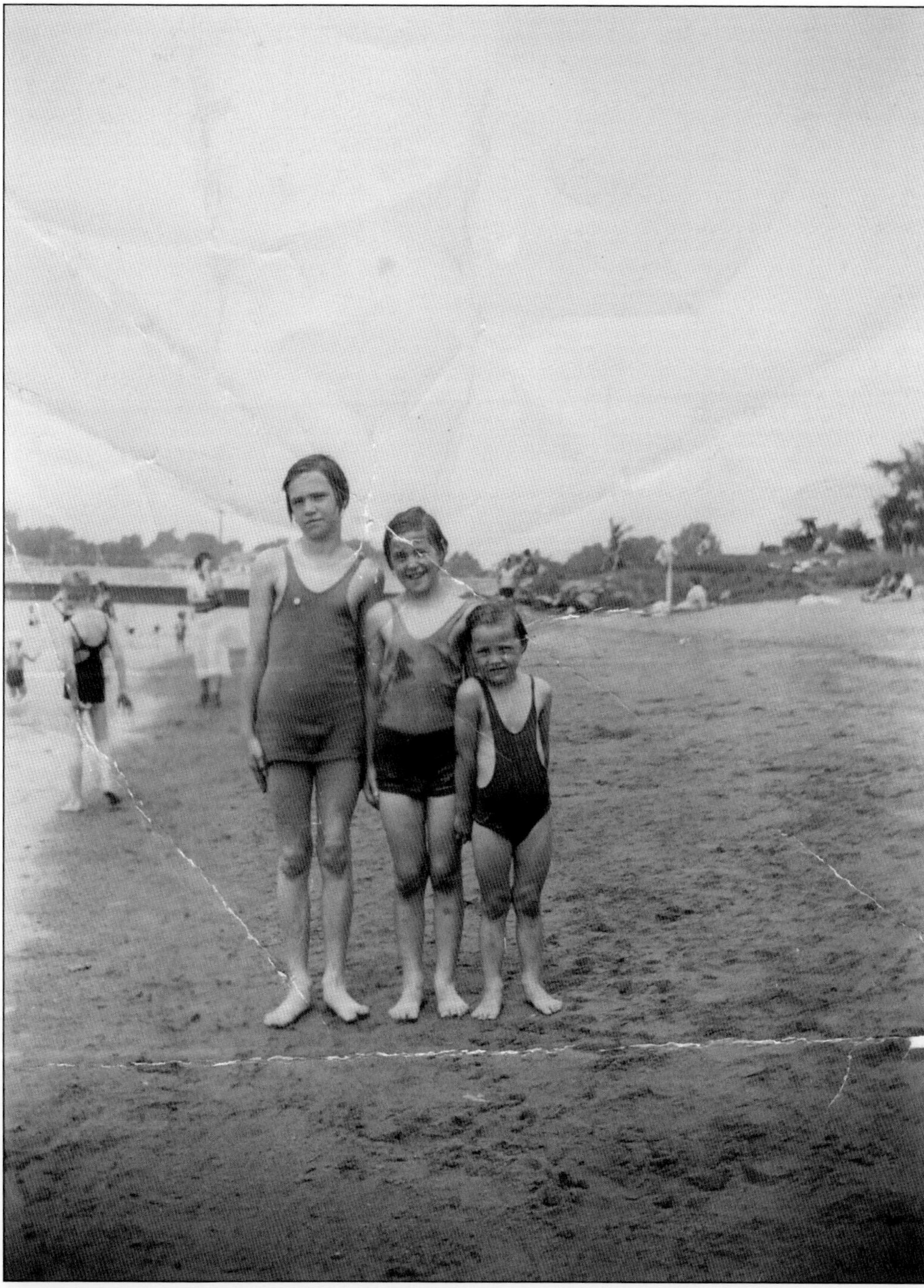

Smith's Pool is an eight-acre tidal pond located between Salem Neck, Winter Island, and Cat Cove. It is named for a local family who bequeathed the pond to the city. Years ago, it was a swimming hole for Salem's children. The Pronska sisters spent a summer day there in the mid-1930s. They are, from left to right, Josephine, Lucy, and Alice. Today, Smith's Pool is open for school visits so children can study the tiny ecosystem. (APW.)

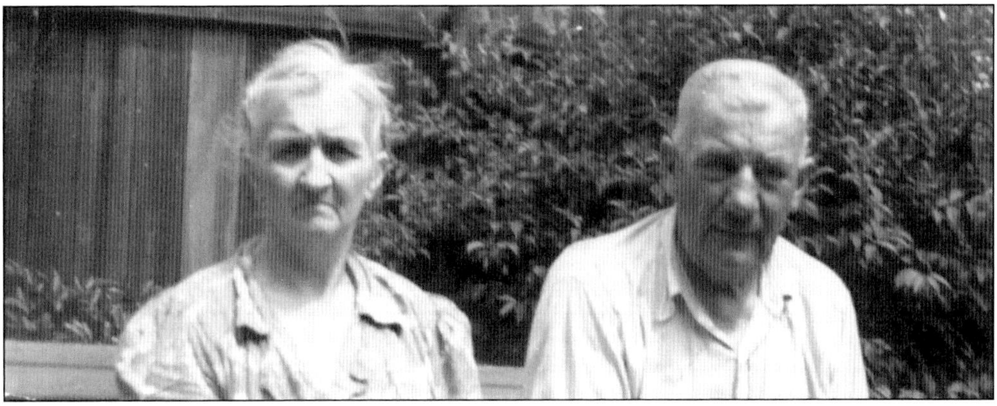

Helen Kobierska and Stanislaw Wilczenski were among the early immigrants who came to the United States as teenagers in the 1890s. They were married in Salem in 1899 and raised a family of five: Julia (Piasecki), J. Louis, S. Albert, Bernard, and John. Minutes of the St. Joseph Society's meetings in the early 1900s recorded Stanislaw as bookkeeper and treasurer. (FLW.)

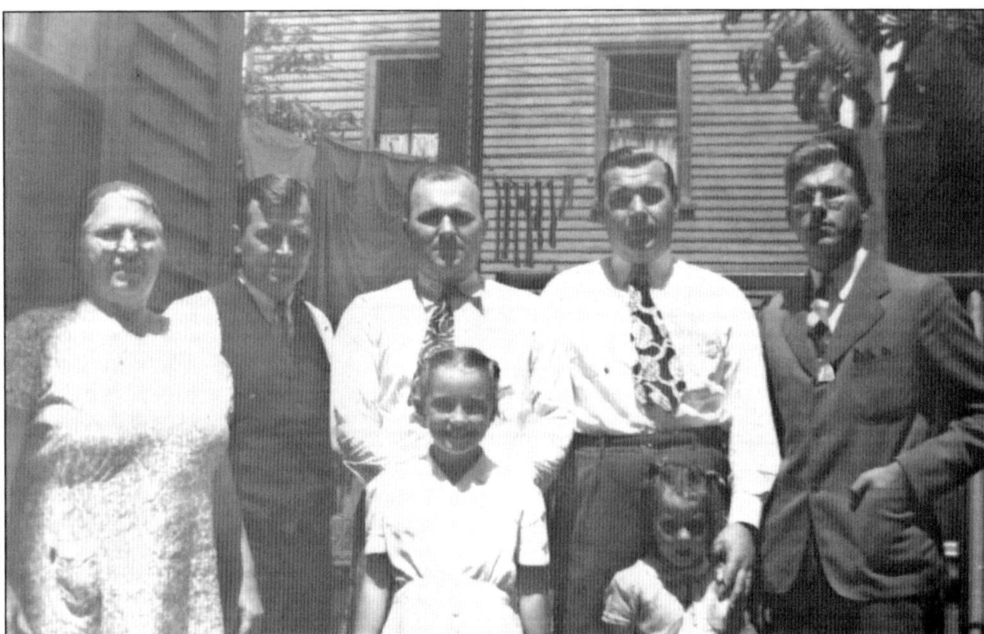

Standing next to their mother for this backyard photograph were (from left to right) sons Bill, Steve, Kay, and Alex Solodiuk, and granddaughters. For many years, Kay hosted a popular Polish music program on WESX radio in Salem. Polka music could be heard every Sunday afternoon in Polish homes throughout the city. (PLAV.)

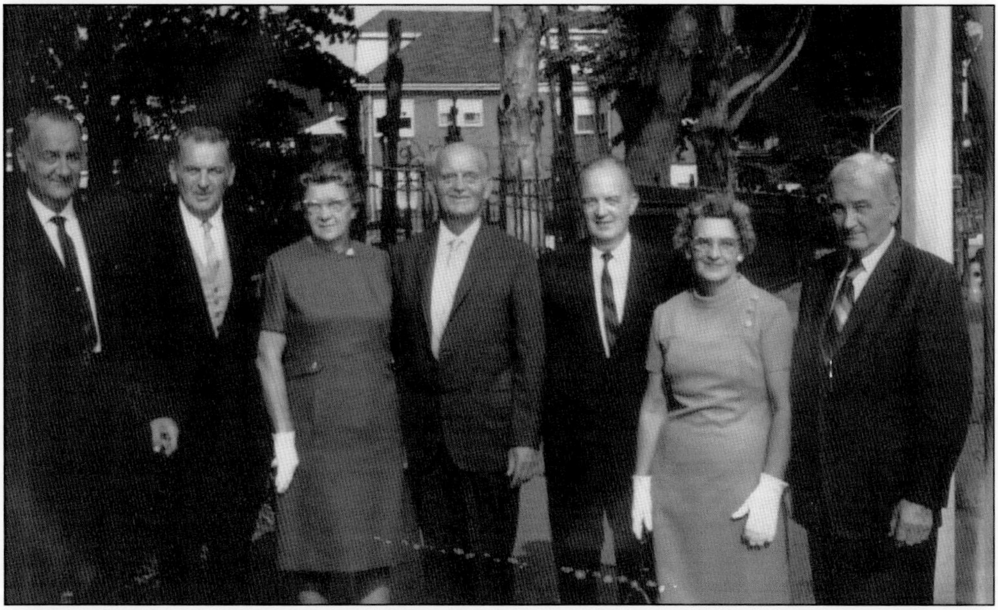

Polish families remained connected after they left the old neighborhood. The Kowalskis grew up on Daniels Street. Family members got together in 1970 to celebrate the marriage of Albert's son Ralph in Newton, Massachusetts. Pictured are, from left to right, Stephen, Albert, Alice (Bachorowski), Edmund, William, Claire (Nowak), and John. (RNC.)

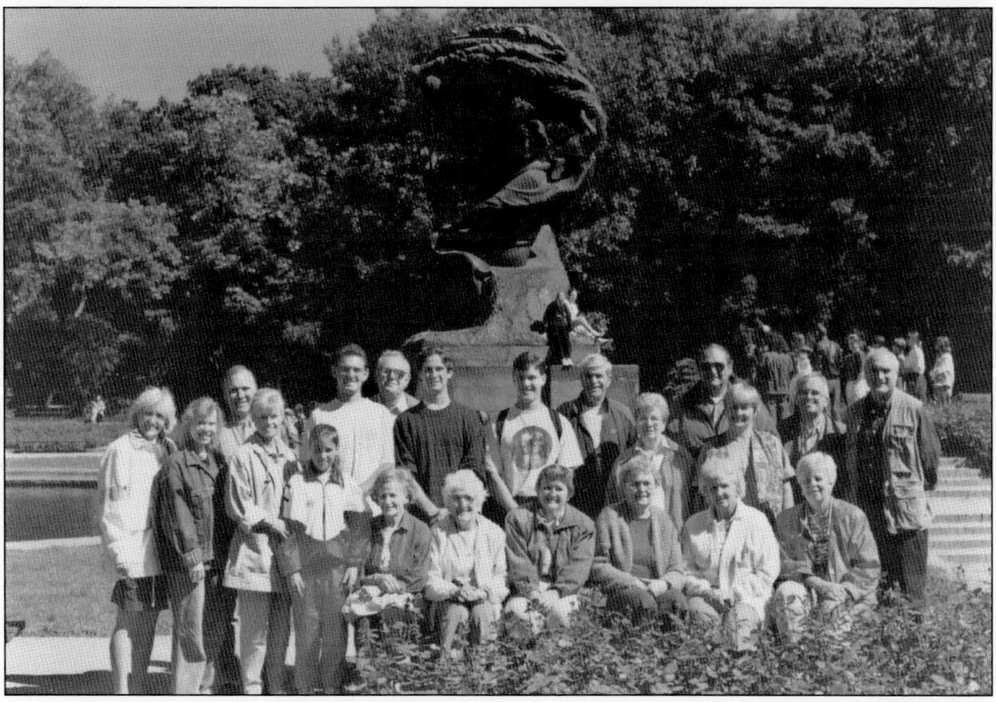

Three generations of Nowaks traced their family roots on a tour of Poland in June 1994. They visited Mary Nowak's hometown of Hnatkowice, which is in southeast Poland near the regional capital city of Rzeszow. This picture was taken in front of the Fredric Chopin monument in Lazienki Park, Warsaw. (RNC.)

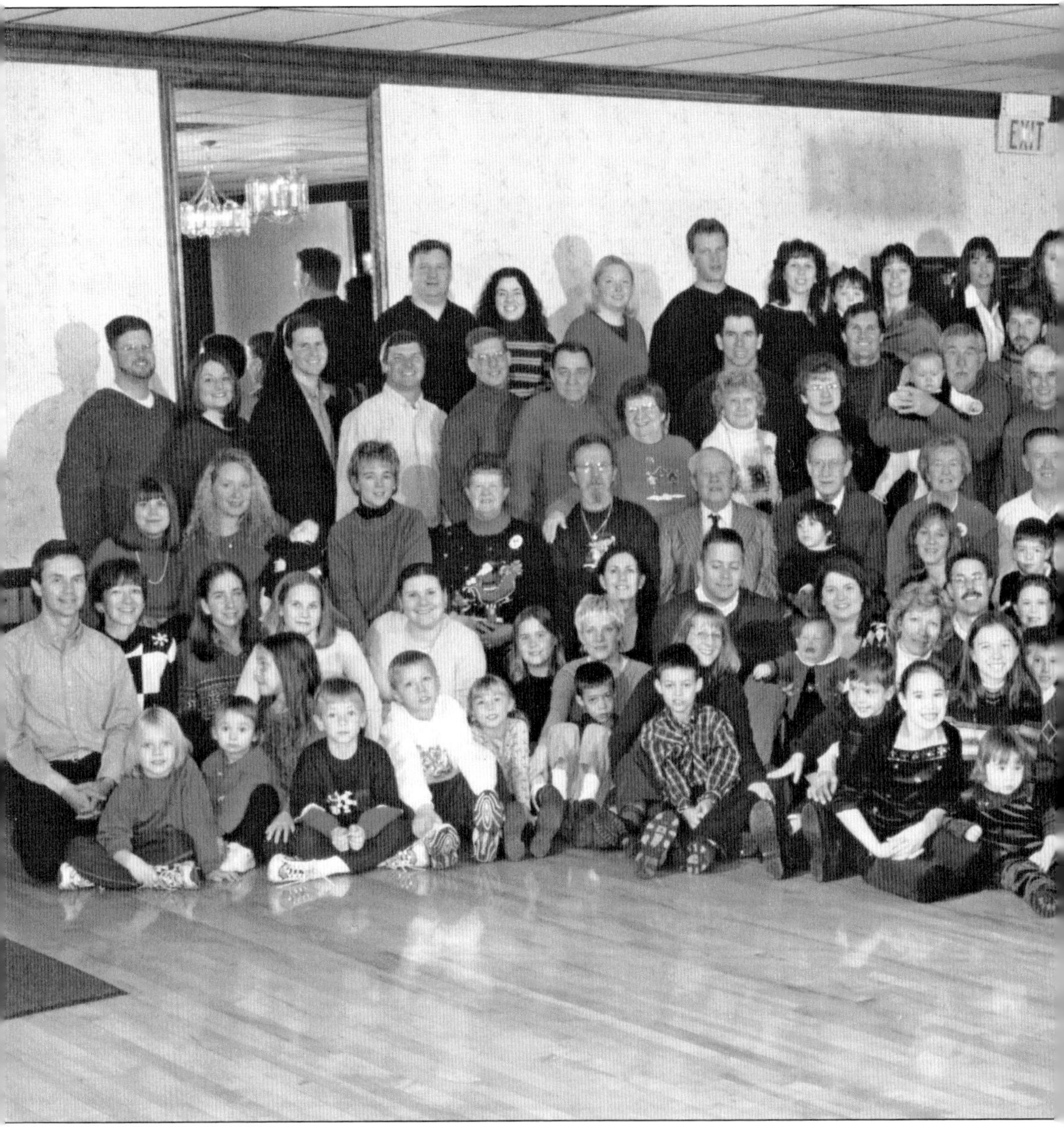

The Malioneks are prominent in Polish Salem. Pictured at their reunion in the millennium year 2000 were four generations of the Malionek family, the offspring of Paul and Tekla Malionek. For the past 40 years, the family has gathered the second Sunday of December at the Knights of

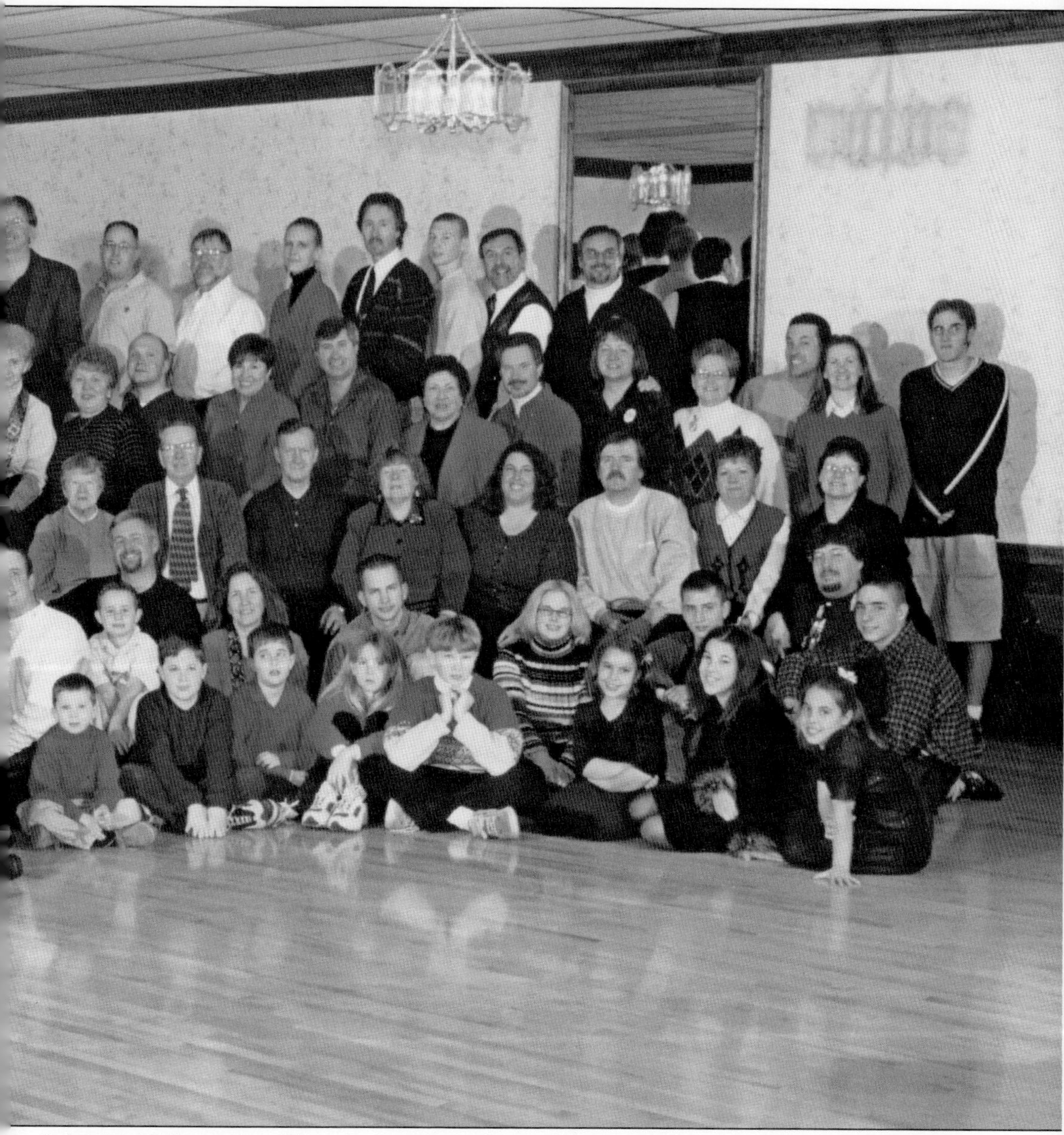

Columbus Hall in Salem. They also continue a longstanding tradition of delightful entertainment by having the children compose original skits, make their own costumes, and present a play, which remains a closely guarded secret to surprise family members at the party. (PM.)

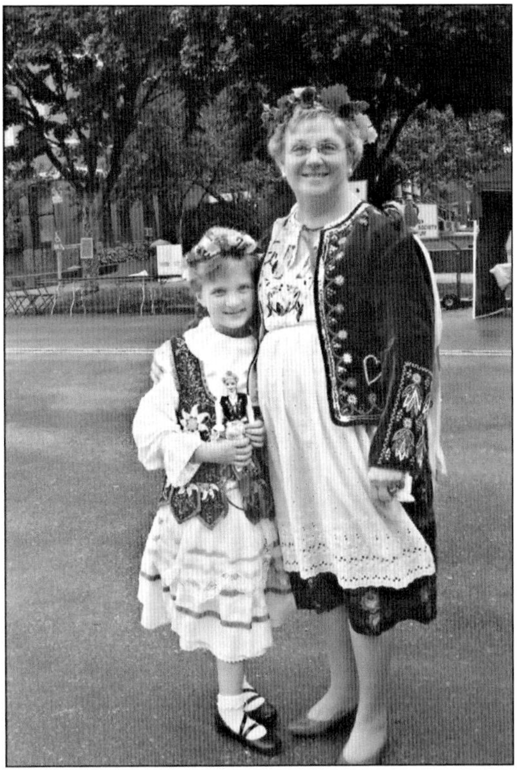

Ethnic and cultural festivals are popular events held yearly in Salem and in many neighboring North Shore communities. Polish participants often dress in brightly colored costumes that are predominantly the red and white colors of Poland. Alice (Sobiesielska) Zujewski and her granddaughter Emily Zujewski posed in traditional Polish outfits. Emily is holding a souvenir doll her grandmother bought during a trip to Poland. Mothers Alicja Reksc (left) and Lucine Wabno Beaurand (right) stood behind their daughters who dressed in Polish costumes for the St. John the Baptist annual Polish picnic in 2010. (Left, MZ; below, RNC.)

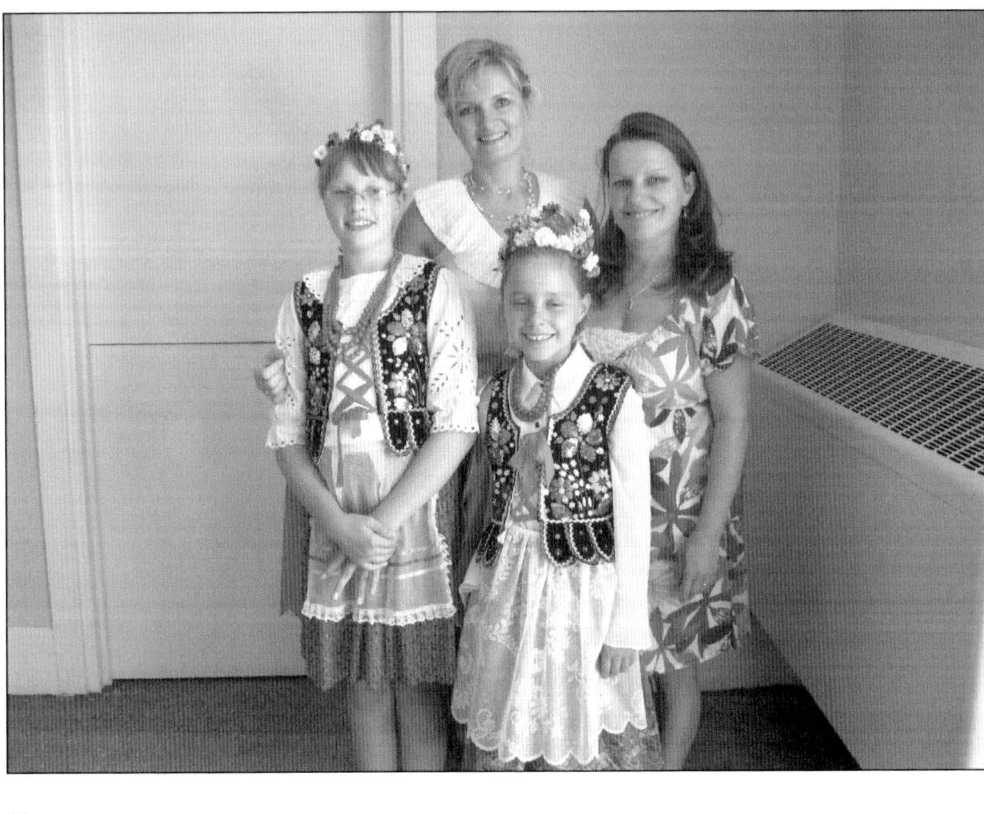

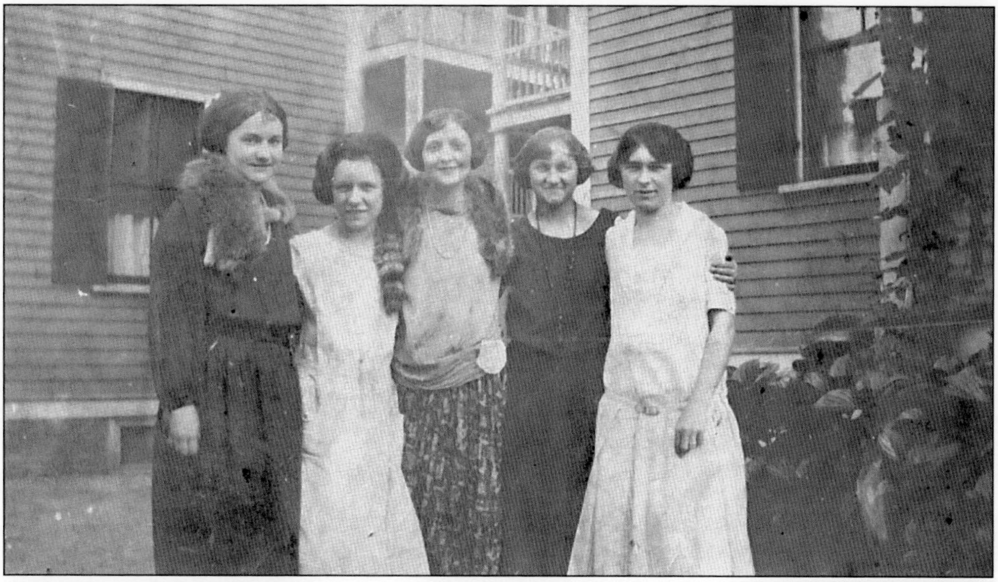

Sophia Jastrzembska Wysocki (right), sister Helen (second from the left), and friends posed in front of the Wysocki's apartment house at 62 Forrester Street. Whole animal fur collars were fashionable around 1920, suggesting the women were dressed for a special event. Zygmunt Wysocki came from Warsaw in 1914 to visit his cousin Alexander Kotarski. At Kotarski's store, he met the fetching bookkeeper, Sophia, married, and never returned to Poland. (MM.)

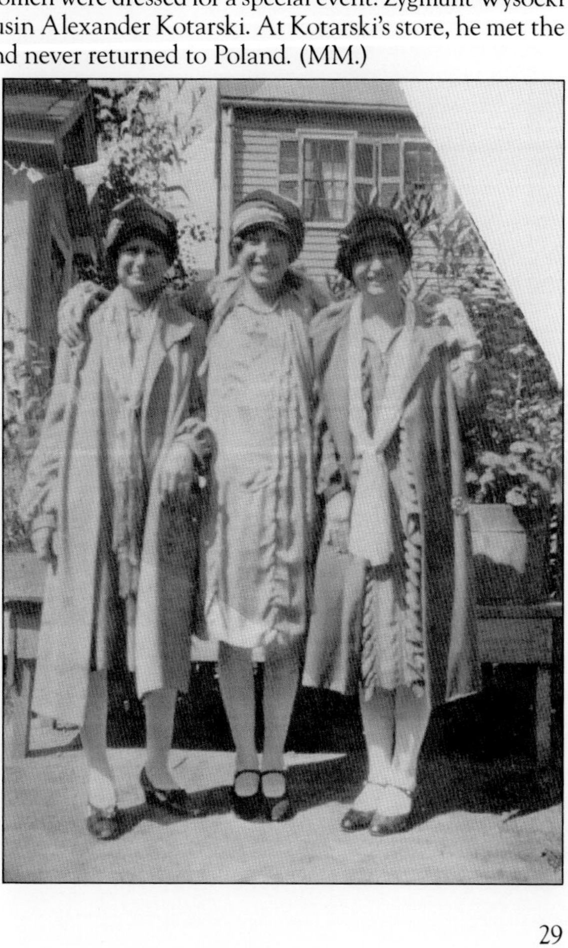

Personal relationships were the heart of the Polish community. Lasting friendships developed among the teenage members of the Polish neighborhood. Activities sponsored by St. John the Baptist Parish and the Gables Settlement House brought them together. In 1926, 16-year-old Genevieve Plutnicki (Wilczenski), pictured in the center, hugs her good friends Josephine Nowak, left, and Stasia Olbrych, right. (RNC.)

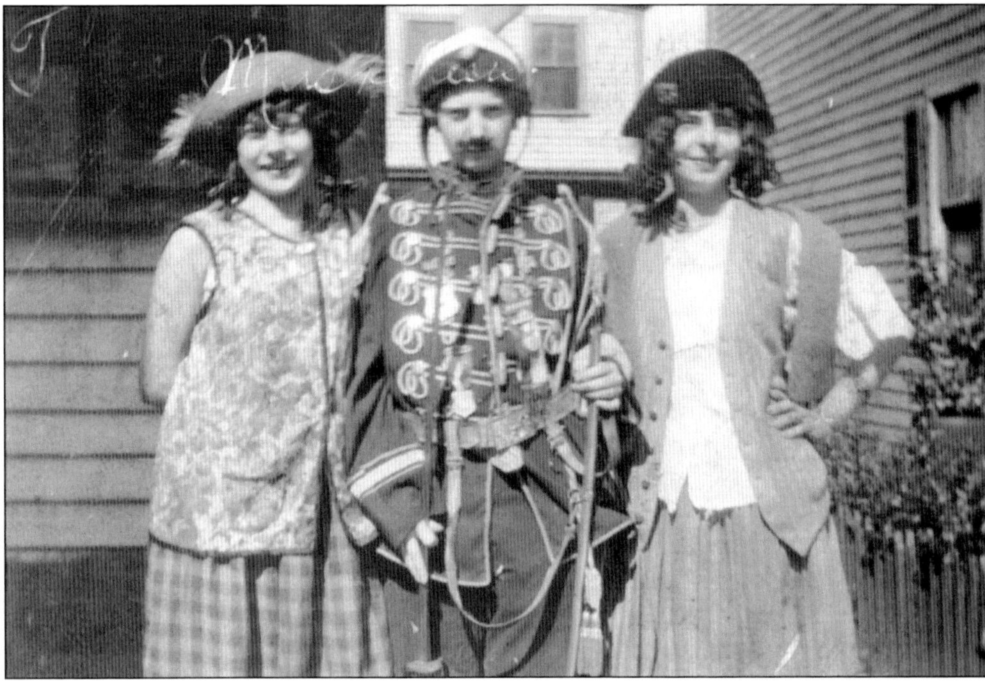

The Polish community had to work hard but also took time for fun. The Bartnicki sisters, Jane, Helen (Olbrych), and Alice (Lepkowski) rummaged through some old clothes to dress as the Three Musketeers in this 1926 photograph. Helen was wearing the St. Joseph's Society drill team uniform of her father, Teofil. (LBM.)

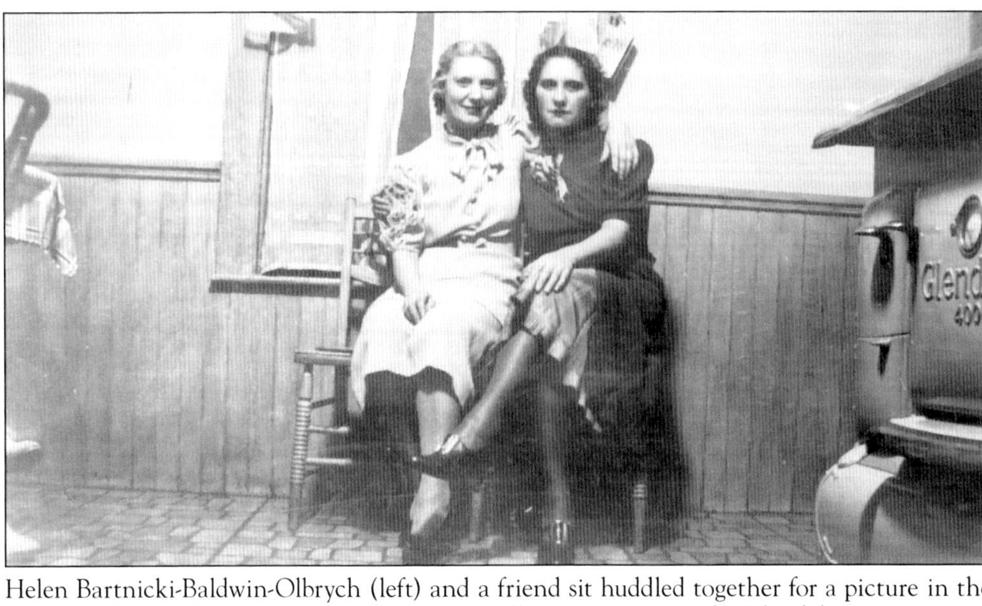

Helen Bartnicki-Baldwin-Olbrych (left) and a friend sit huddled together for a picture in the kitchen of Helen's Bentley Street house. Now a collector's item, note the Glendale cast iron wood and gas stove from the 1920s that would have provided a source of warmth to heat the home for the family in the cold winter months. (LBM.)

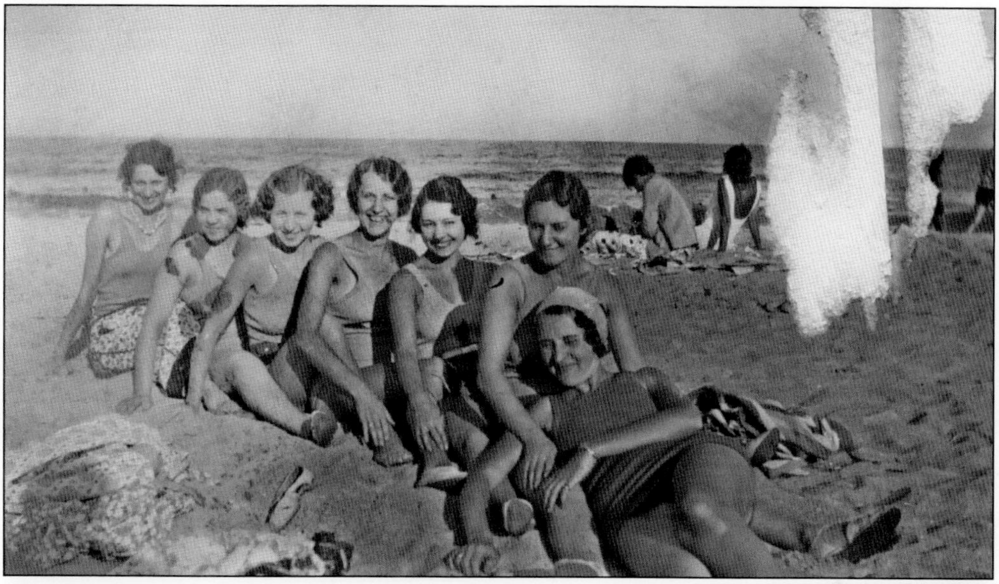

The New England coastline has many beautiful beaches. Besides the sand and sea, Hampton Beach, New Hampshire, had many restaurants, arcades, dance halls, and other amusements for visitors in the 1920s. Helen and Jane Bartnicki (second and third from the right) and a group of their Ward One friends from Salem traveled to Hampton for a day in the sun. (LBM.)

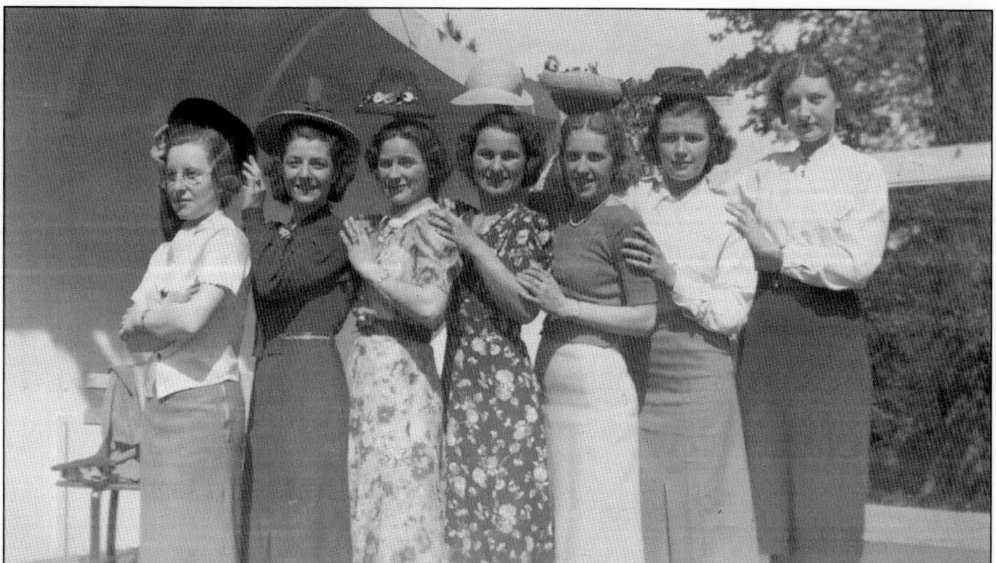

Good friends, who were often described as "attached at their hips," appeared to be connected in this mid-1930s picture! Standing in the line up from left to right were: Monica Gesek Ozireko, Jane Pszenny Sarnowski, Margie Nowak Kowalski, Xaviera "KiKi" Hincman Kable, Regina Plutnicki Wharff, Hedwig Drankowski Gavenda, and Sophie Wroblewski Warcholik. (JKW.)

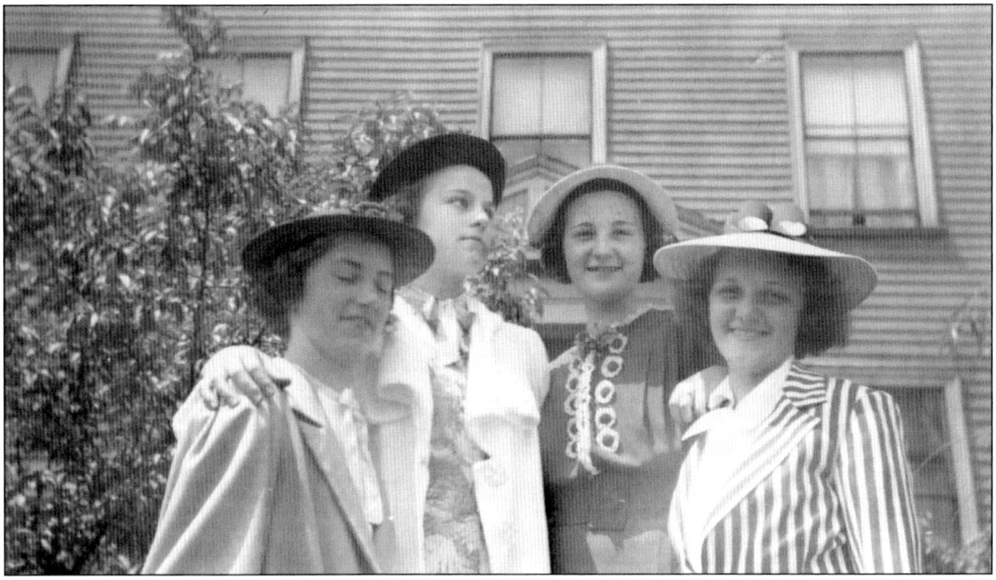

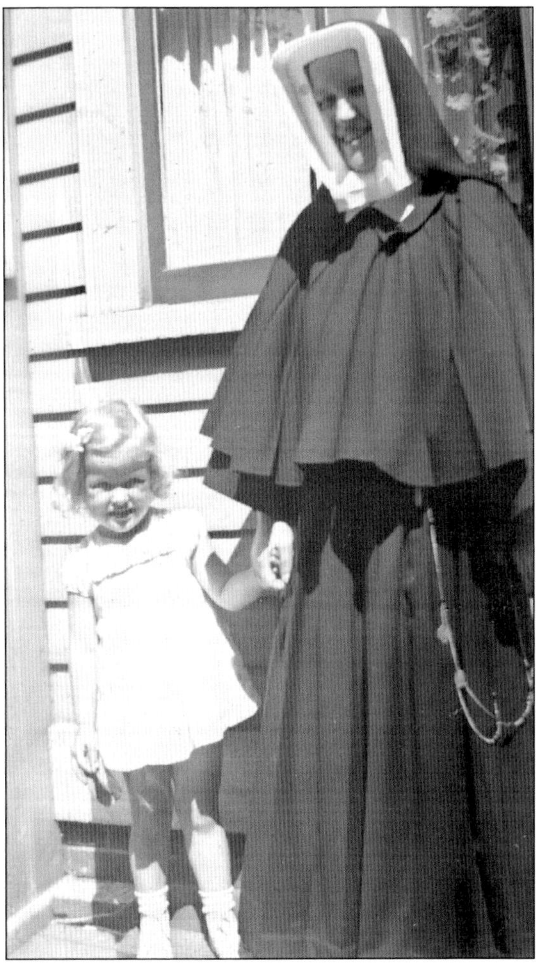

From left to right, Sabina "Sally" Sumska (Kuva), Irene Palmer (Bochynska), Hyacinth Pszenny (Dobrosielska), and Frieda Dobrosielska (Kobos) were photographed in 1938 in front of the Capt. Simon Forrester House at 188 Derby Street across from Central Wharf, then owned and occupied by Peter Mysliwy, a local grocer, and his family. (PD.)

Albina Nestor's daughter Claudia was photographed with her aunt Sister Mary, a member of the Immaculate Conception religious order, at the family home in Salem in the summer of 1941. The religious order had a primarily educational ministry. Sister Mary's elaborate wimple and habit must have been quite warm for this July photograph! (LBM.)

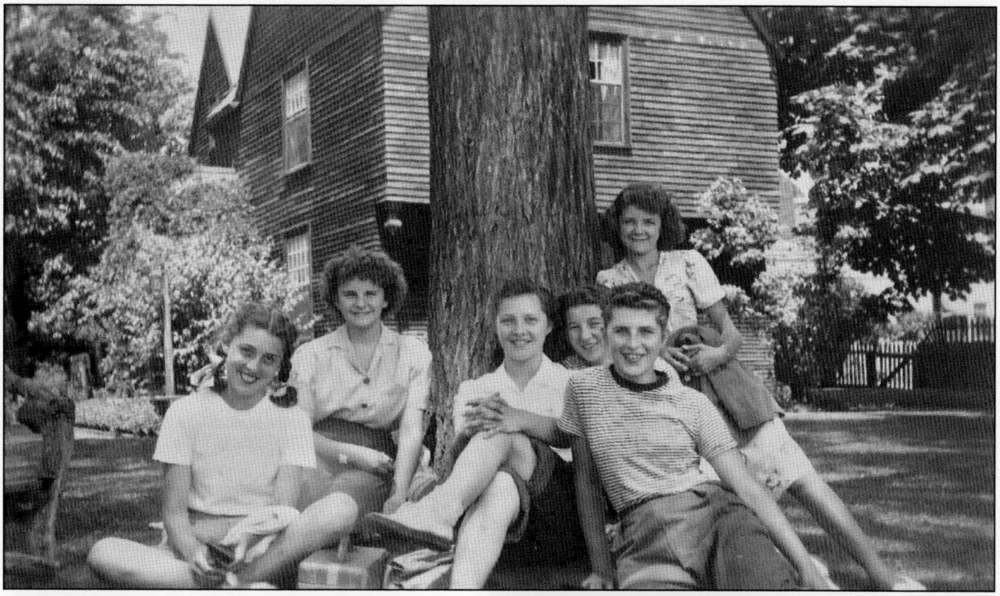

The "Jolly Jelly Beans," a group that included Polish teenagers from Ward One, were photographed around 1945 sitting outside the House of Seven Gables as members of Mrs. Chapin's "cultural club." Youth activities sponsored by the Gables in the 1940s were arranged to teach an appreciation of civic culture in order to promote good citizenship among the children of immigrants. (APW.)

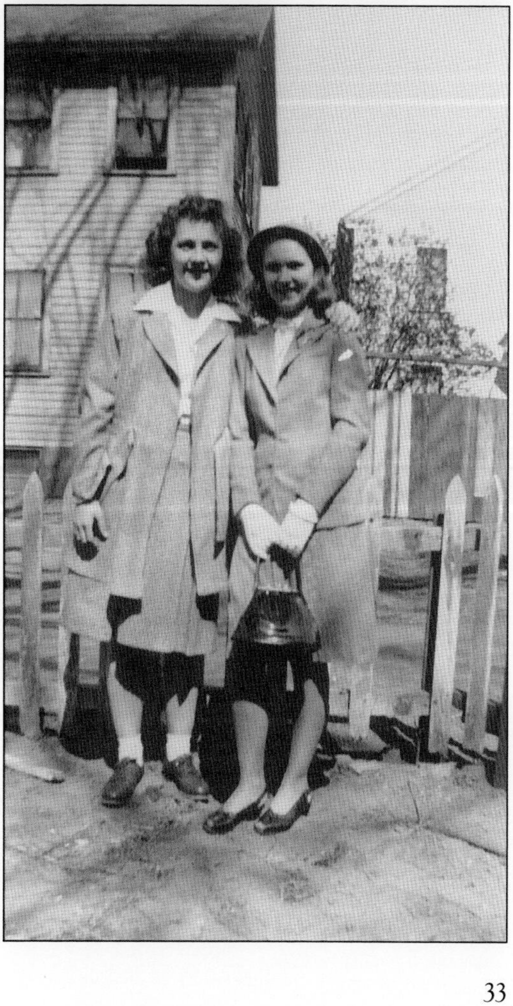

Friends Alice Pronska (left) and Geraldine Nowak (right) got together on Easter Sunday in 1946. The picture was taken in the backyard of the Nowak home on Essex Street. Alice and Geraldine met as children while attending youth activities sponsored by the House of Seven Gables, and they remained lifelong friends. (APW.)

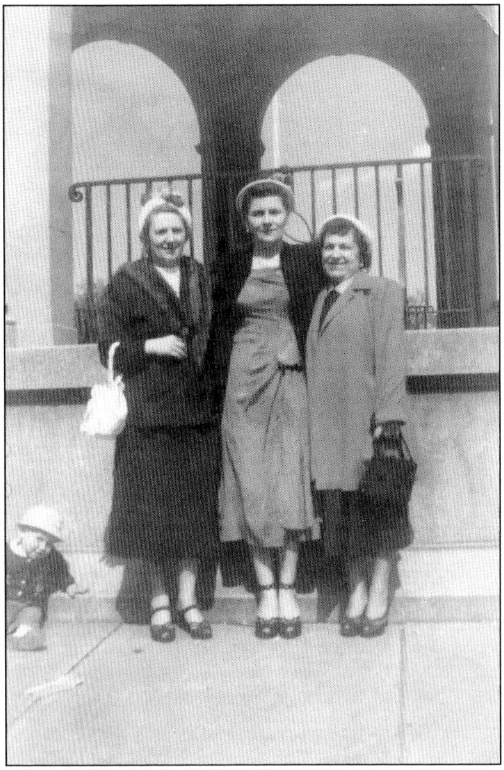

The Salem Common Bandstand, which was erected at the time of Salem's tricentennial Celebration in 1926, provided the background for this early-1950s picture of three friends; standing are, from left to right, Helen (Bartnicki-Baldwin) Olbrych, Charlotte (Agacinska) Negri, and Mary (Plutnicki) Wroblewski. The Salem Common was in close proximity to the Polish Ward One district. (LBM.)

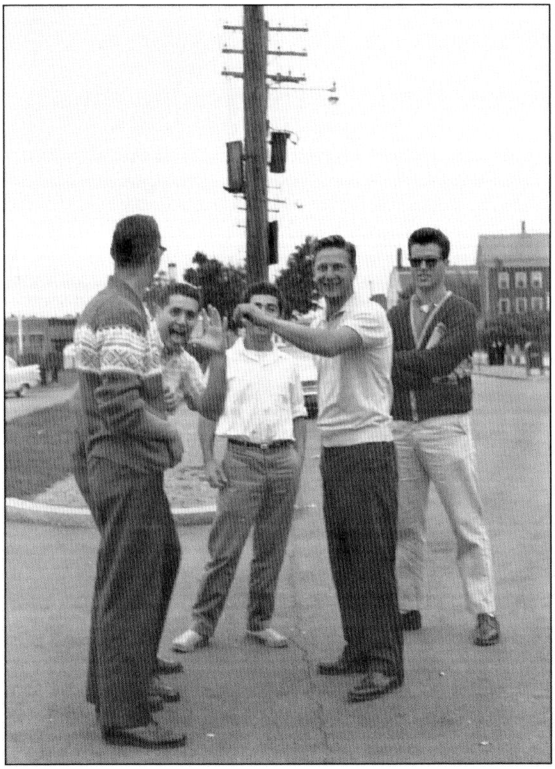

Hamming it up for the camera in 1960 were, from left to right, the following Derby Street buddies: Richard Iwanowicz, Richard Smith, William Davis, Ralph Stankiewicz, and Kenneth Carpenter. Such gatherings were usually impromptu, and the boys chat about everything from dates to the meaning of life. Sometimes they would head to a local club for cold beer. (RC.)

Three

Traditions

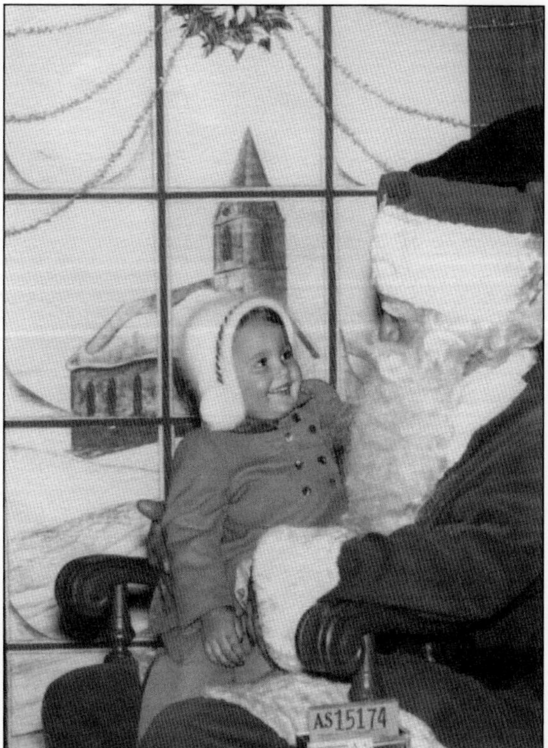

A visit to Santa Claus in the lower level of Almy's Department Store on Essex Street was a holiday tradition for Salem's children. Each child was photographed with Santa and received a present from his elves. Julie Kowalski is pictured telling Santa her Christmas wishes in 1954. (JKW.)

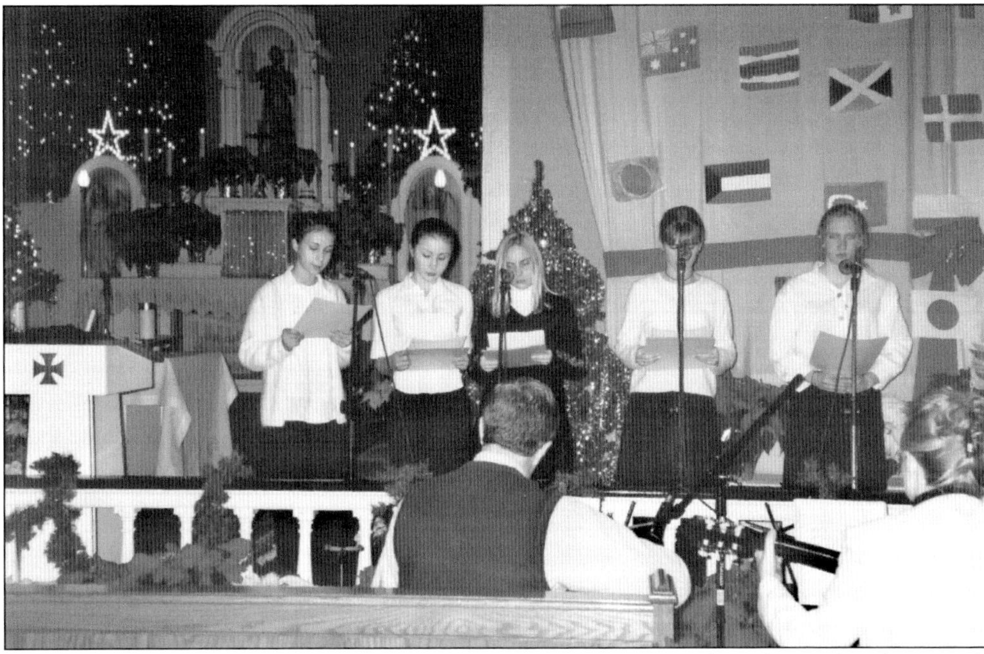

Religious rituals were always part of the Christmas celebration among the Poles. In this photograph, the St. John the Baptist children's choir sang *kolendy* (carols) during a Christmas service at the church in 1998. "Dzisiaj w Betlejem" ("Today in Bethlehem") was always a favorite piece for the parishioners to sing along. (SJB.)

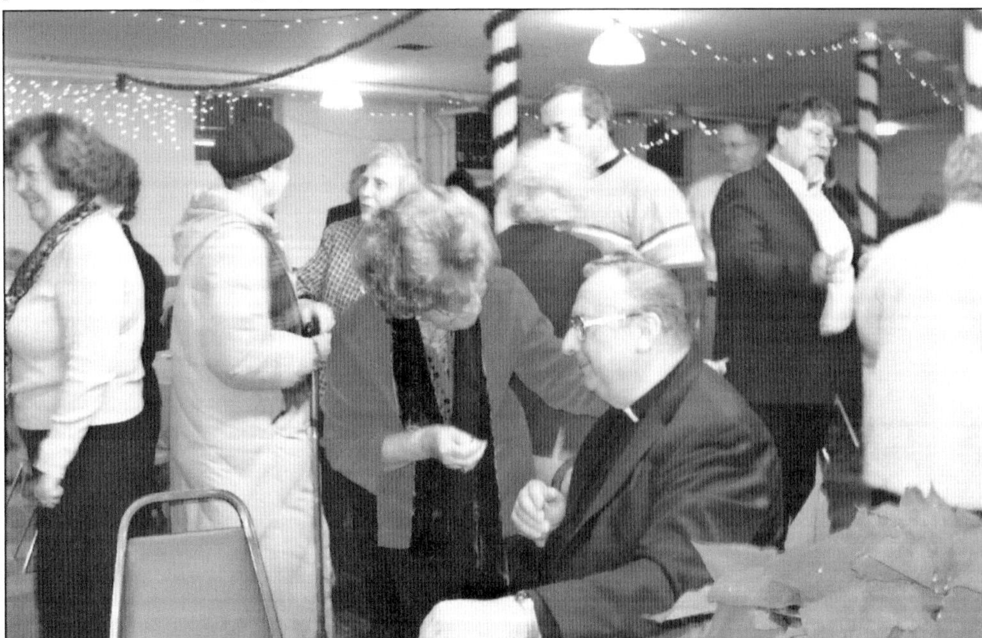

Msgr. Stanley Parfienczyk hosted the 2010 annual St. John the Baptist community *oplatek* at the parish hall. Following tradition, parishioners break off a piece of each other's oplatek (an unconsecrated Christmas wafer) as they extend forgiveness for offenses over the past year and good wishes for the New Year. (RNC.)

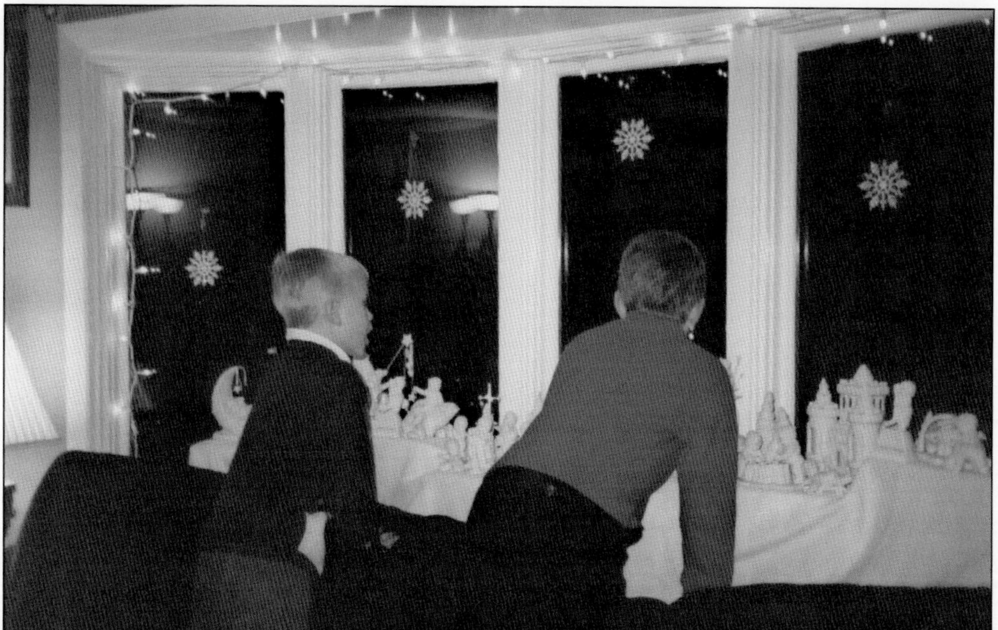

In 2008, Christmas Eve celebrations, the *wigilia* (meaning "vigil" or "watch"), began at the Ciampa house after the *pierwsza gwiazda* (first star) of the evening was sighted. Nicholas (left) and Andrew Carter were eager to find the star so the festivities could begin. The custom recalls the story of the Star of Bethlehem that led the three wise men to the manger. (RNC.)

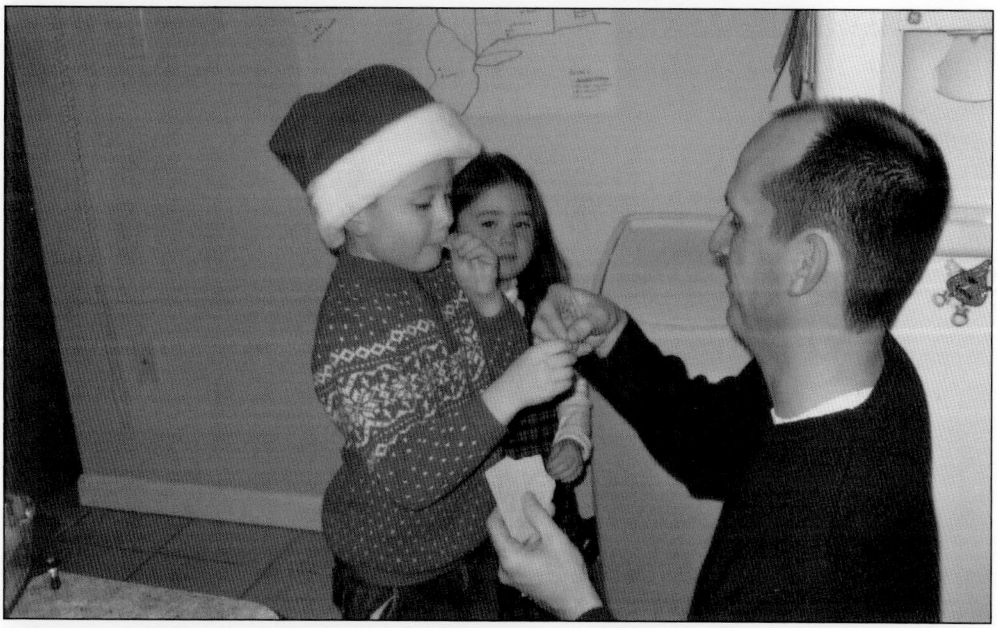

Jeff Carter passed on the tradition of oplatek to son Eric and daughter Mia in 2008. After breaking off a piece of each other's wafer and sharing a kiss with wishes for good health in the coming year, the wafer is eaten. Everyone is now ready for a meatless meal that may include mushroom *barszcz* (borscht), *kapusta* (sauerkraut), pierogi (dumplings), and fish. *Kolendy* (carols) are sung and gifts are exchanged. (RNC.)

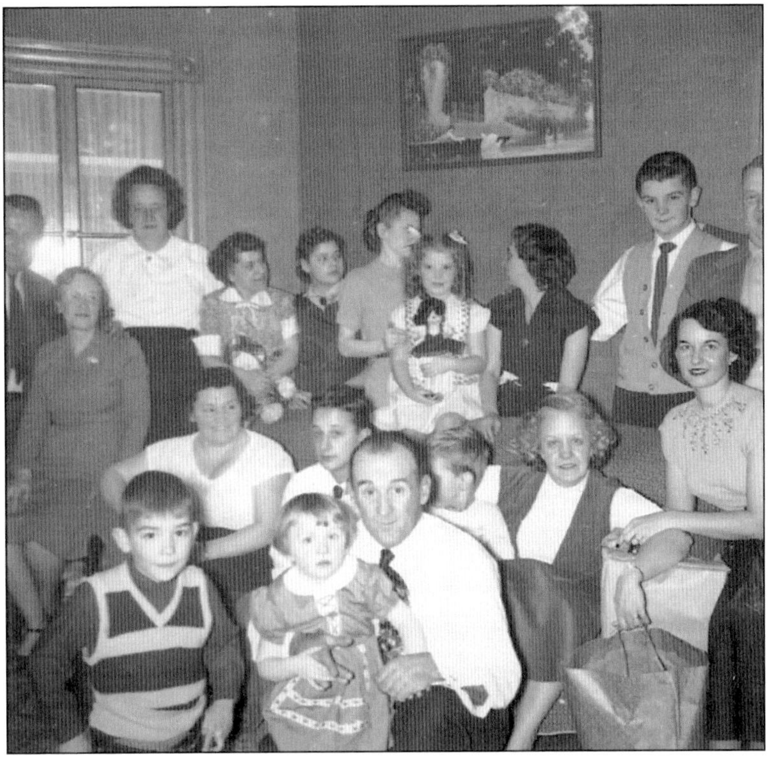

Three generations of the Plutnicki and Wilczenski families gathered to celebrate Christmas Eve, though the camera only captured half of those present in 1950! After dinner, oplatek, and gift giving, most of the family members headed out to midnight mass at St. John the Baptist Church. (FLW.)

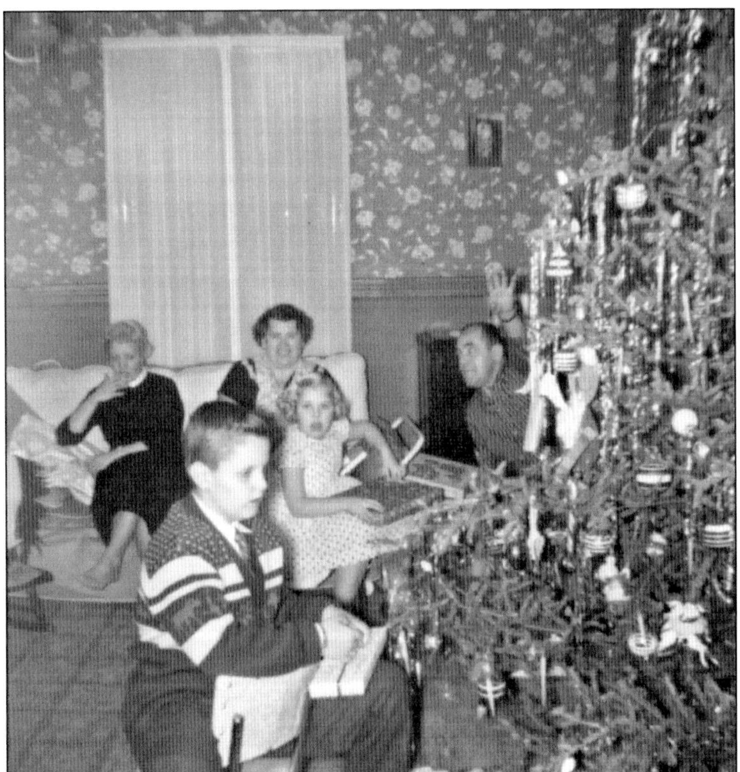

For Julianna and Joseph Plutnicki's grandchildren, cousins Larry and Felicia, opening presents was the highlight of *babcia* (grandmother) and *dziadzia's* (grandfather) Christmas Eve *wigilia* in the 1950s. Watching their son and daughter are Beatrice Plutnicki (left) and Genevieve (Plutnicki) Wilczenski (right). Uncle Matthew Plutnicki waved to the camera from behind the tree. (FLW.)

Following the Polish custom, Mary Nowak's Swieconka (Easter) food was blessed by the parish priest visiting her home on Holy Saturday in 1950, the day before Easter Sunday. The next day, Polish families carefully arranged an Easter table with blessed ham, kielbasa, decorated eggs, salt, butter, and homemade bread (*babka*). No one was allowed to cook on the holiest of holidays. (GNC.)

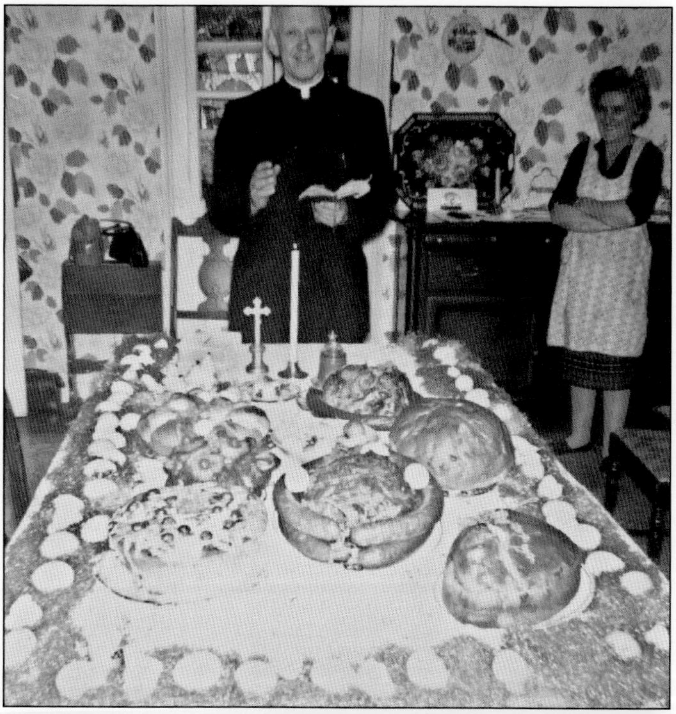

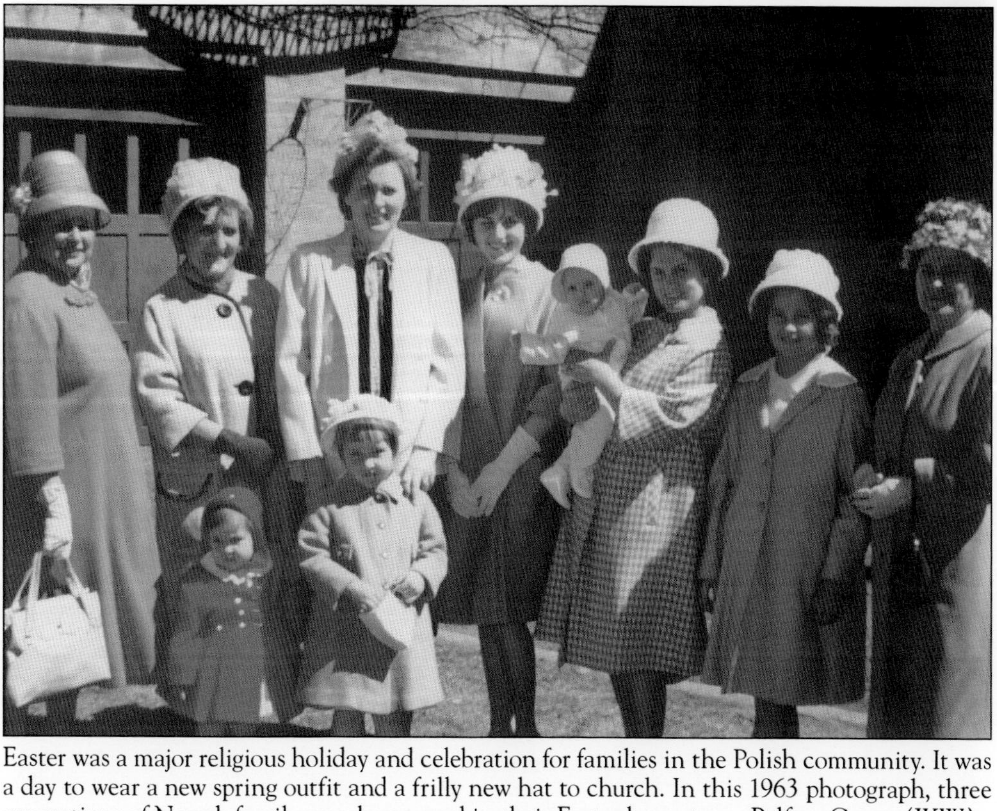

Easter was a major religious holiday and celebration for families in the Polish community. It was a day to wear a new spring outfit and a frilly new hat to church. In this 1963 photograph, three generations of Nowak family members posed in their Easter bonnets on Palfrey Court. (JKW.)

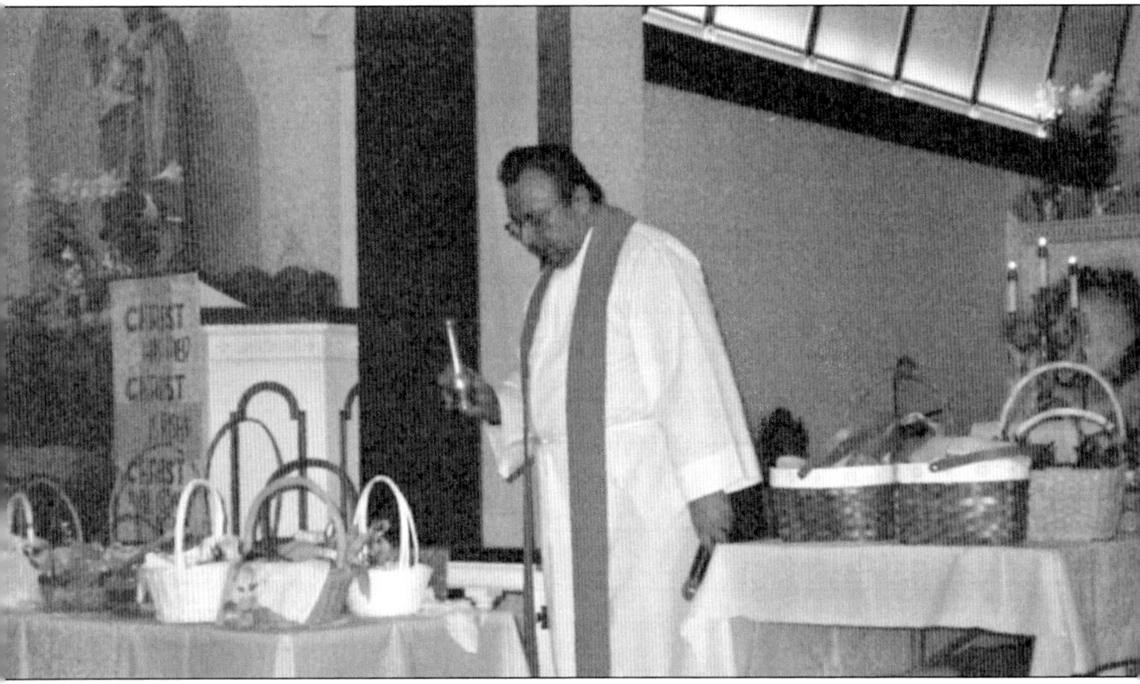

The Swieconka tradition now takes place at the church. The blessing of the Easter baskets is one of the most beloved Polish folk traditions. Families bring baskets of food to be blessed in gratitude to God for His gifts. Often the baskets are decorated with pussy willows, which is a symbol of Easter in Poland. In the picture, an array of baskets containing a sampling of Easter foods was blessed by Msgr. Stanislaw Parfienczyk at St. John the Baptist Church on Holy Saturday in 2009. The food items included in the baskets have symbolic meaning; for example, eggs (*jajka*) represent the renewal of life through the Resurrection, horseradish (*chrzan*) recalls the bitterness of Christ's death on the cross, salt (*sol*) represents purification, butter (*maslo*) molded as a lamb is a reminder of Christ as the Lamb of God, ham (*szynka*) is symbolic of abundance, and bread (*babka*) symbolizes the staff of life. (RNC.)

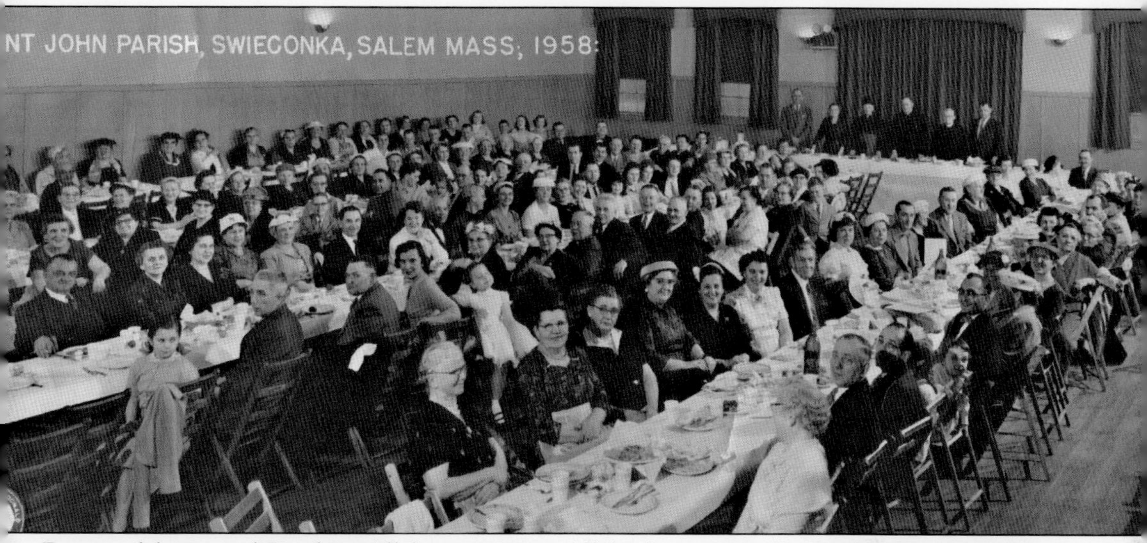

Easter celebrations (Wesolego Alleluja or Happy Alleluia) are generally family affairs, but the parishioners of St. John the Baptist also considered themselves as a family bonded by religious ties. After holiday festivities concluded within their own homes, the parishioners gathered for a Swieconka party at the church, usually the week after Easter. After fasting, meatless meals, and denial of treats through Lent (Wielki Post), a big part of the celebration of Easter was to eat the restricted foods. One tradition is to remove the shell of the blessed eggs and cut them into pieces to be shared among the "family" members to ensure good health. Eating the blessed foods was also supposed to bring good luck. Following those traditions, Easter 1958 was observed with a large community meal at the St. John the Baptist Parish Hall. (MMC.)

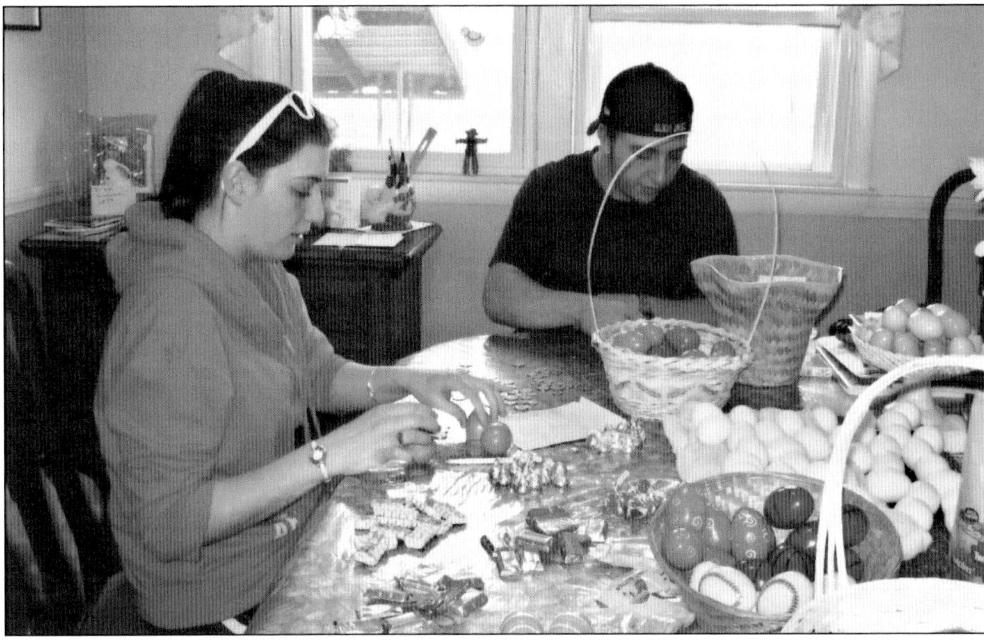

Decorating Easter eggs is a longstanding tradition in Poland, and there are different techniques to the art. Stephanie and Steve Ciampa used a vegetable dye of red onion skins to color hard-boiled eggs (*kraszanki*) and then drew designs on the eggs with wax (*pisanki*) in preparation for the Carter family 2010 Easter celebration. (RNC.)

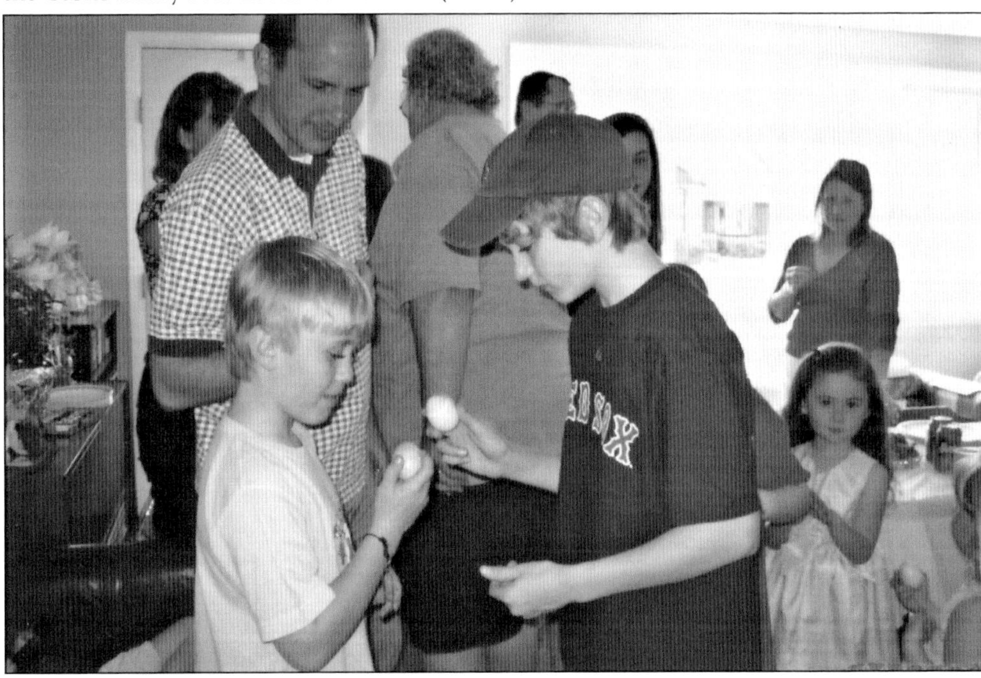

Brothers Nicholas (left) and Andrew Carter played *wybitki* (also known as *walatka*) in 2010. Wybitki is a traditional Easter challenge of hitting hard-boiled eggs against each other until one breaks. After the competition, the holder of the intact egg is the winner. An egg-rolling contest (*kulanie jajec*) is another Polish tradition and a Carter family favorite. (RNC.)

Four

Milestones

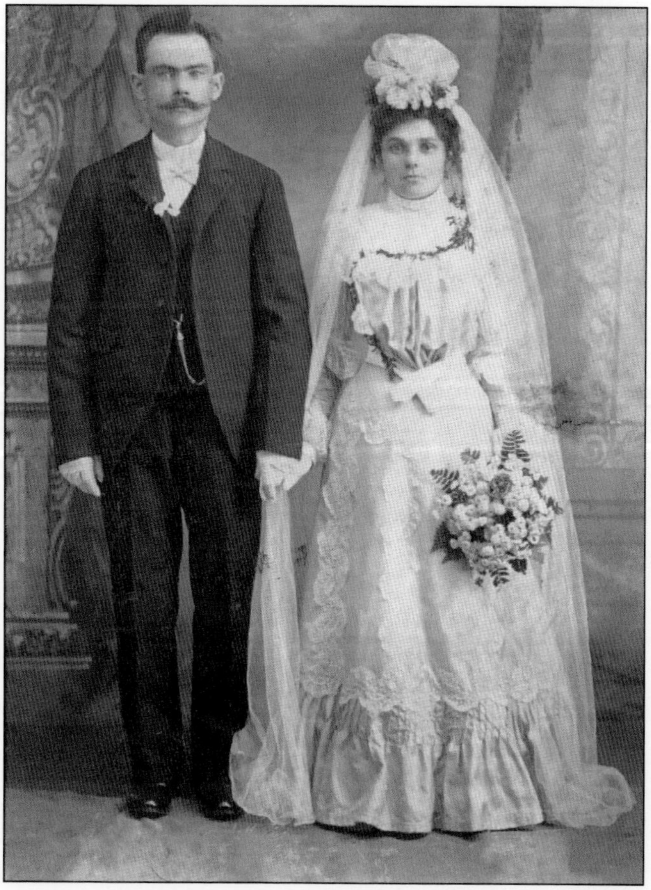

Here is a photograph of Teofil and Anastasia Bartnicki from their wedding day, June 15, 1902. Weddings were eagerly anticipated social events in Polish Salem. Receptions could go on for days with lots of food, drink, and dancing to feed and entertain the many guests who attended. (LBM.)

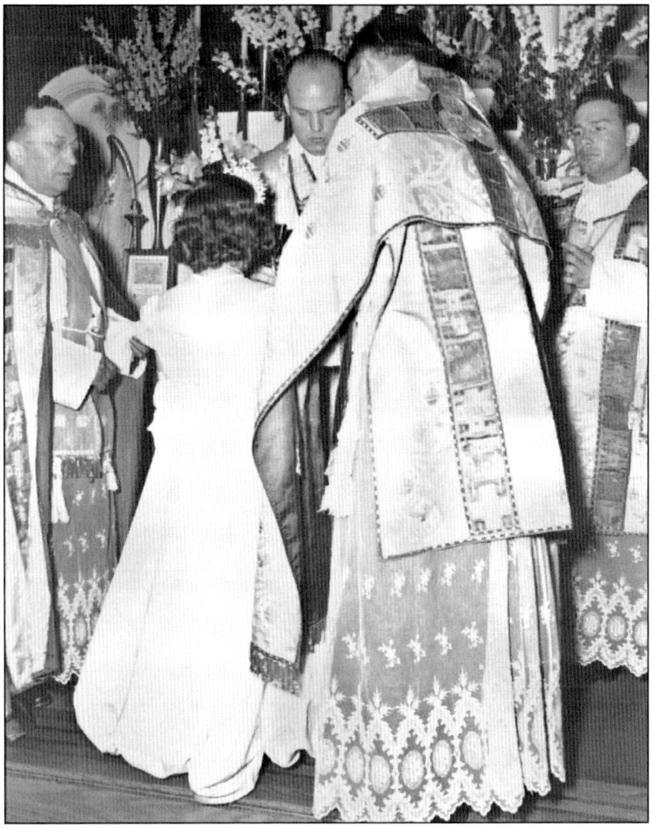

After ordination, the next major event in priestly life is celebrating the first mass. Alicia Wroblewski (Maguire) presented the chalice to newly ordained Fr. Louis Bilicky as he officiated at his first mass before family, friends, and well-wishers at St. John the Baptist Church in 1949. (AWM.)

Pamela Ann Czypryna (Indra) was baptized by Rev. Ladislaus Sikora in the sacristy of St. John the Baptist Church in 1951. Her uncle Thomas Meler and aunt Helen Meler Manning were godparents. Pamela's godmother made her christening dress from a silk parachute given to her husband, John F. Manning, a Merchant Marine, by a paratrooper rescued from the ocean during World War II. (MMC.)

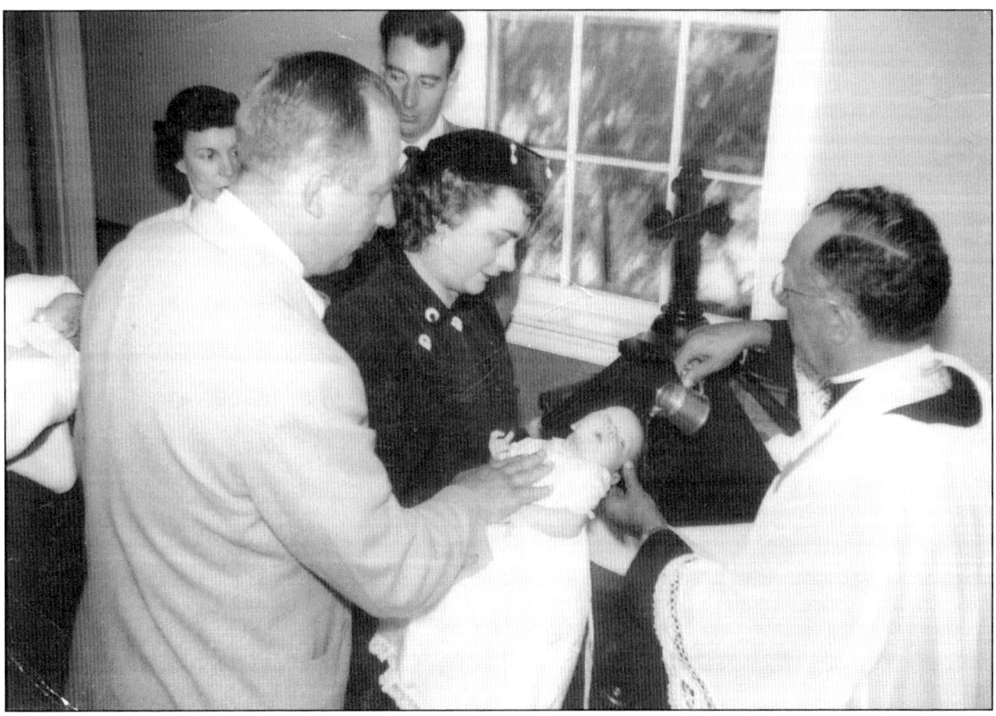

Education was important in the Polish community, and even very early school accomplishments were recognized. Pictured in academic regalia, Margaret Zdancewicz (Wilkens) was a member of the graduating kindergarten class from the old St. John the Baptist School in 1960. The picture was taken at the Boltrukewicz family home on Herbert Street. (MZW.)

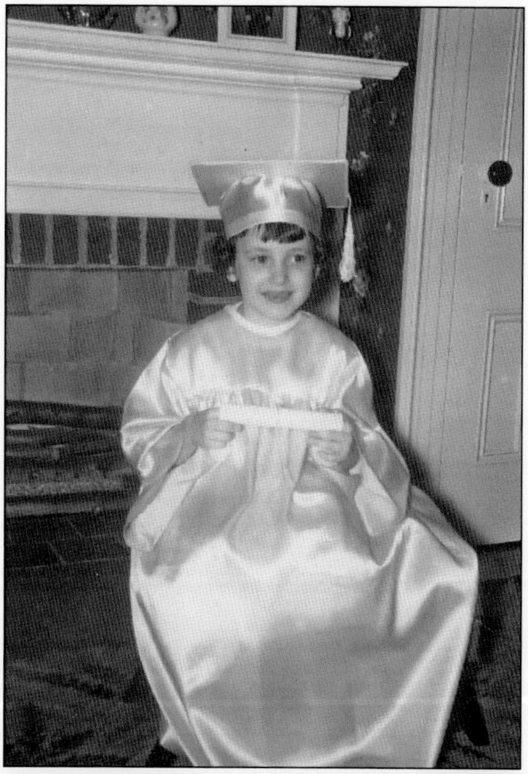

School transitions were always marked with traditional academic rituals and a church service for children in the Polish community. After receiving their diplomas from Father Sikora, smiling St. John the Baptist kindergarten students posed for a picture with him to celebrate their promotion to first grade. This class was among the first to attend the new school on St. Peter Street in the early 1960s. (SW.)

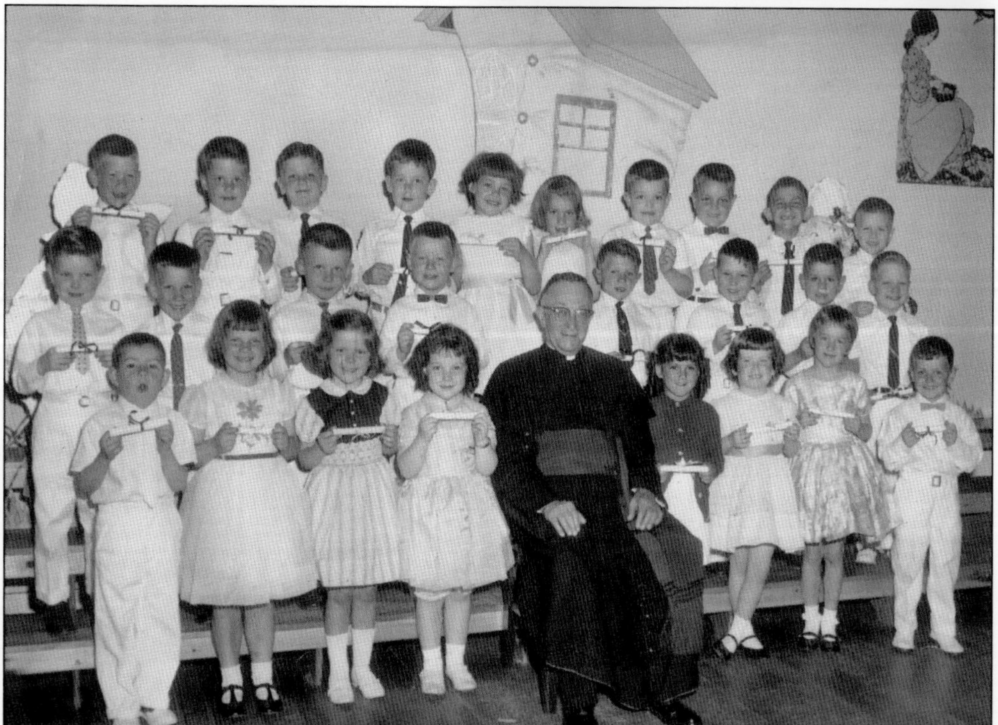

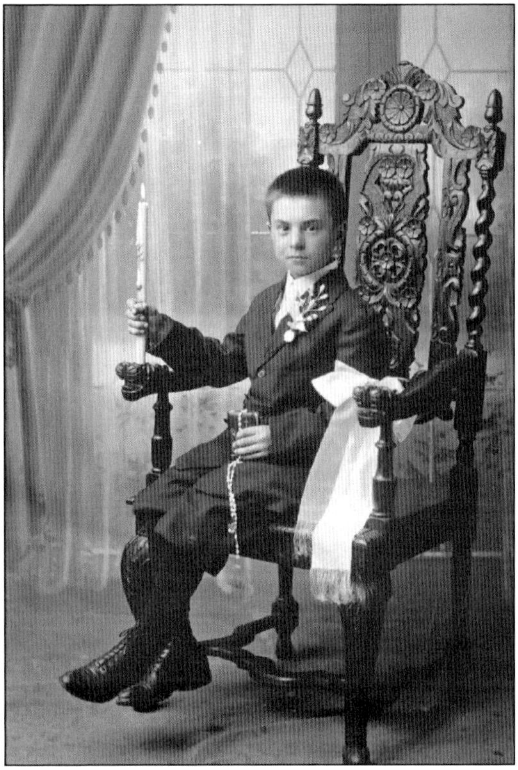

Looking angelic, Edmund Bartnicki was dressed in his First Holy Communion finery for this portrait taken around 1917. Eddie was the son of Teofil and Anastasia Bartnicki. He remained an active parishioner at St. John the Baptist throughout his life, leading the choir with his beautiful tenor singing voice. (LBM.)

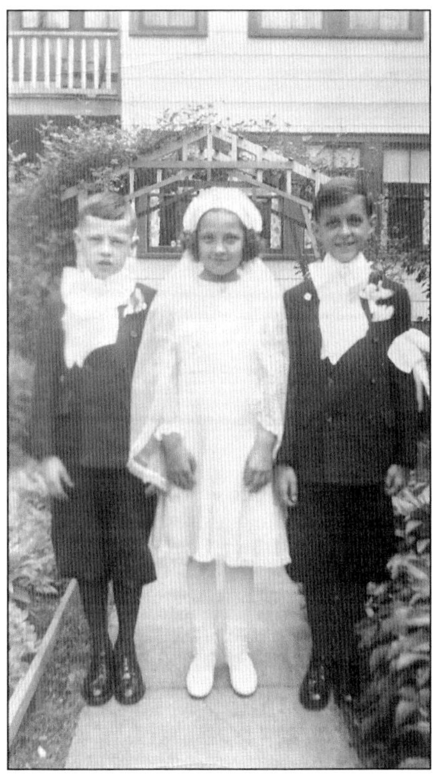

Pictured from left to right, Fred Beaupre, Alice Pronska, and Clarence Wojciechowski were decked out in their best clothes for First Communion services at St. John the Baptist Church. Parents took many pictures to record all the events of their children's special day. Childhood sweethearts Alice and Clarence, pictured here about 1940, were married years later. (APW.)

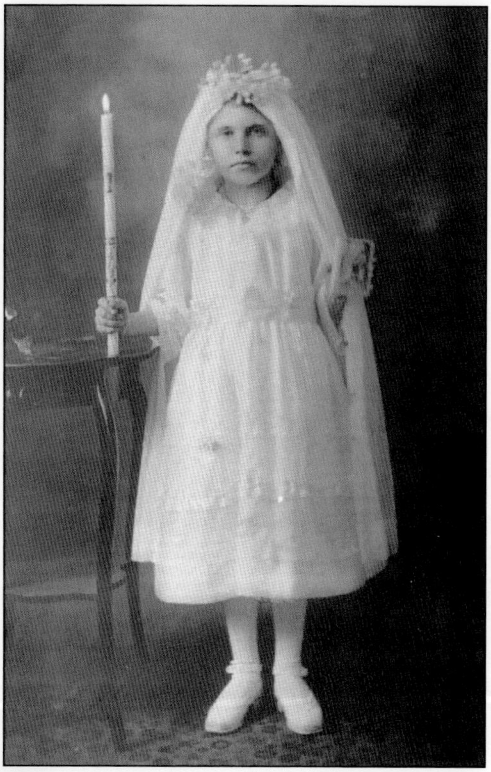

First Communion was a significant event in the Polish community and a major milestone in the lives of the children. The occasion was marked with elaborate and standing room–only church services. After the religious ceremonies, families celebrated at home, and the new communicants received gifts. Girls wore fancy white dresses and veils. Parents often arranged for formal photographs to be taken to record the event. Standing with a candle and prayer book, Genevieve Plutnicki (Wilczenski) was photographed for her First Communion on May 30, 1920. Thirty-seven years later, First Communion dress styles were quite different when Genevieve's daughter, Felicia, posed for her picture on May 18, 1957. (Both, FLW.)

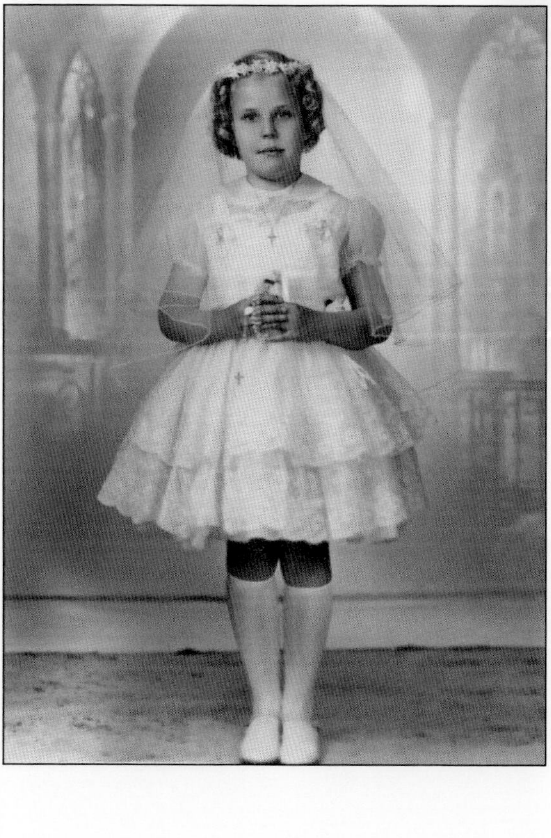

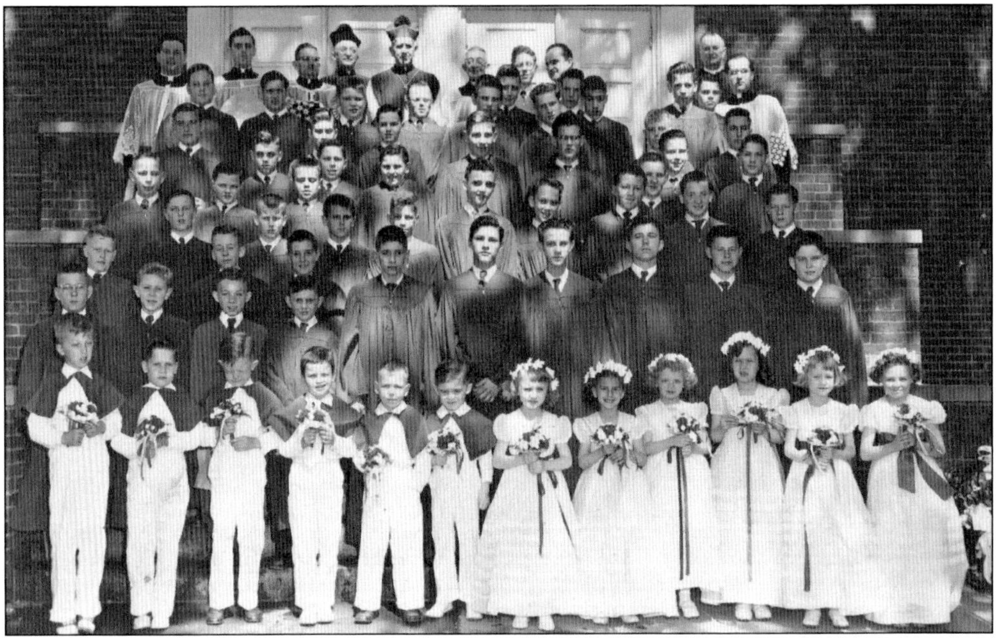

Confirmation is one of the seven sacraments and a major rite of passage from adolescence to adulthood for Catholics. In Confirmation, the Holy Spirit is called upon to continue the gifts of Baptism and to bind the newly confirmed to a deeper commitment to the life of the church. The Bishop makes a sign of the cross on the person's forehead using chrism oil with the following words: "Be sealed with the gifts of the Holy Spirit." Boys in an early 1950s St. John the Baptist Confirmation class, dressed in scarlet robes, were photographed after leaving the church ceremonies. Ann Szybiak prepared to attend her Confirmation service in 1966. Girls wore white robes with red collars and caps. (Above, PLAV; below, CSB.)

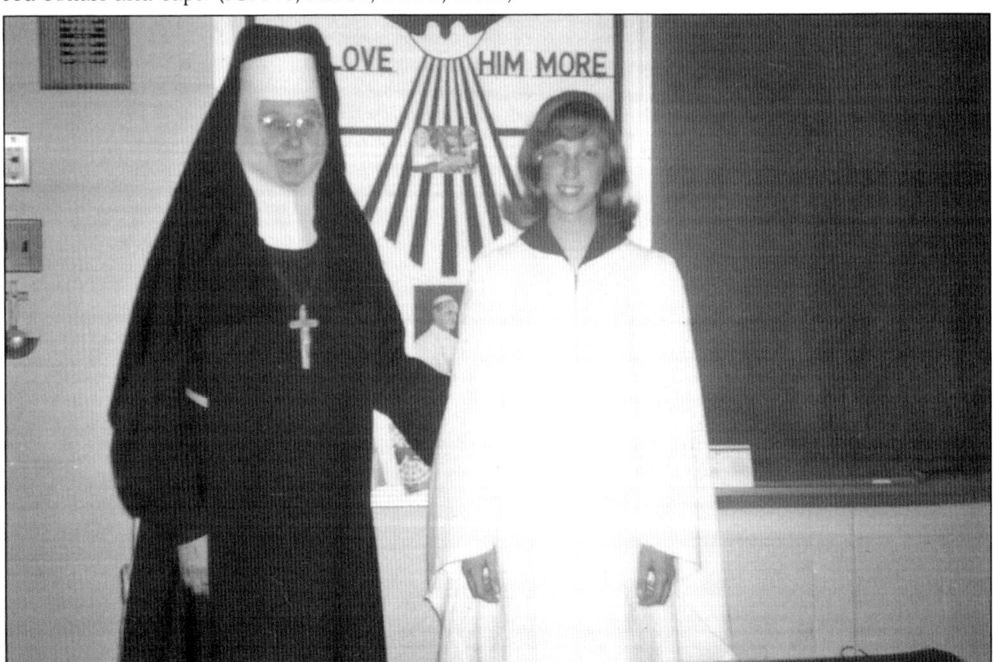

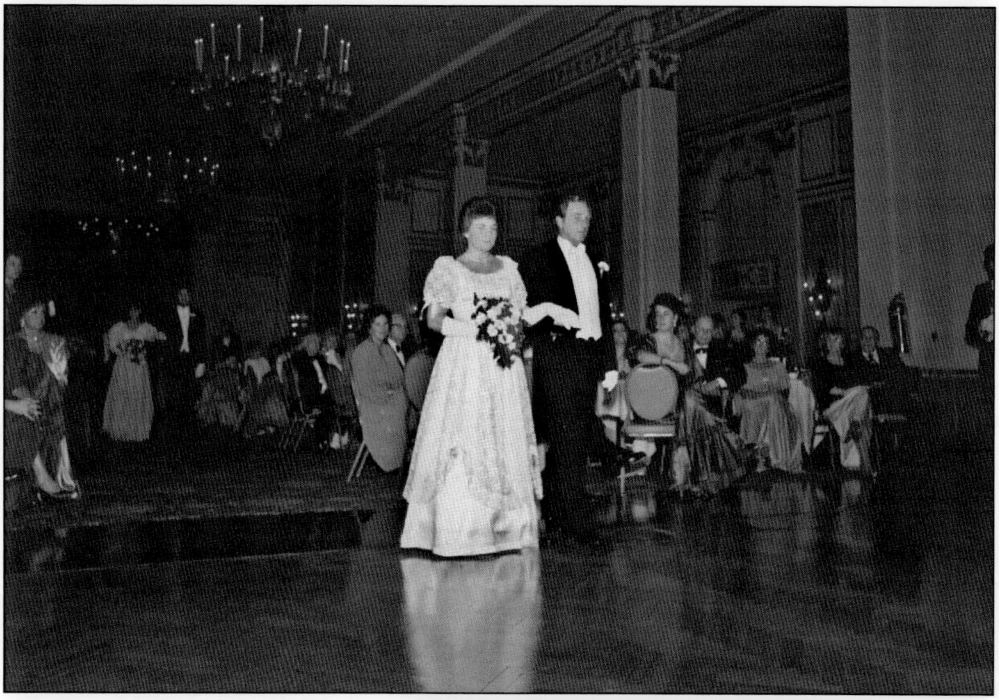

Debutante Jill Zujewski was presented to society and the community by her father, John, at the 21st Biennial Kosciuszko Foundation Presentation Ball in Boston, Massachusetts, on November 29, 1985. The event was jointly sponsored with the Massachusetts Federation of Polish Women's Clubs. For over 70 years and continuing to this day, the Kosciuszko Debutante Council invites applications from young women with a background of scholastic achievement and community service to be honored at the ball. Jill's sister Julianne Zujewski also made her debut in 1985 and is pictured dancing with her father at the Presentation Ball. (Both, ASZ.)

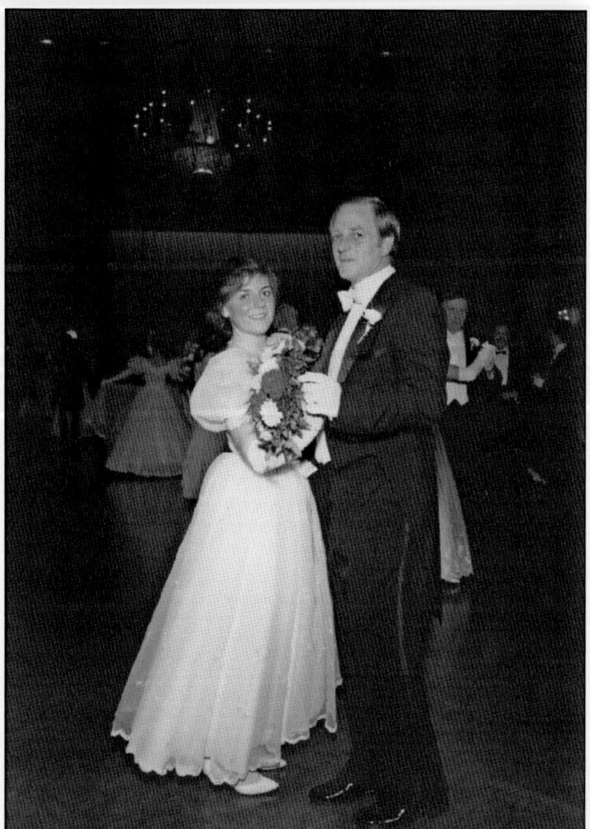

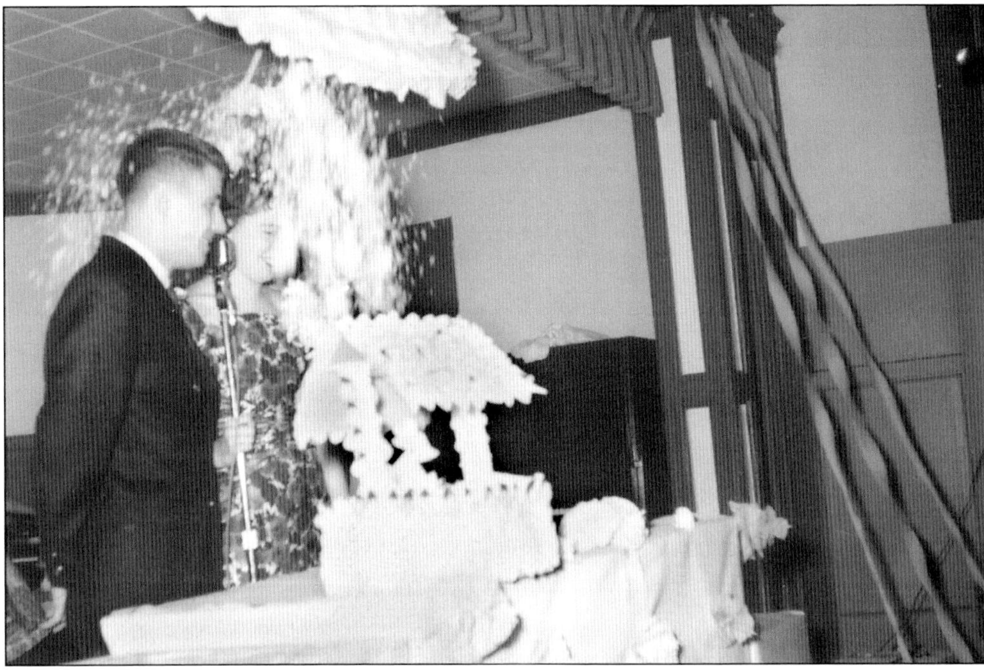

Falcons' Hall was the site of many bridal showers and weddings for members of the Polish community. Bridal showers were spectacular affairs. Engaged to be married in August 1959, Dorothy Hincman and Stanley "Sammy" Semenchuk stood under the umbrella to be showered with confetti. Rows of guests were seated to admire the gifts as they were opened. Family and friends of the bride-to-be prepared the sandwiches and *paczkis* for dessert. At Polish bridal showers, the men arrived after all the gifts were opened. There would be a meal and often an open bar with an orchestra playing polkas for dancing. (Both, DHS.)

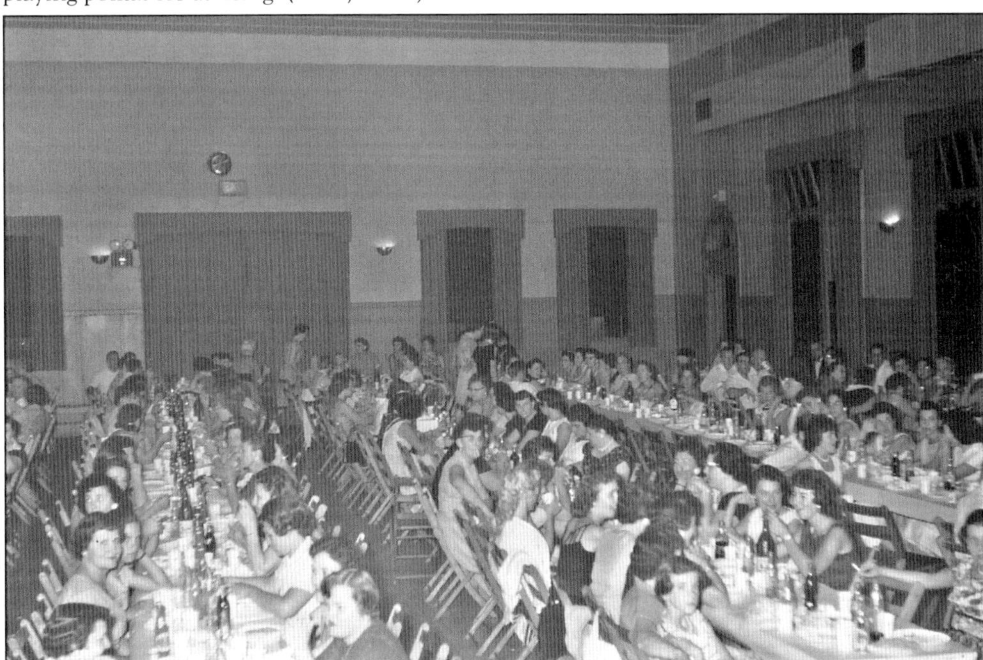

Emigrating from the Galicia in Poland, Polish Austrians John Furtek and Apolonia Wojnarowicz came to the United States in the early 1900s and married about 1907. The Furteks raised a family of four children: Cecilia, Stanley, Wanda, and Julian. They lived on Daniels, Hardy, and English, which were side streets off of Derby, moving around to acquire more room for their growing family or to find more affordable housing. (RNC.)

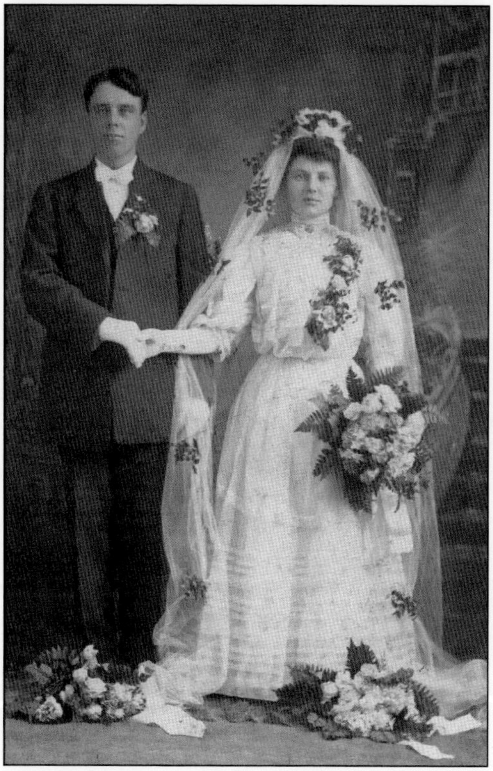

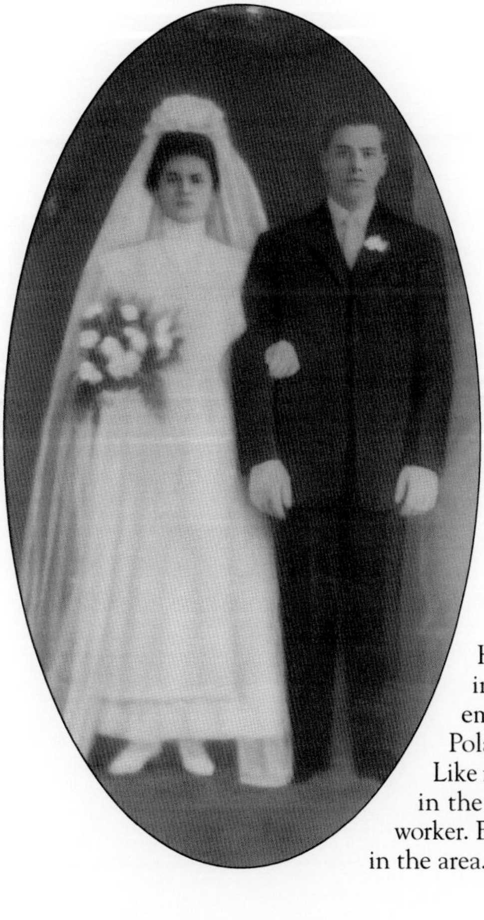

Honorata Burda and Victor Szczuka were married in 1919 when she was 16 and he was 23. Honorata emigrated from the Southern Galician region of Poland and Victor from Russian-occupied Poland. Like many of their Polish community peers, she worked in the Naumkeag (Pequot) Mill, and he was a leather worker. Both came to Salem to join other family members in the area. (RC.)

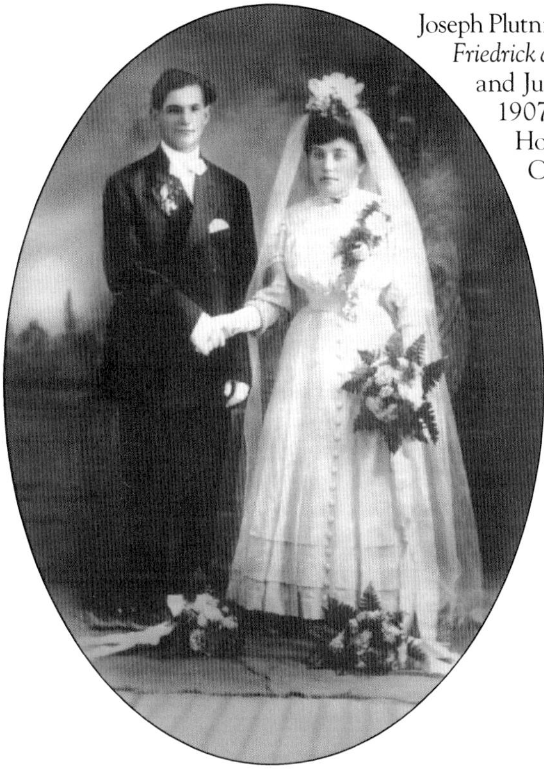

Joseph Plutnicki emigrated from Poland in 1906 aboard the *Friedrick der Grosse* steamship out of Bremen, Germany, and Julianna Nidzgorski arrived at Ellis Island in 1907 aboard the *Ryndam* out of Rotterdam, Holland. They married at St. John the Baptist Church on September 19, 1909. (FLW.)

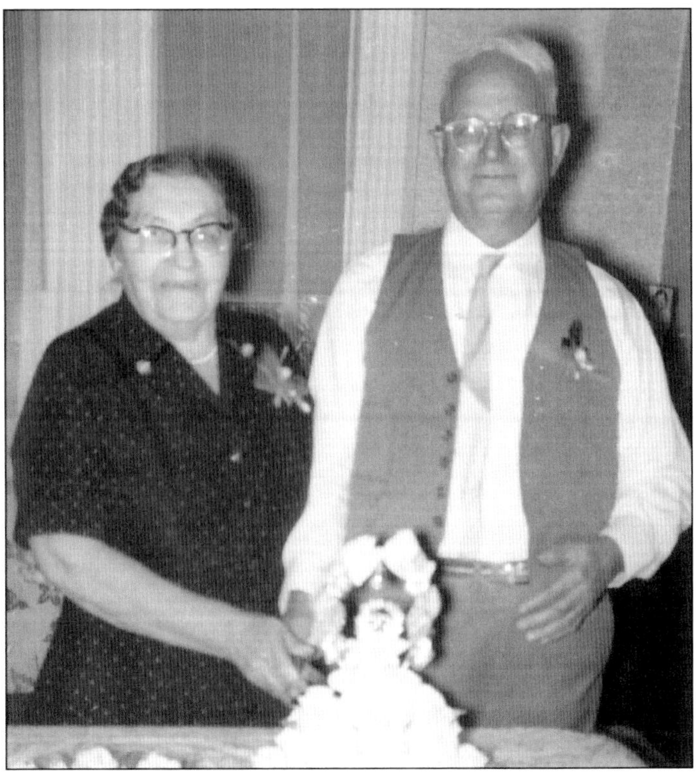

The *Salem Evening News* reported the occasion of Joseph and Julianna Plutnicki's 25th wedding anniversary in 1934 with 200 family and friends in attendance at the Falcons' Hall. Frank Wroblewski was master of ceremonies. By the time of celebrating their 50th wedding anniversary in 1959 (pictured), they had moved away from the Polish neighborhood to a home in a predominantly Irish section of North Salem. (FLW.)

St. Joseph's Hall was the site of many parties and wedding receptions for the Polish community. Over 200 family and friends received an invitation to the nuptials of Genevieve Plutnicki and Louis Wilczenski on September 17, 1933. The guests returned to continue the celebration the next day! (FLW.)

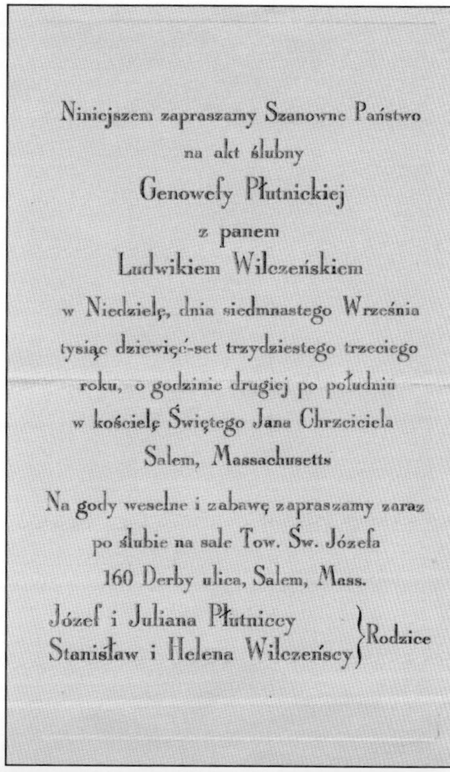

Niniejszem zapraszamy Szanowne Państwo
na akt ślubny
Genowefy Płutnickiej
z panem
Ludwikiem Wilczeńskiem
w Niedzielę, dnia siedmnastego Września
tysiąc dziewięć-set trzydziestego trzeciego
roku, o godzinie drugiej po południu
w kościelę Świętego Jana Chrzciciela
Salem, Massachusetts

Na gody weselne i zabawę zapraszamy zaraz
po ślubie na sale Tow. Św. Józefa
160 Derby ulica, Salem, Mass.

Józef i Juliana Płutniccy
Stanisław i Helena Wilczeńscy } Rodzice

Here, the Plutnicki-Wilczenski 1933 wedding party members are, from left to right, (seated) Sophia Zmijewska, Stella Welenc, Genevieve (bride), Mary Plutnicki (maid of honor), and Sophie Kocialka; (standing) John Wilczenski, Matthew Plutnicki, Louis Wilczenski (groom), Stanley Wroblewski, and William Kowalski. (FLW.)

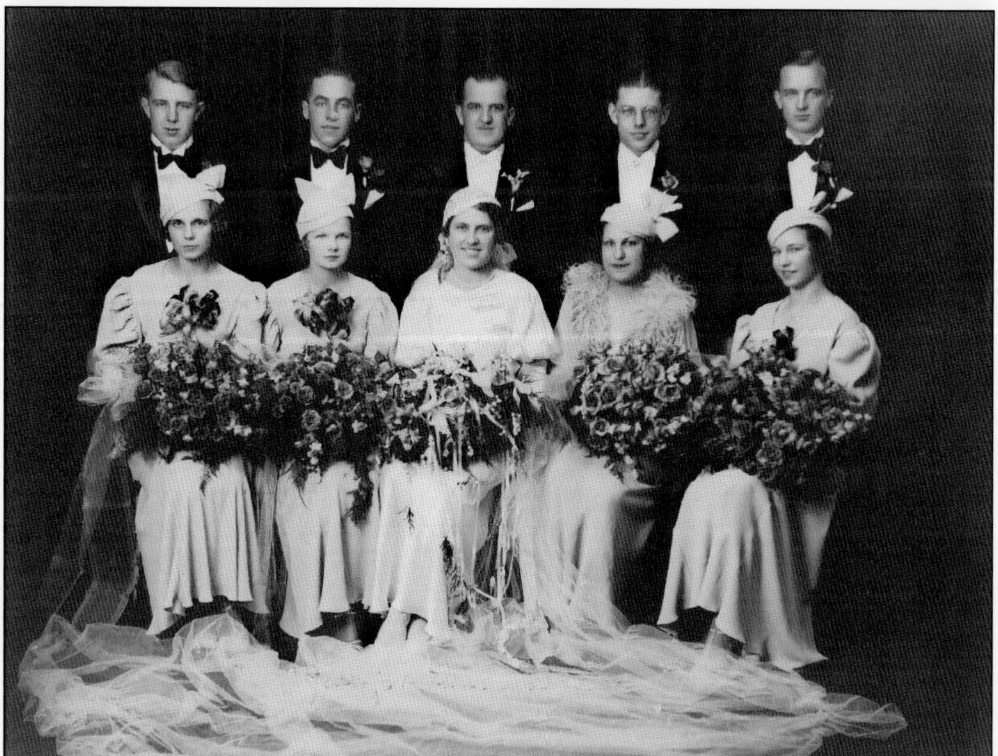

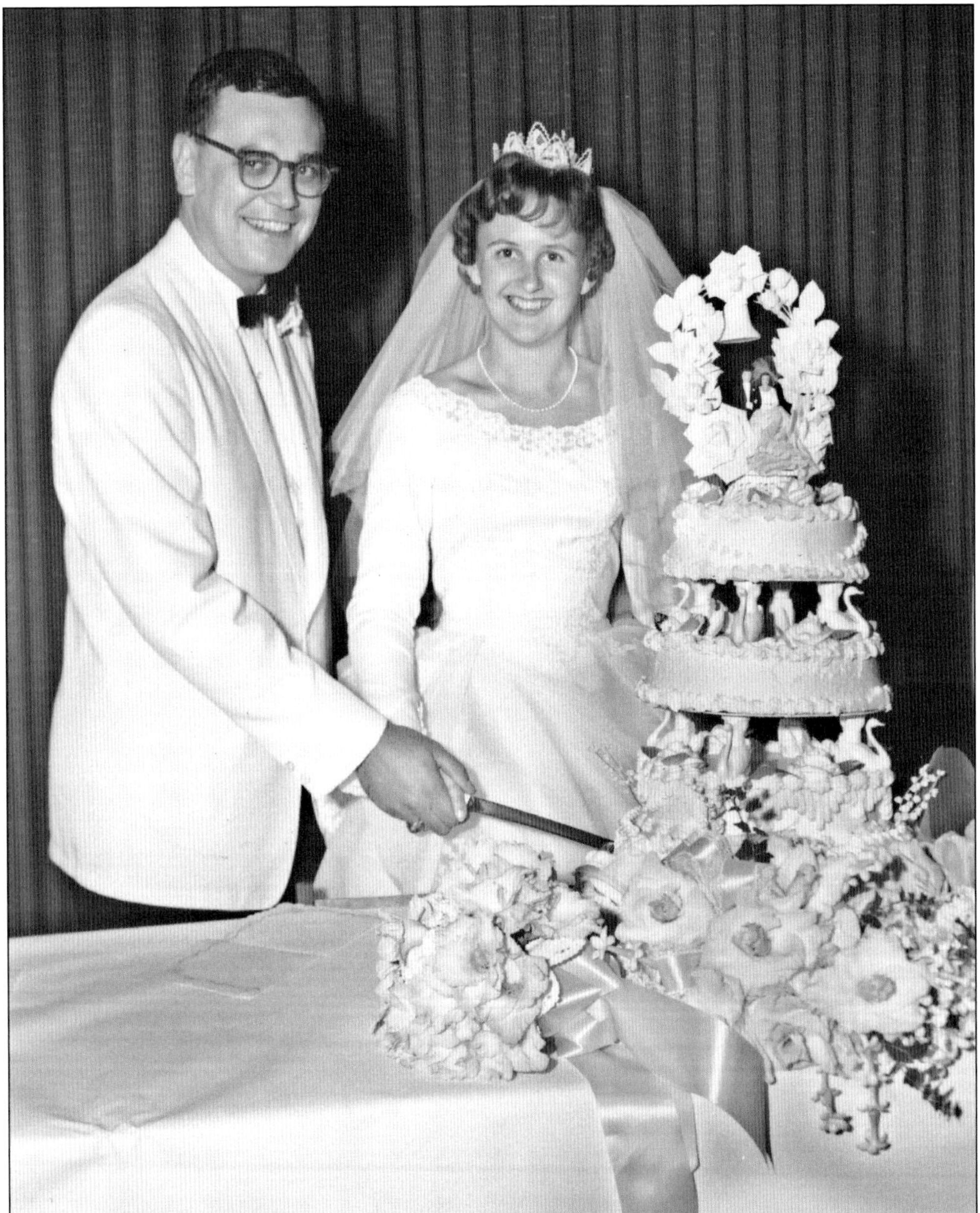

Many Polish weddings were held at Falcons' Hall on Cousins Street in Salem, the former headquarters of the Polish Falcons Nest No. 188. Leroy Carter and the new Rita Nowak Carter are pictured cutting the cake during their reception on September 15, 1963. Over 300 people attended the wedding celebration. Grabas, the caterer, served his specialty family-style turkey dinner, quickly refilling every plate as soon as it was emptied. Later, Buddy Walker's Warszawicki Orchestra played polkas so folks could dance off the calories! At the time of his marriage, Roy was an ensign in the Navy with orders to report for duty. The wedding was almost postponed! Luckily, Roy's naval destroyer, the USS *Davis*, needed last minute repairs and was delayed in deploying to the Caribbean to monitor compliance with agreements ending the Cuban missile crisis. The newlyweds were able to take few days off for a Canadian honeymoon. (RNC.)

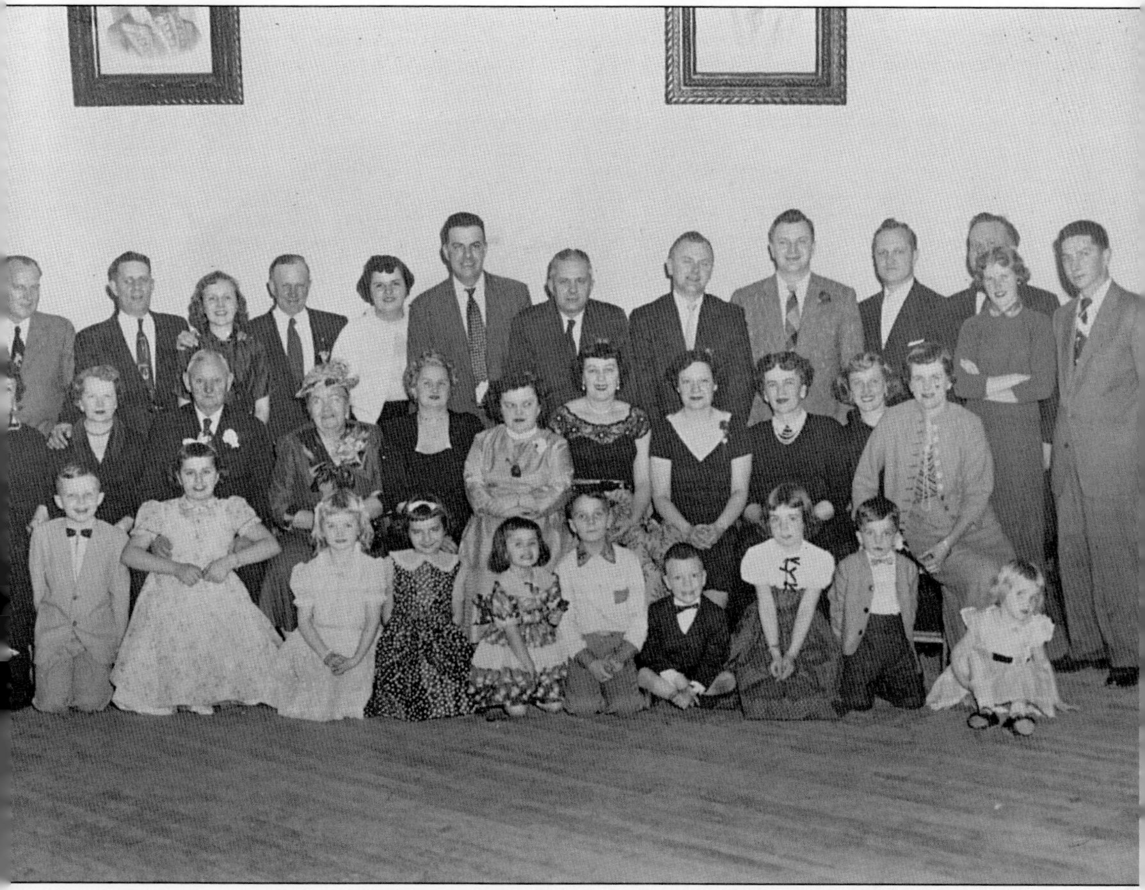

Wedding anniversaries were a reason to celebrate long-lasting marriages and to reunite growing extended families. Family members would all pitch in to make sure the occasion was a very special and memorable one. In the 1950s, St. Joseph's Hall was still a central meeting place for celebrations that brought together family members who lived within the Salem Polish community as well as those who had moved away from the neighborhood. Several generations of the Welenc family met again at St. Joseph's to mark a significant golden wedding anniversary milestone. Pictured here, Ignatius and Marianna Welenc, seated in the second row, third and fourth from the left, observed their 50th year of marriage in 1953 at a party given by their eight children and sixteen grandchildren. (BPR.)

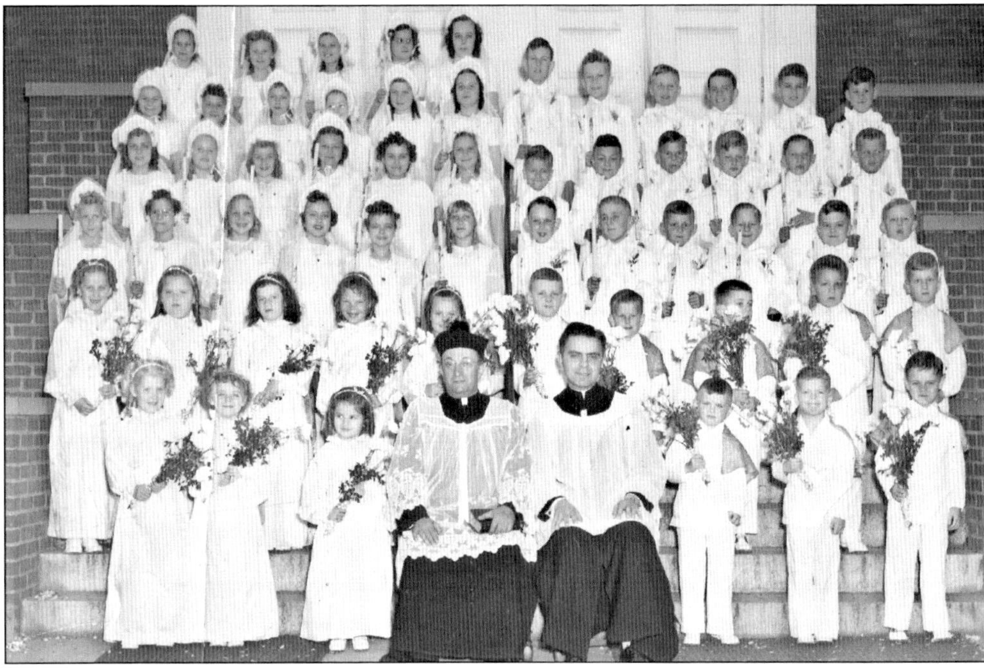

These pictures show children growing up in St. John the Baptist Parish and reaching major religious and educational milestones in their Catholic upbringing. Family and friends attended ceremonies to recognize those important events in their children's lives. First Communion was a highlight of childhood that Catholics always remember. Holy Communion recipients in 1947 were photographed following the church service at St. John's. Five years after that 1947 Communion photograph, a number of those same children were photographed in 1952 as the eighth-grade graduates of St. John the Baptist School. Fathers Sikora and Lucas presided at their graduation ceremony. (Above, PLAV; below, PP.)

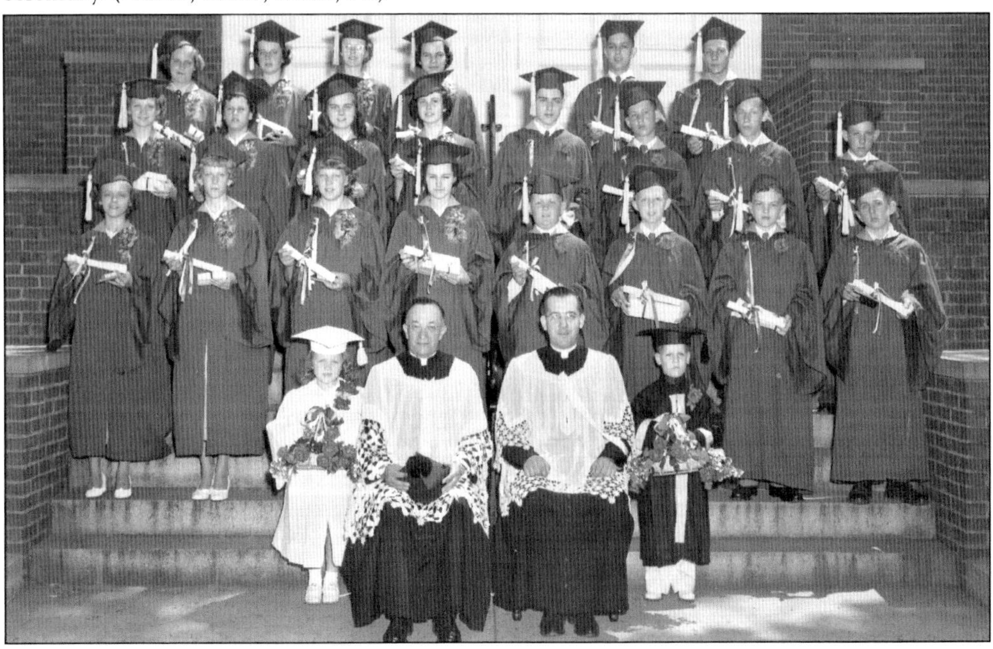

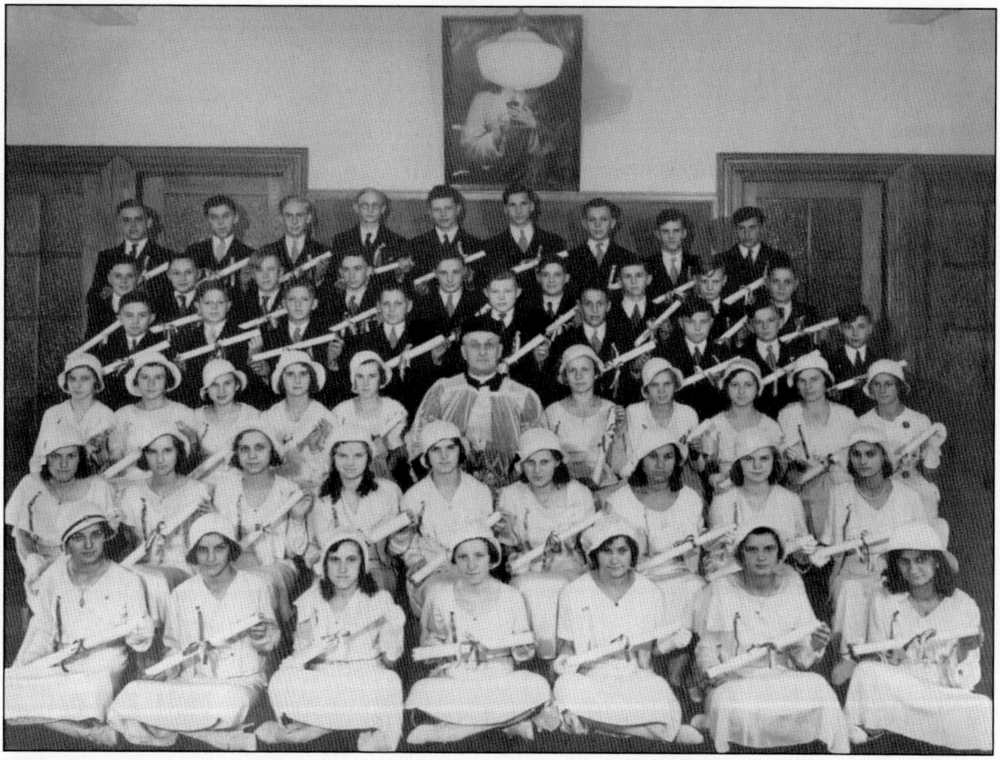

The class of 1932 of St. John the Baptist School was photographed with Father Czubek for its graduation picture. Rev. Joseph Czubek was the first pastor of St. John the Baptist Parish, serving the parish from its inception in 1903 until his death in 1940. (MZW.)

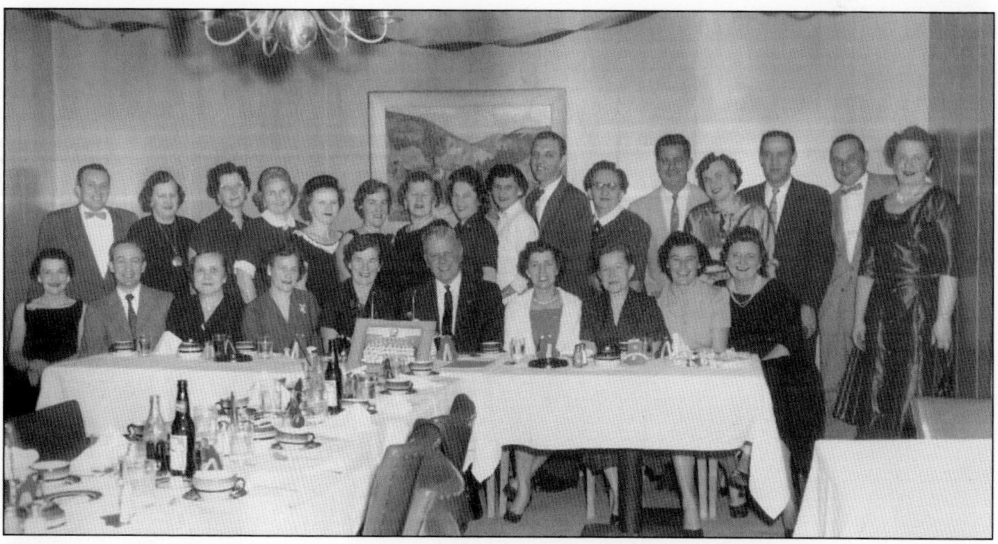

Elementary school reunions are quite an event. The relationships formed during those early years between the St. John the Baptist schoolchildren endured over time. Twenty years later in 1951, many members of the class of 1932 met again to reconnect and renew their friendships. (DO.)

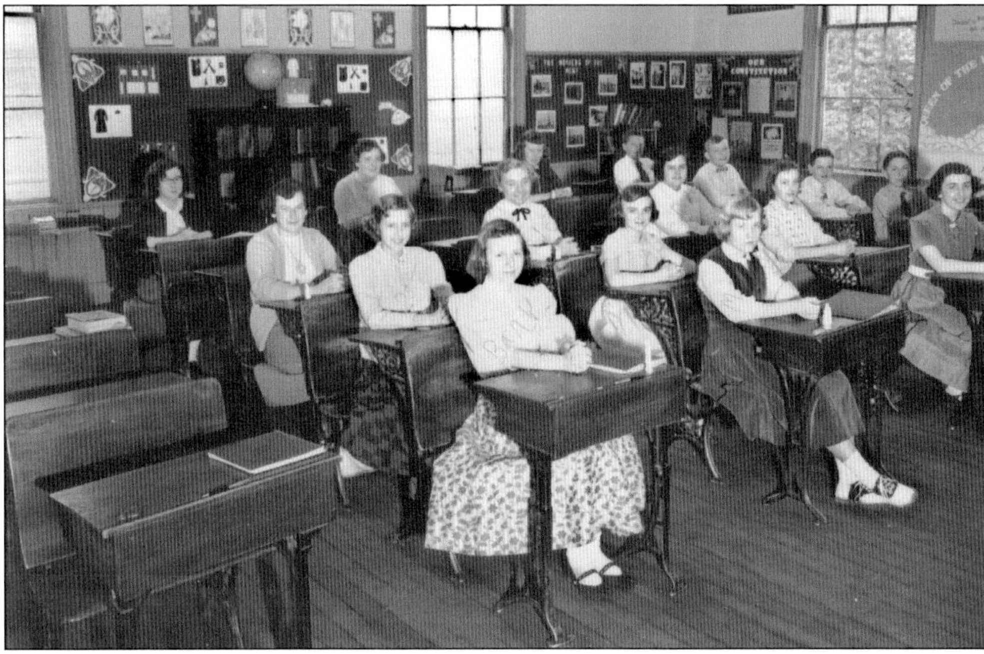

For this class picture, eighth-graders were seated at attention at their desks in the old St. John the Baptist School. Students are, from front to back, (first row) Barbara Pszenny, Dorothy Kufchinska, Celia Carter, and Mary Watis; (second row) Marijane Plecinoga, Alice Sobiesielska, Alicia Mendalka, and Clare Foley; (third row) Celia Negri, Linda Baldwin, Diane Marquis, and Lori Szezechowicz; (fourth row) Ronald Ouellette, unidentified, Thomas Meler, and Charles Kozlowski. At the end of the school year, in the spring of 1954, those eighth-grade students completed their grammar school studies and celebrated their graduation with a class photograph. (Above, LBM; below, ASZ.)

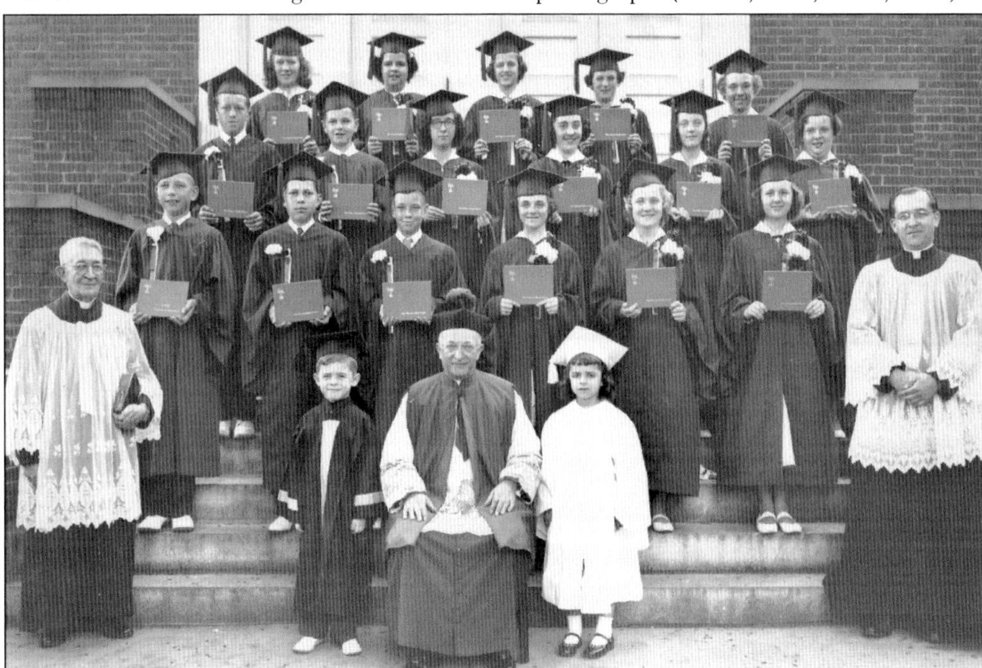

Five

St. John the Baptist Parish

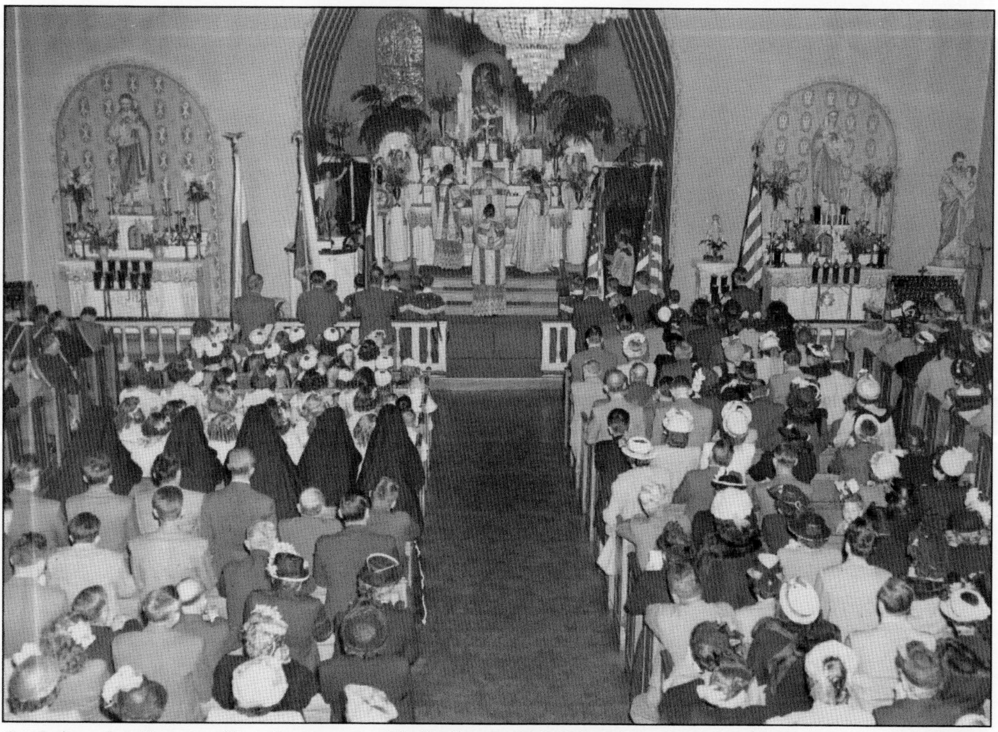

St. John the Baptist Parish was established in 1903. The present church building, purchased in 1908 from the Central Baptist Church, still conducts masses in Polish. The church filled to capacity on May 4, 1949, for the first mass of one of its own parishioners, Fr. Louis Bilicky. Other parishioners ordained to the priesthood were Rev. L. Ciesinski (1927), Rev. F. Miaskiewicz (1937), Rev. S. Miaskiewicz (1947), and Rev. F. Slejzer (1953). (PP.)

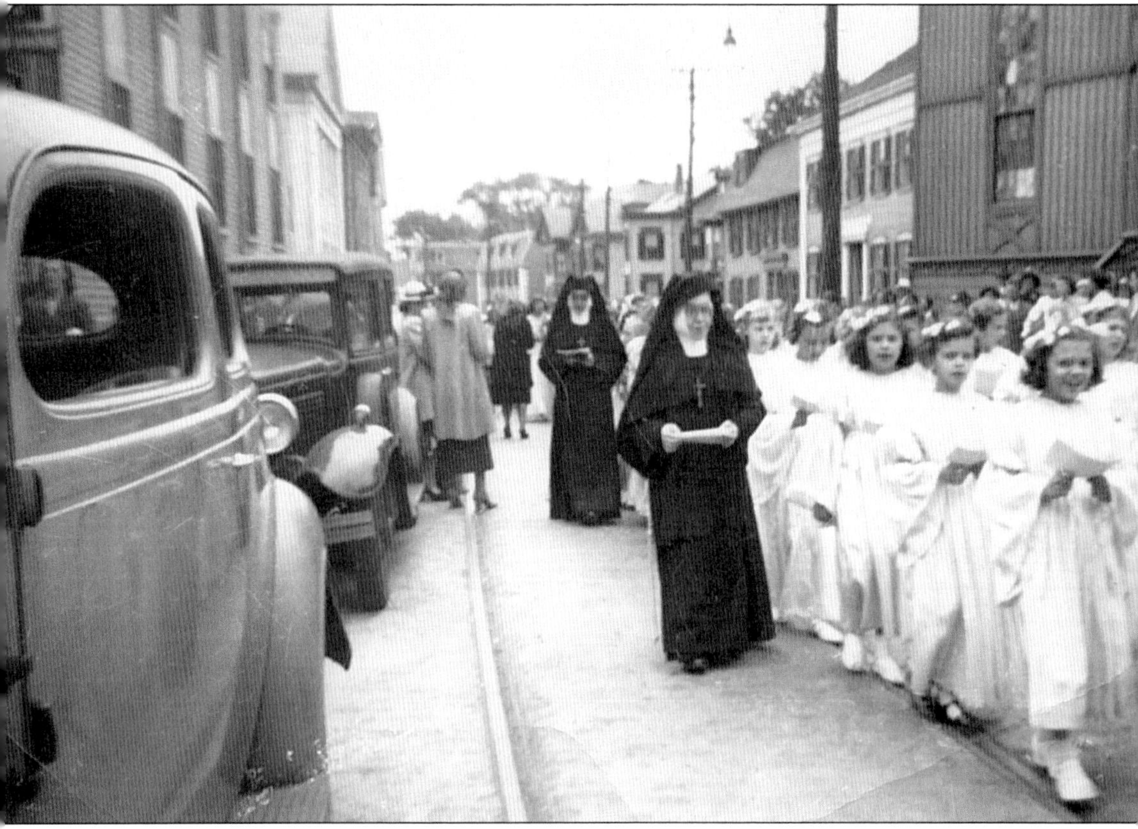

Catholicism was an especially important aspect of Polish identity in the late 19th century and first half of the 20th century. May processions were exciting events for all the schoolchildren in Salem's Polish community. The procession, usually held on a Sunday at the beginning of May, actually encompassed a number of the month's important occasions for the parishioners: the religious admiration for the Mother of God, Polish Constitution Day, Mother's Day, and First Communion. A musical band led the procession that started at St. John the Baptist School on Herbert Street, paraded around Federal, Washington, and Church Streets, and ended at St. John the Baptist Church on St. Peter Street to honor the Blessed Mother Mary by placing a crown on her statue. In the picture are the Felician nuns, who had a special devotion to Mary, directing the 1947 May procession as it started its march from Herbert Street onto Essex Street. (LBM.)

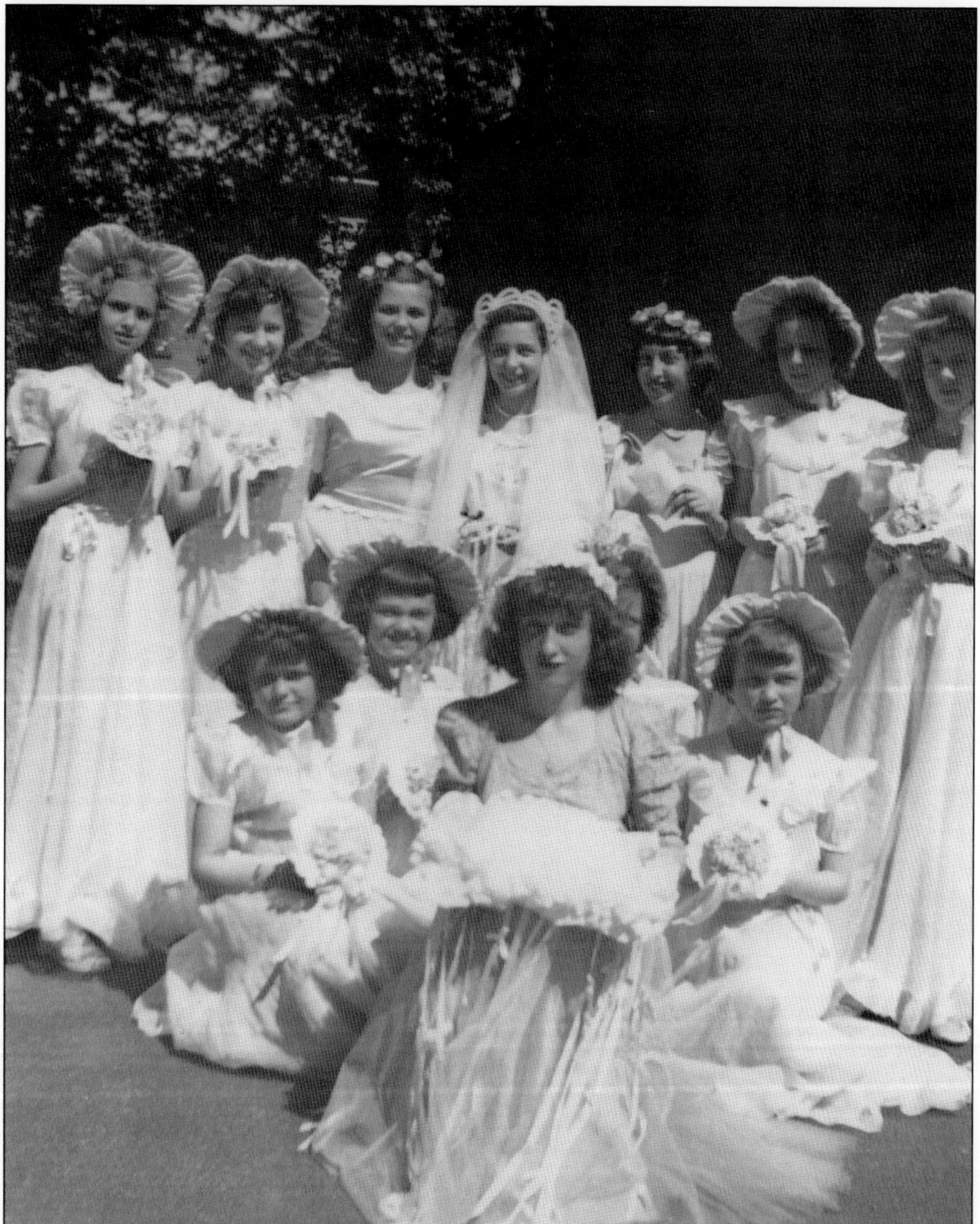

It was a source of great family pride and a great honor for the girl selected as the queen to lead the May procession and to crown the Blessed Mother Mary at Church Street. Every spring, St. John the Baptist schoolgirls vied to become the May queen. Winning a position as a member of the queen's court was also an important recognition. The queen often wore a borrowed wedding gown, and the girls in her court often wore fancy bridesmaids' dresses for the occasion. For the May procession in 1951, the queen and her court were, from left to right, (first row) crown bearer Barbara Dubiel; (second row) Theresa Witkos, Frances Hale, Joan Klus (barely visible), and Joan Colatos; (third row) Barbara Lipka, Rita Stupakiewicz, Louise Kozlowski, Dorothy Hincman (queen), Marie Dupuis, Pauline Carter, and Sandra Baldwin. (DHS.)

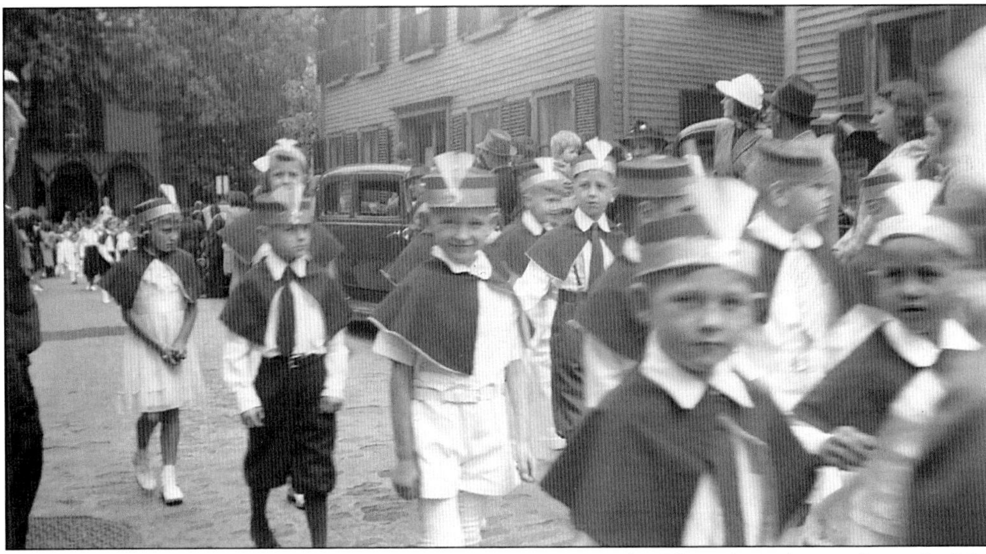

Although the girls were the center of attention in crowning the Blessed Mother at the end of the ritual, the boys also played important supporting roles. In 1947, a young Tom Sobocinski (center, wearing white shorts) looked directly at the camera as he marched among the St. John the Baptist Crusaders children's group in the May procession. (PSP.)

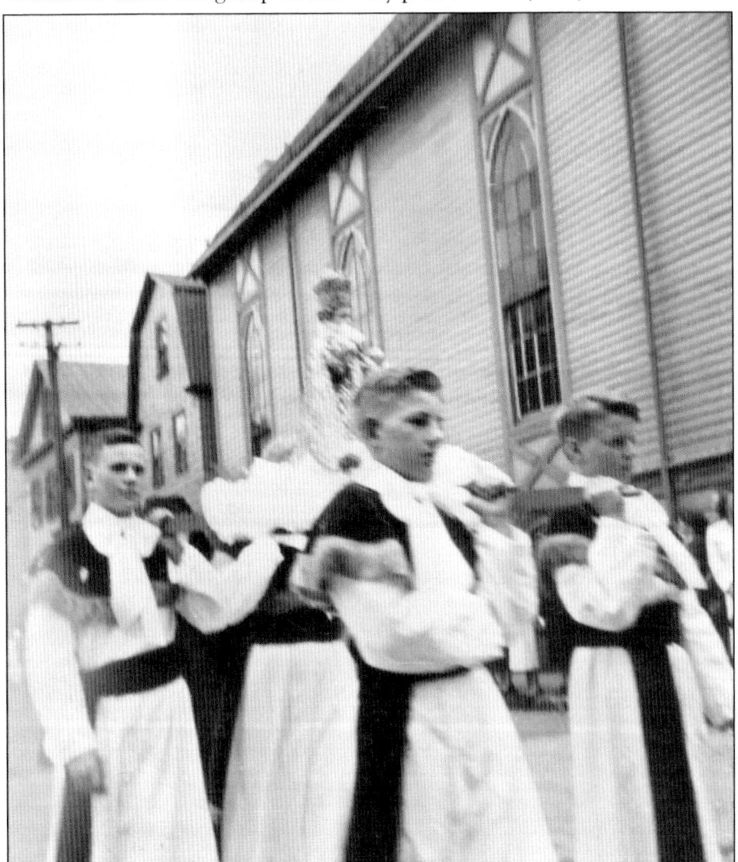

It was also a great honor for boys to be selected for a leading role in the May procession. St. John the Baptist altar boys Leroy Carter, John Trojak, and Gerald Szczehowicz were chosen to carry the Infant of Prague statue in the May procession of 1949. (RNC.)

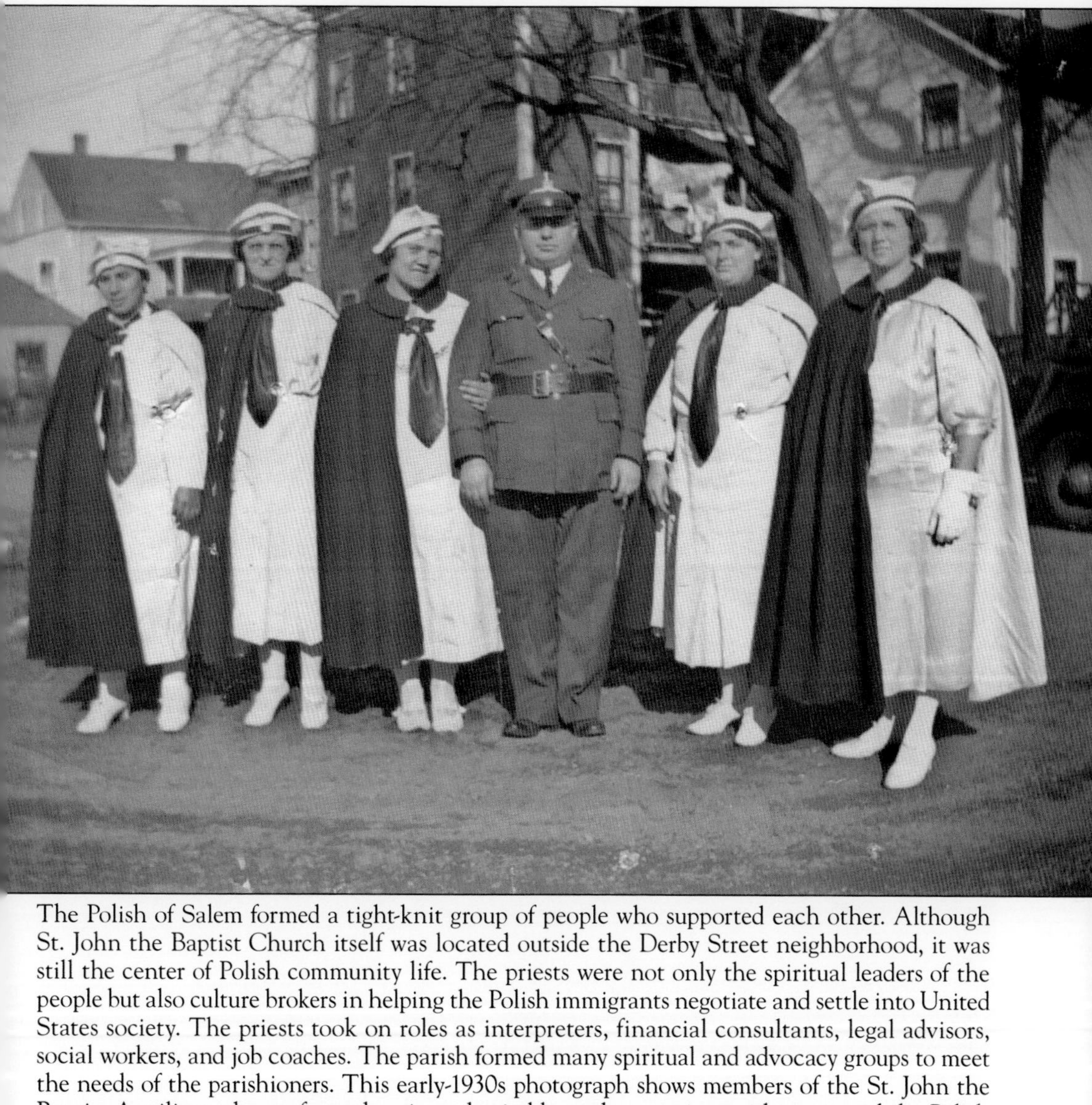

The Polish of Salem formed a tight-knit group of people who supported each other. Although St. John the Baptist Church itself was located outside the Derby Street neighborhood, it was still the center of Polish community life. The priests were not only the spiritual leaders of the people but also culture brokers in helping the Polish immigrants negotiate and settle into United States society. The priests took on roles as interpreters, financial consultants, legal advisors, social workers, and job coaches. The parish formed many spiritual and advocacy groups to meet the needs of the parishioners. This early-1930s photograph shows members of the St. John the Baptist Auxiliary who performed various charitable works to assist parishioners and the Polish community at large. Pictured third from the left is Genevieva Protasewicz Pronska standing next to her husband, Gabriel Pronski. (APW.)

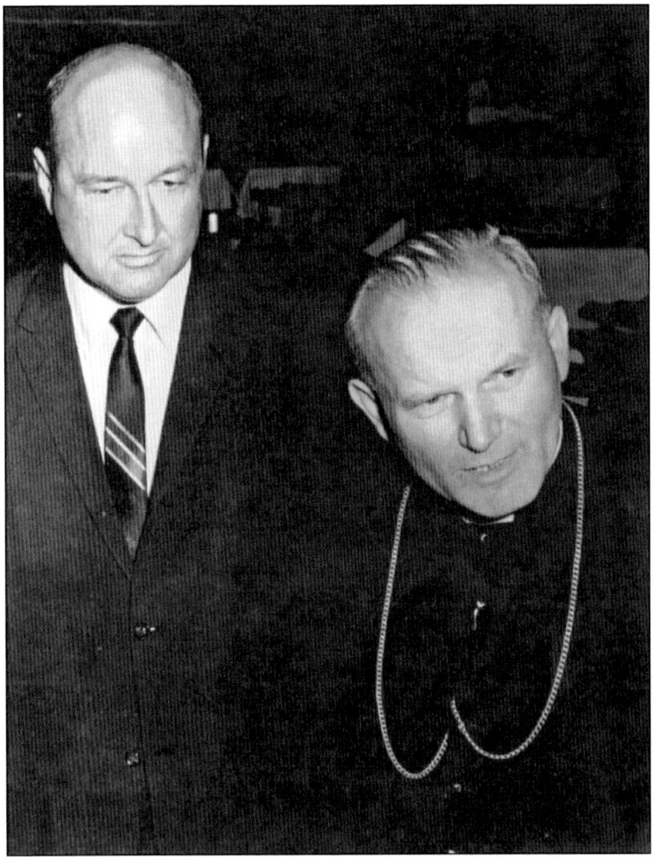

Thaddeus Buczko, Massachusetts state auditor at the time, arranged a luncheon for then-cardinal Karol Wojtyla, Archbishop of Krakow, at Jimmy's Harborside Restaurant on the Boston waterfront in 1969. It was the cardinal's first taste of lobster. The cardinal suggested that one day Buczko might be president of the United States. Buczko returned the compliment predicting that one day the cardinal would be the pope! (TB.)

Parishioners at St. John the Baptist Church were exuberant when Cardinal Karol Wojtyla was elected the first Polish pope. Julia Liszka met Pope John Paul II at the Vatican Gardens in Rome. Father Strykowski was next in line to greet the pope. The parish sponsored the trip in June 1979. (APW.)

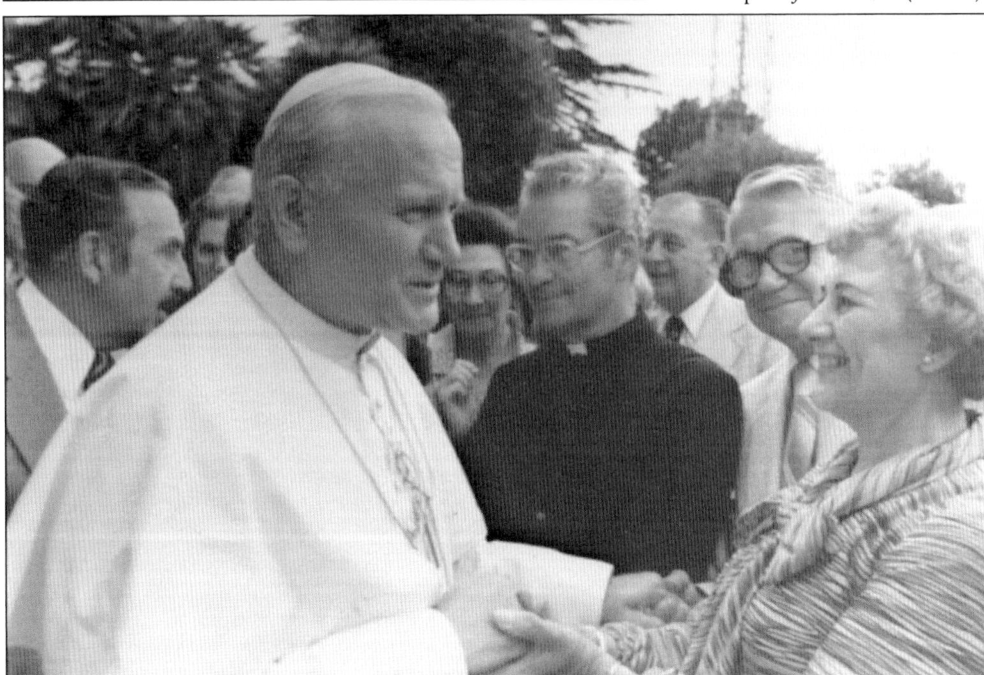

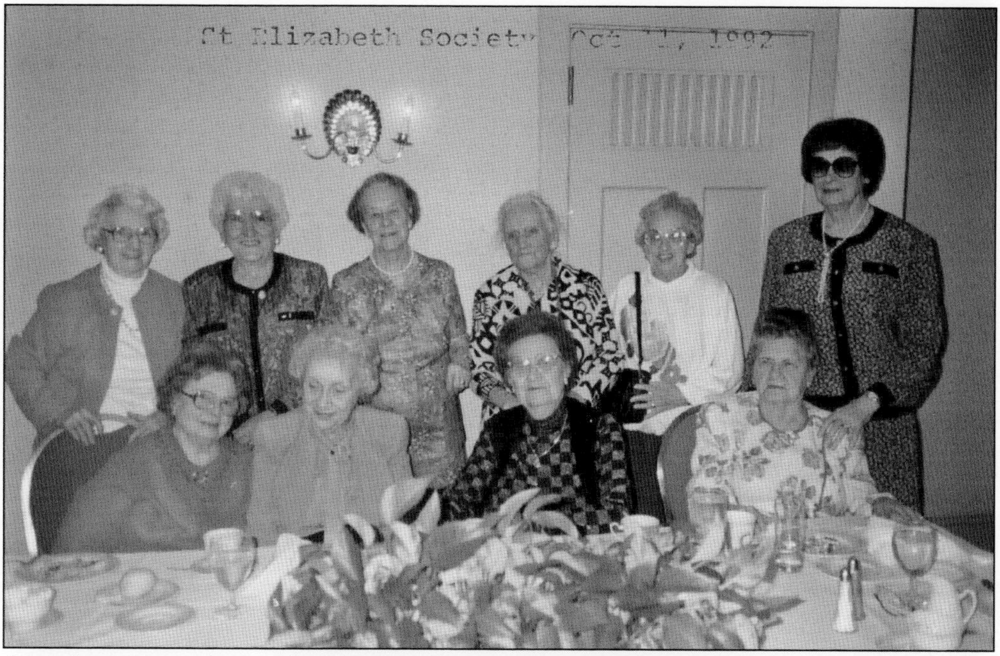

A mothers' group, the St. Elizabeth's Society, which honors the mother of St. John the Baptist, met for lunch on October 11, 1992. The parish also sponsored other groups, such as the Holy Rosary Society and St. Anthony Society, which served various social and religious purposes for the church. (LBM.)

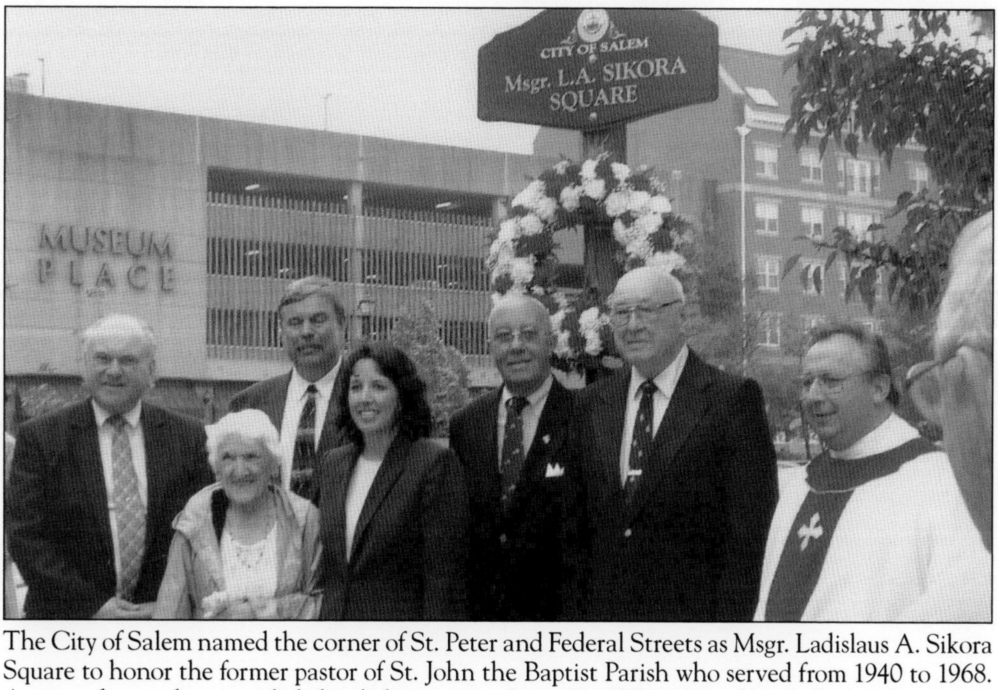

The City of Salem named the corner of St. Peter and Federal Streets as Msgr. Ladislaus A. Sikora Square to honor the former pastor of St. John the Baptist Parish who served from 1940 to 1968. Among those who attended the dedication on June 24, 2006, were, from left to right, David Gonet, Mary Nowak, Mike Bencal, Mayor Kim Driscoll, Walter Sikora, Thaddeus Buczko, and Fr. Stanley Parfienczyk. (PP.)

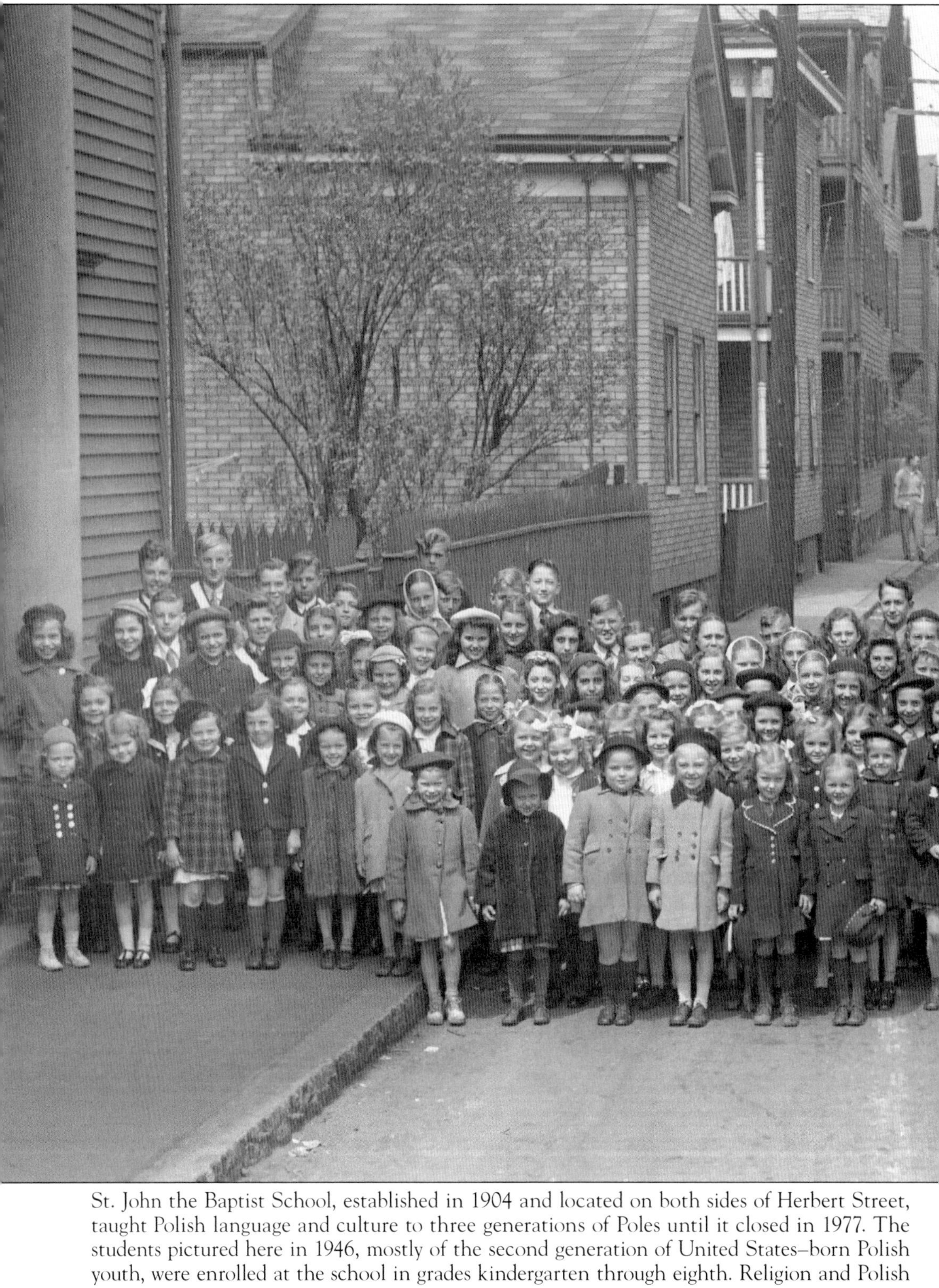

St. John the Baptist School, established in 1904 and located on both sides of Herbert Street, taught Polish language and culture to three generations of Poles until it closed in 1977. The students pictured here in 1946, mostly of the second generation of United States–born Polish youth, were enrolled at the school in grades kindergarten through eighth. Religion and Polish

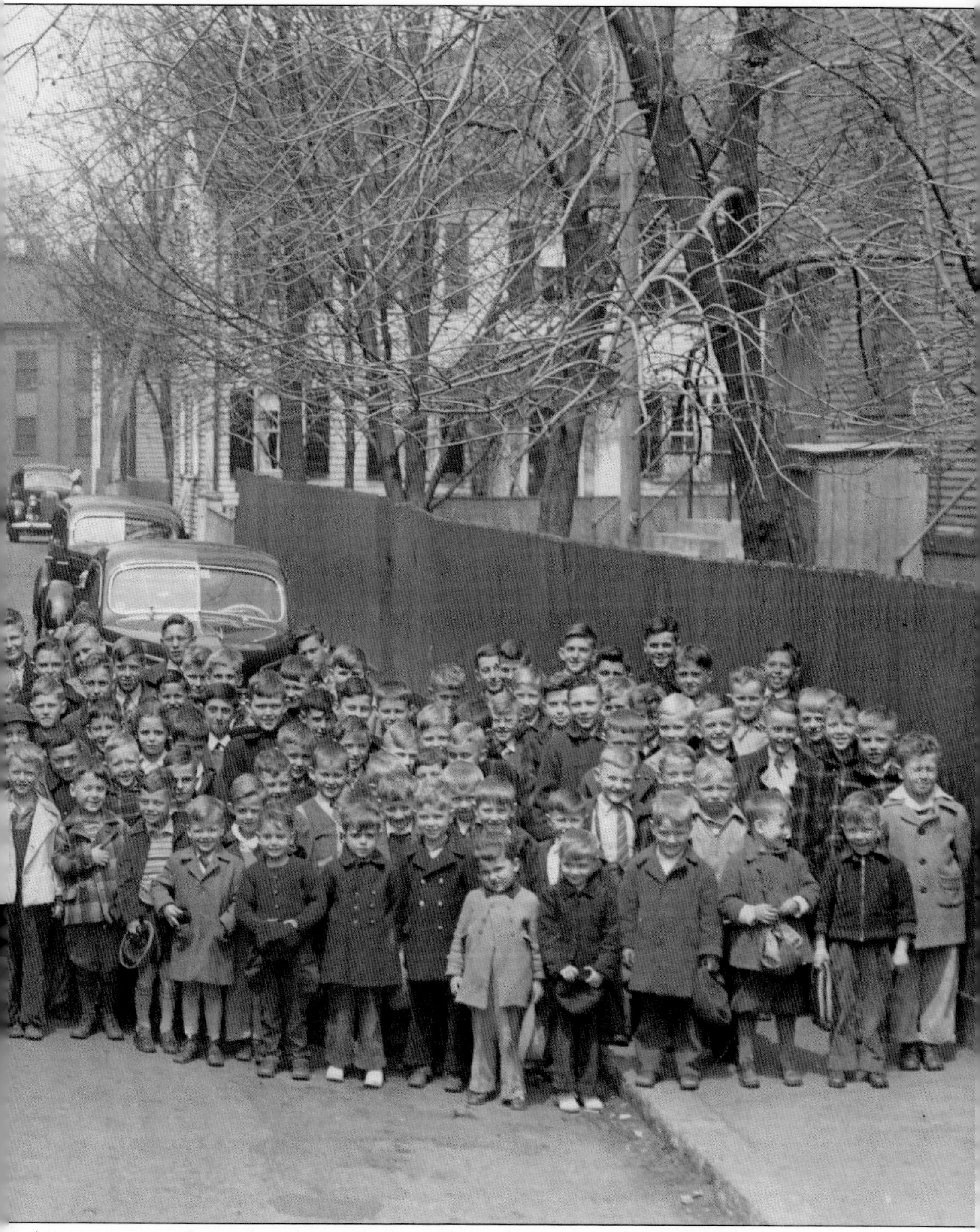

history were emphasized in the curriculum. Given the needs of the immigrants' children and grandchildren to survive in an English-speaking country, English replaced Polish as the primary language of instruction by the early to mid-1950s. The Felician Sisters from the Province of Enfield, Connecticut, directed the school. (LBM.)

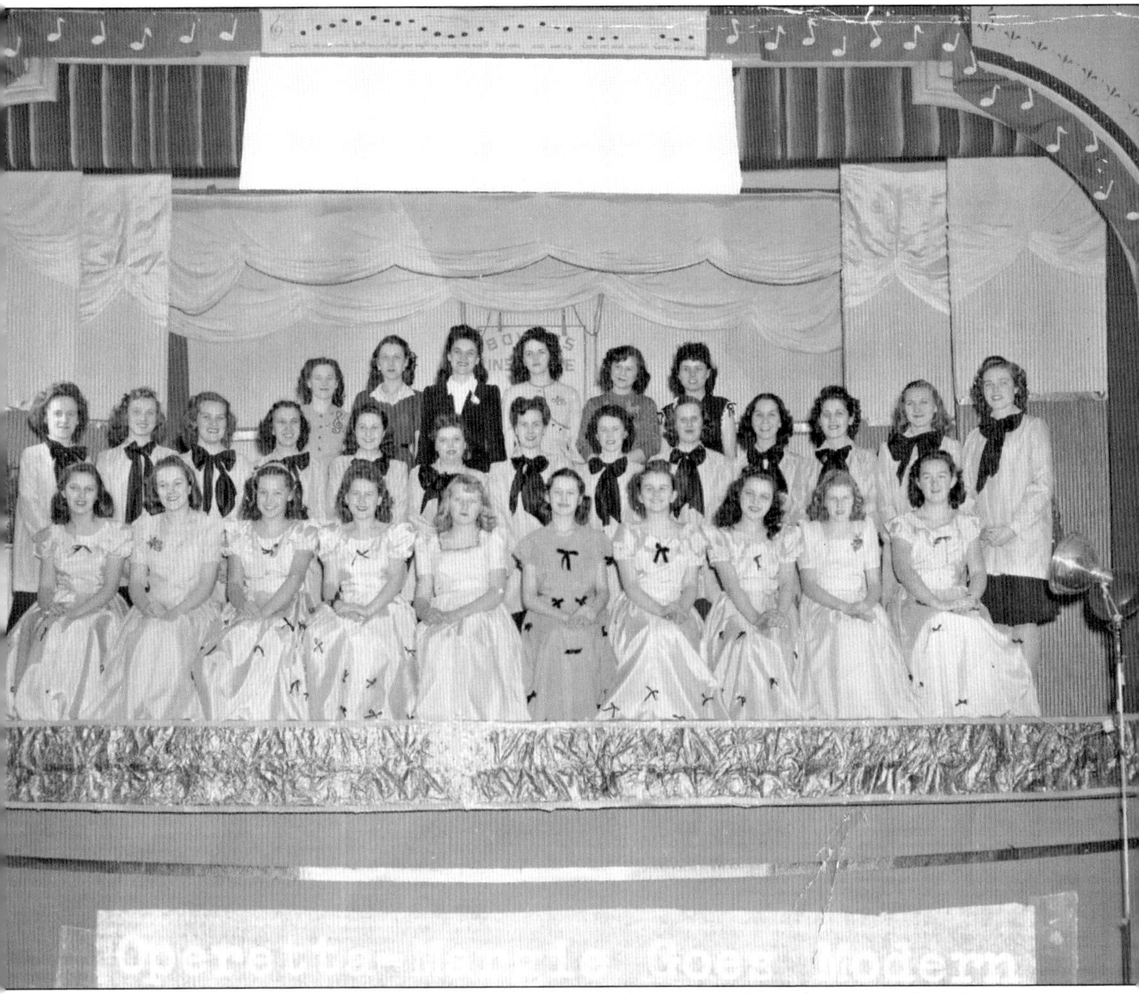

Musical theater was very popular in the 1930s and 1940s in the Salem area. Otis Carrington, a renowned music teacher in California, composed the music and lyrics for a number of amusing one-act operettas that were adaptable for school productions. Students performed his operettas across the nation, and the students at St. John the Baptist School on Herbert Street in the mid-1940s were no exception. A mixed-age group of girls presented one of his operettas, "Margie Goes Modern," written in 1935 for an all-female ensemble. The cast members were all dressed in pink tops with big black bows tied under their chins. The school produced annual plays, and this operetta called on alumnae to help with the performance. Proud of their grammar school alma mater, St. John the Baptist graduates were honored to be included in the production with the younger students. (AKJ.)

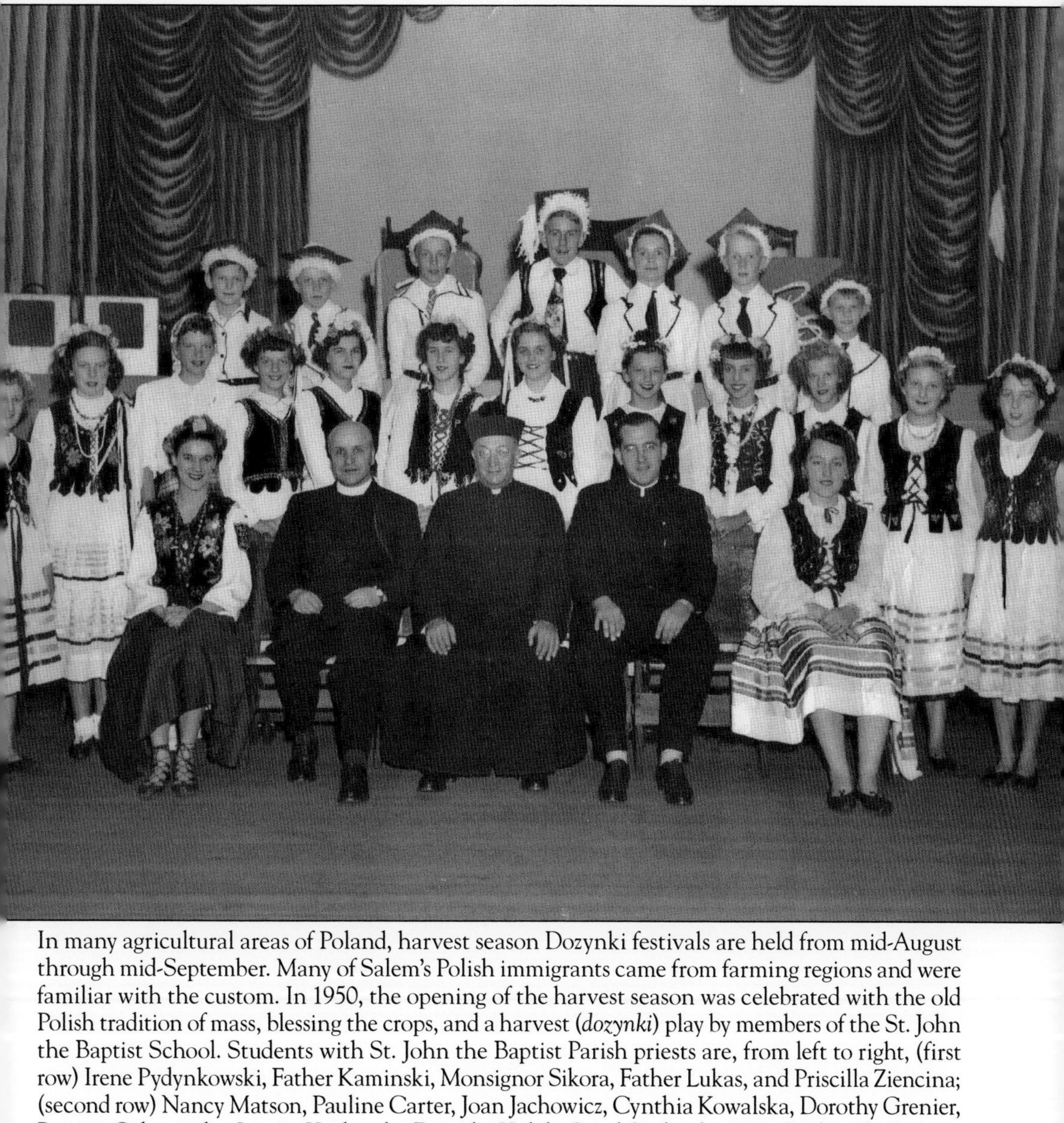

In many agricultural areas of Poland, harvest season Dozynki festivals are held from mid-August through mid-September. Many of Salem's Polish immigrants came from farming regions and were familiar with the custom. In 1950, the opening of the harvest season was celebrated with the old Polish tradition of mass, blessing the crops, and a harvest (*dozynki*) play by members of the St. John the Baptist School. Students with St. John the Baptist Parish priests are, from left to right, (first row) Irene Pydynkowski, Father Kaminski, Monsignor Sikora, Father Lukas, and Priscilla Ziencina; (second row) Nancy Matson, Pauline Carter, Joan Jachowicz, Cynthia Kowalska, Dorothy Grenier, Patricia Sobocinska, Louise Kozlowski, Dorothy Kulak, Carol Stefanski, Mary Malionek, Patricia Trojanowski, and Dorothy Hincman; (third row) Daniel Witkos, Paul Laski, Joseph Swiniarski, Donald Brennan, Paul Burda, George Plecinoga, and Richard Malionek. (PSP.)

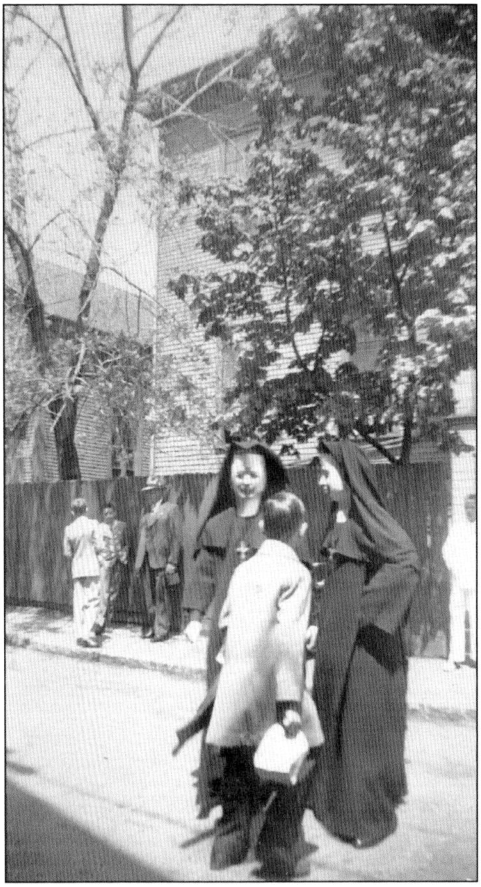

This picture, taken about 1948, caught Sister Benjamin (principal) on the left and middle school teacher Sister Regina talking to a student outside St. John the Baptist School on Herbert Street. The school, staffed by the Felician sisters, taught the basic educational curriculum mandated by the Commonwealth of Massachusetts but also included ethnic studies of Polish language and history. (DSF.)

In 1955, students at St. John the Baptist School helped celebrate the 100th anniversary of the founding of the Felician sisters, a religious order established in Warsaw by Blessed Mary Angela Truszkowska. Although their numbers are declining, Felician sisters are dedicated to educational and social work in Polonia communities across the United States. (KNE.)

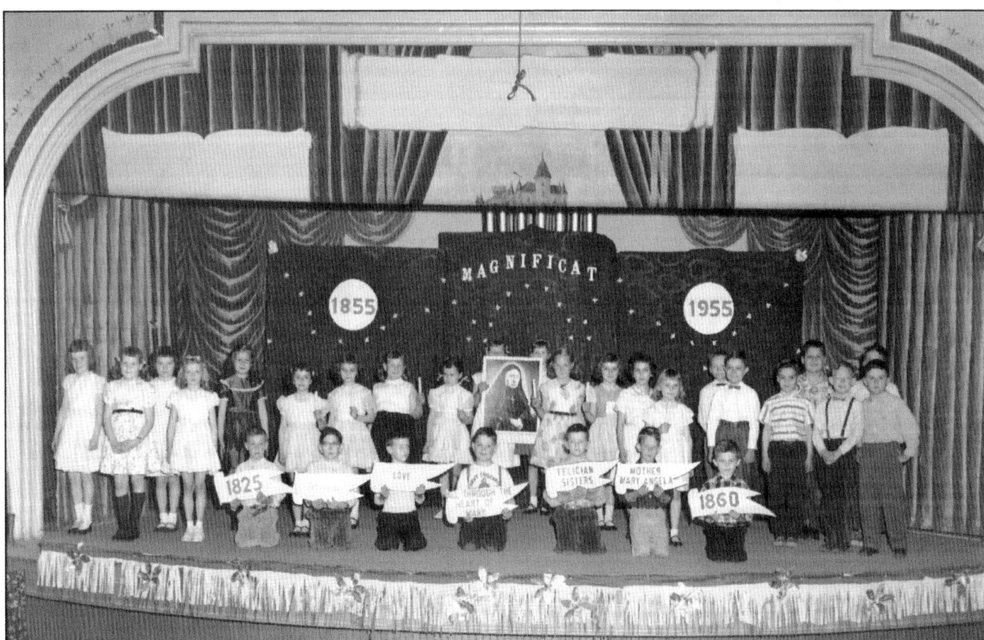

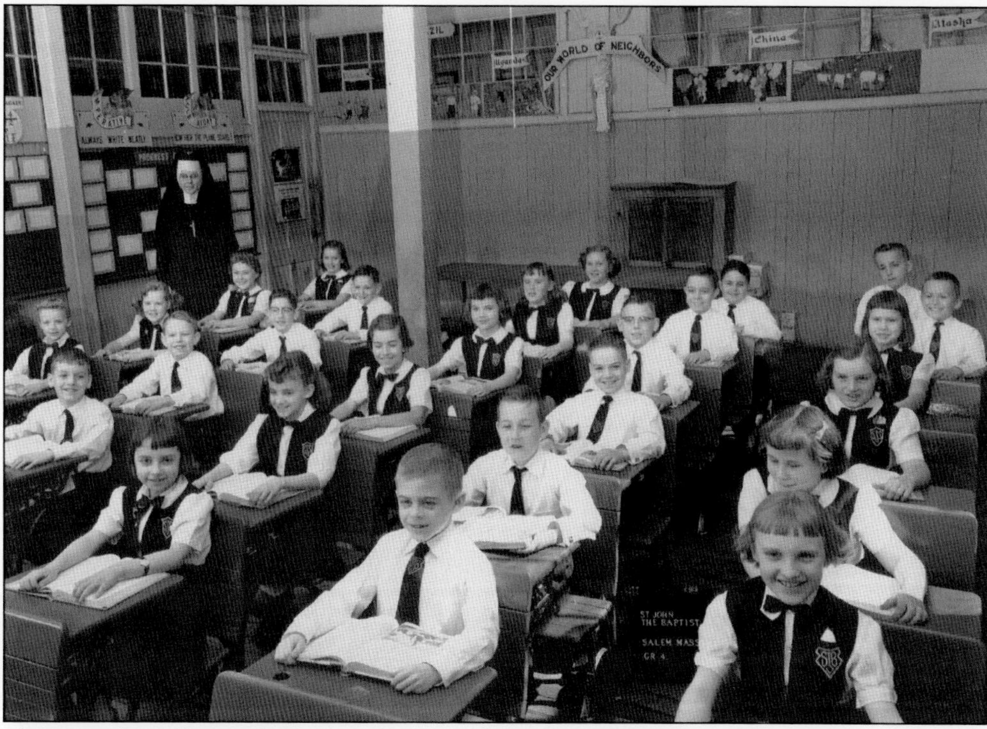

This snapshot of Sister Anthony's classroom will bring back memories for graduates of the old St. John the Baptist School and others who attended parochial schools. These fourth graders—dressed in their neat school uniforms, sitting in straight rows of desks and waiting patiently for lessons to begin—were visited by a photographer for a class picture in 1957. (KNE.)

St. John the Baptist schoolgirls were members of the Falcons' Krakowiakian dancers in the 1960s. Carol Kobierski is shown demonstrating a dance step for the group. Seated are, from left to right, Barbara Rogalski and Cynthia Day. Standing are, from left to right, Doris Szybiak and Marianne Kilczewski. (CSB.)

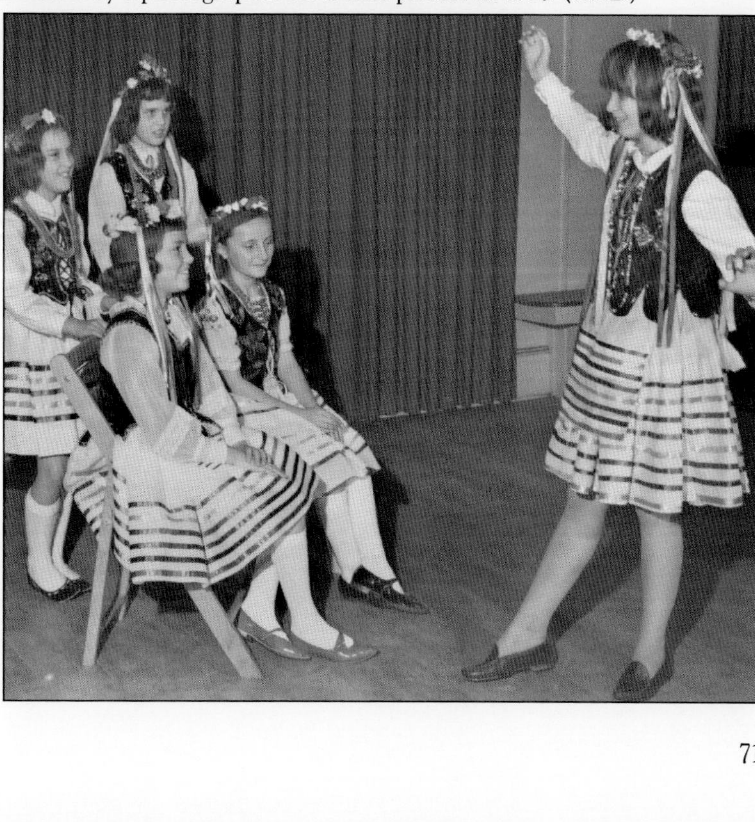

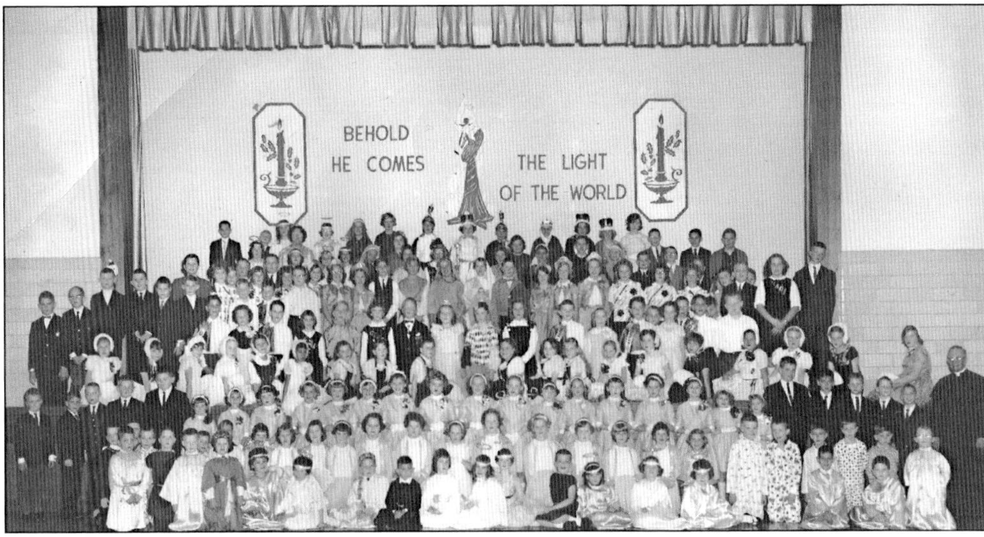

Students at St. John the Baptist School participated in annual Christmas variety shows performed for family and friends in the parish hall. Each grade was responsible for a different song, skit, or dance. While assembling for the grand finale, the entire cast of schoolchildren was photographed in 1962. (SW.)

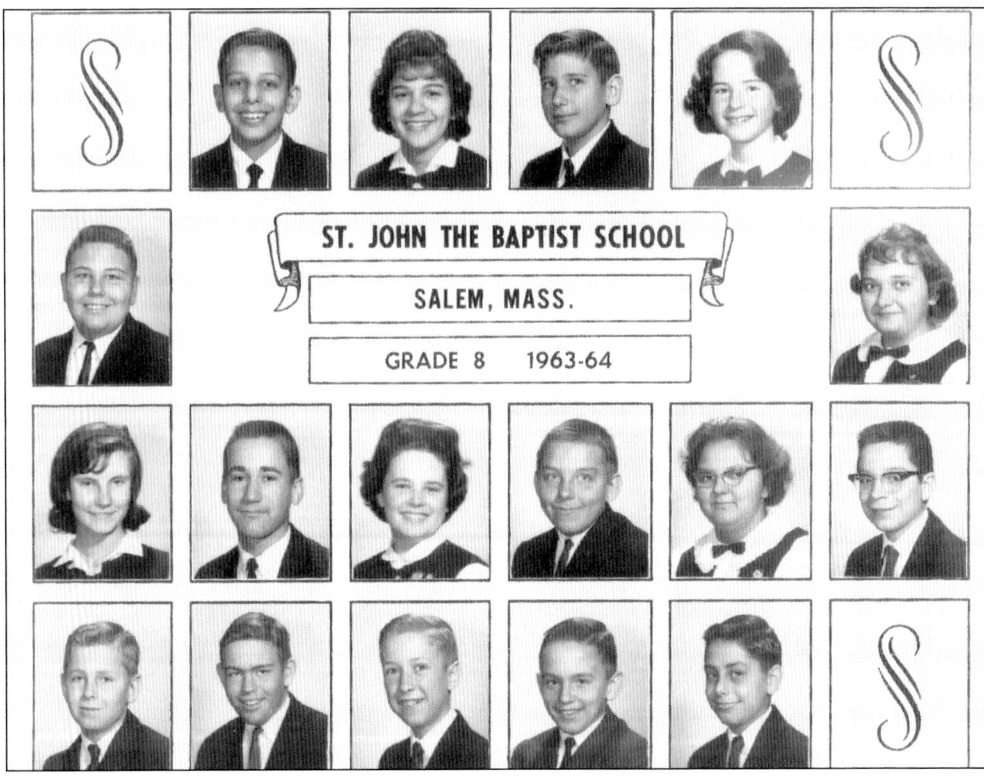

St. John the Baptist School on Herbert Street served two generations of Polish youth. A new school was built to replace the deteriorating building and to provide up-to-date educational facilities. These students were members of one of the first classes to graduate from the new St. John the Baptist School that opened in 1961 on St. Peter Street. (PP.)

Six

St. Joseph Society

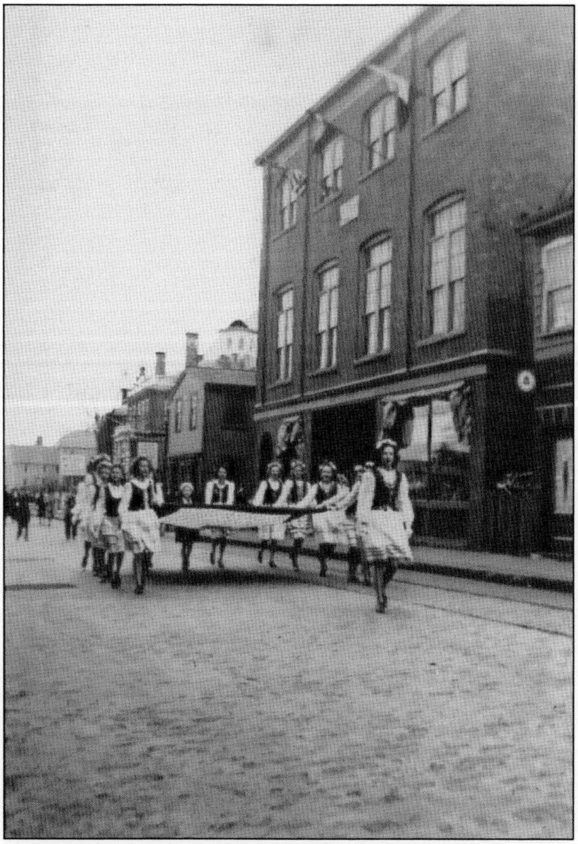

St. Joseph's Hall was built in 1909 and is pictured here in the 1940s. The first floor was rented out as retail space to provide income for the building's upkeep. The second floor was a hall with a stage where dances, weddings, and other celebrations took place. The third floor consisted of small apartments that were rented to Polish immigrants until they could establish themselves in Salem. (NPS.)

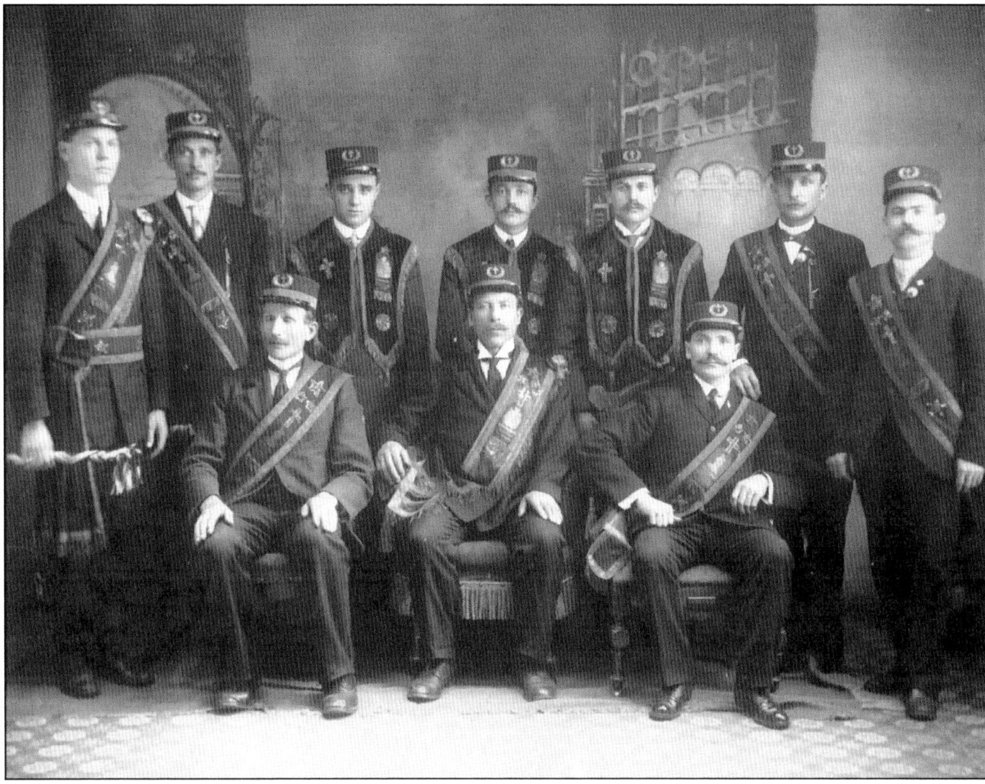

Pictured at the turn of the 20th century, these officers of the St. Joseph's Society were the early organizers of the Polish community in Salem. They were distinguished by the Catholic symbol of the cross and military-like regalia that befit their leadership roles. These uniforms were worn at formal society meetings and ceremonial civic functions. (NPS.)

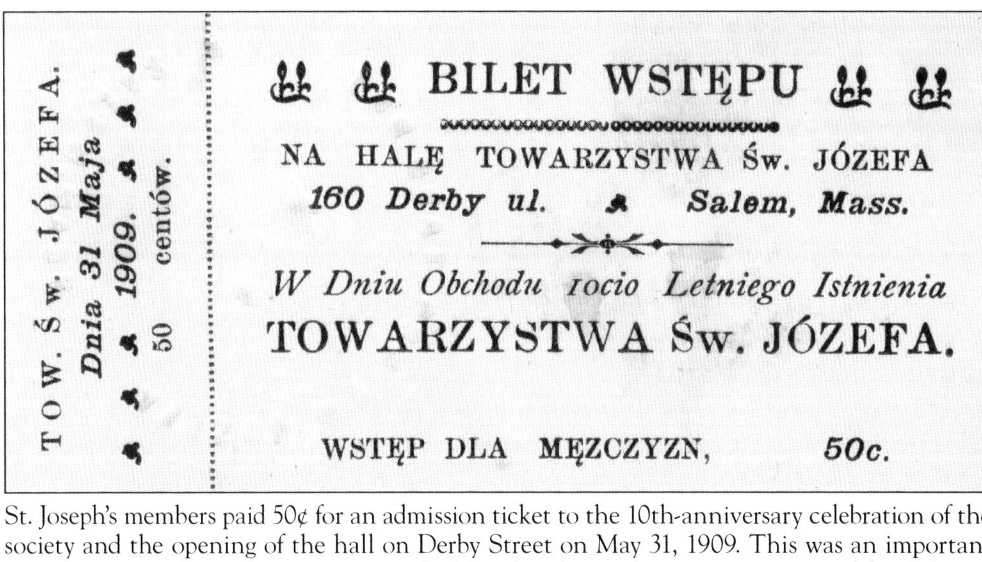

TOW. Św. JÓZEFA.
Dnia 31 Maja 1909.
50 centów.

BILET WSTĘPU

NA HALĘ TOWARZYSTWA Św. JÓZEFA

160 Derby ul. *Salem, Mass.*

W Dniu Obchodu 10cio Letniego Istnienia

TOWARZYSTWA Św. JÓZEFA.

WSTĘP DLA MĘZCZYZN, *50c.*

St. Joseph's members paid 50¢ for an admission ticket to the 10th-anniversary celebration of the society and the opening of the hall on Derby Street on May 31, 1909. This was an important landmark structure in the community and, after a decade in existence, a statement of the enduring Polish presence in Salem. (NPS.)

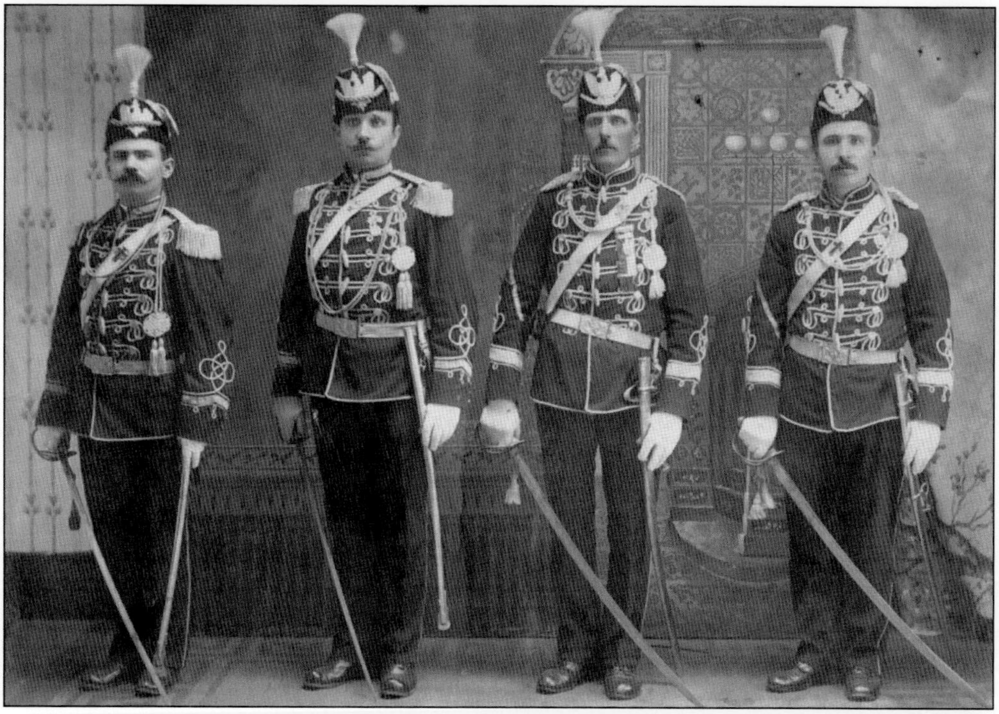

Pictured are a few leading members of the St. Joseph's Society Drill Team, or "Hussars." Between 1907 and 1921, the society fielded a paramilitary drill team of about 25 members that participated in parades and other formal civic activities on behalf of the Polish community. Their uniforms were quite impressive. (LBM.)

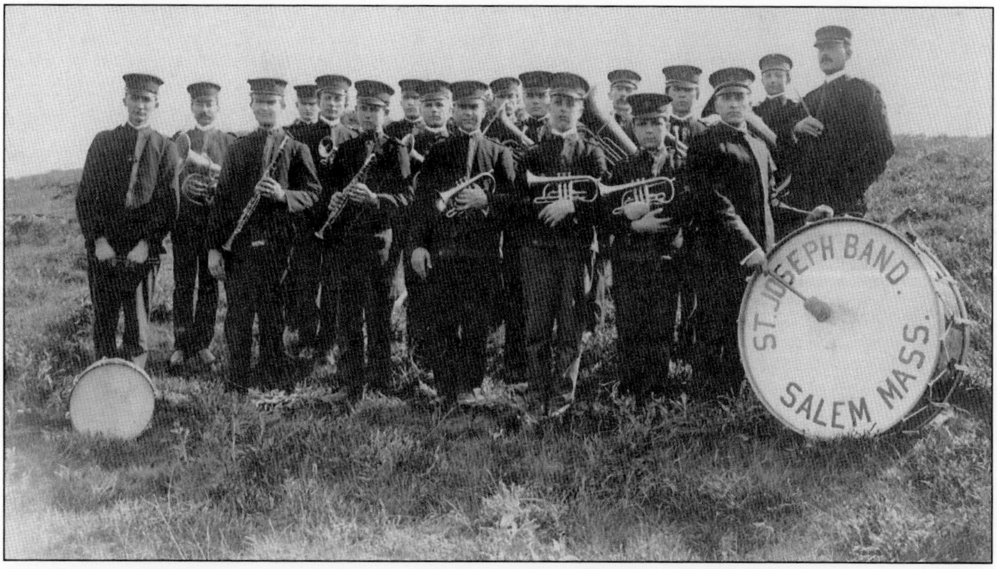

The St. Joseph's Society organized a marching band in 1904 to represent the Polish community in parades and other civic and social events. Society members contributed toward the purchase of instruments and music lessons. The band was a source of pride and conflict within the society. The band unionized and refused to play at certain events that involved nonunion participants, including the opening of its own sponsor's building, St. Joseph's Hall, in 1909! (ND.)

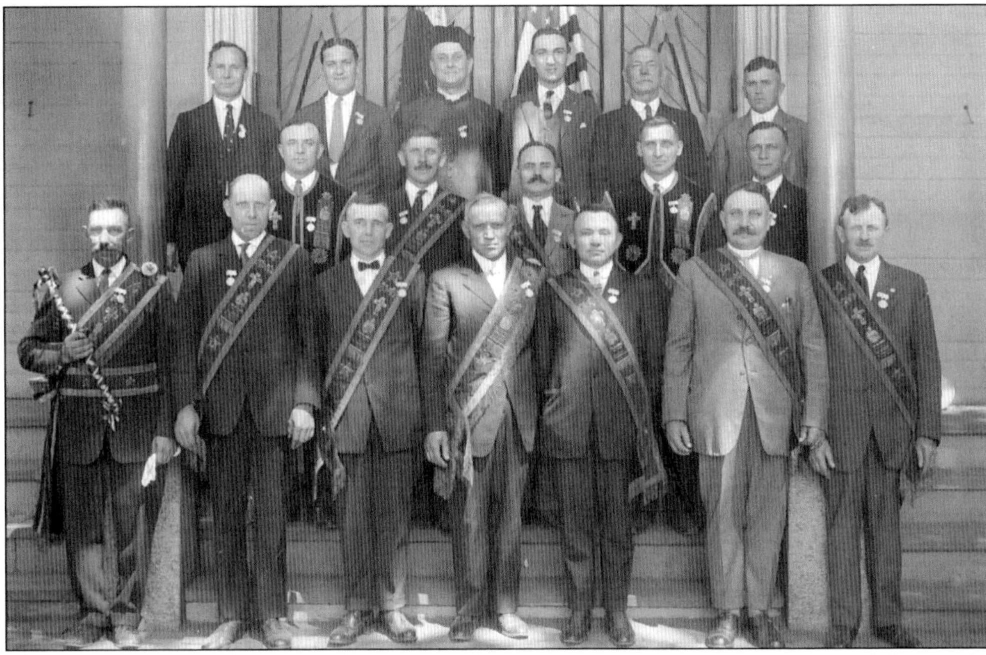

Members of the St. Joseph's Society Honor Guard in the mid-1920s included, from left to right, (first row) A. Nidzgorski, F. Wroblewski, W. Dolmat, J. Kamienski, J. Boltrukiewicz, W. Sowinski, and K. Nidzgorski; (second row) F. Agacienski, S. Proczewski, T. Bartnicki, S. Graczyk, and S. Groszek; (third row) F. Kibiersza, L. Kotarski, Father Czubek, A. Bacharowski, W. Sobocinski, and A. Wilenski. (NPS.)

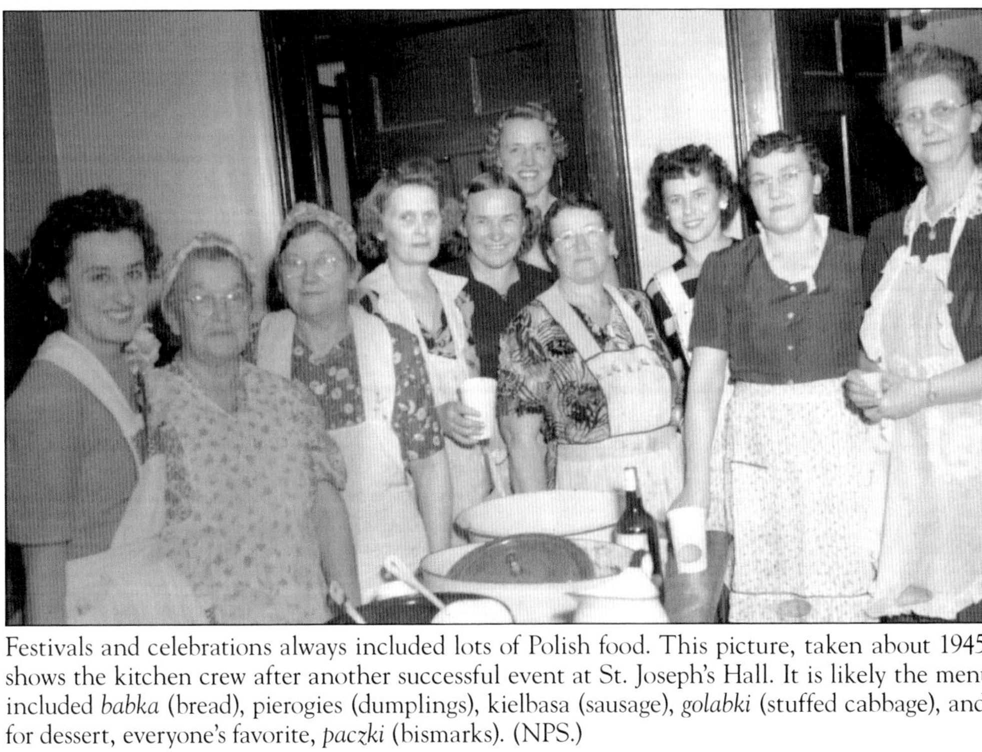

Festivals and celebrations always included lots of Polish food. This picture, taken about 1945, shows the kitchen crew after another successful event at St. Joseph's Hall. It is likely the menu included *babka* (bread), pierogies (dumplings), kielbasa (sausage), *golabki* (stuffed cabbage), and, for dessert, everyone's favorite, *paczki* (bismarks). (NPS.)

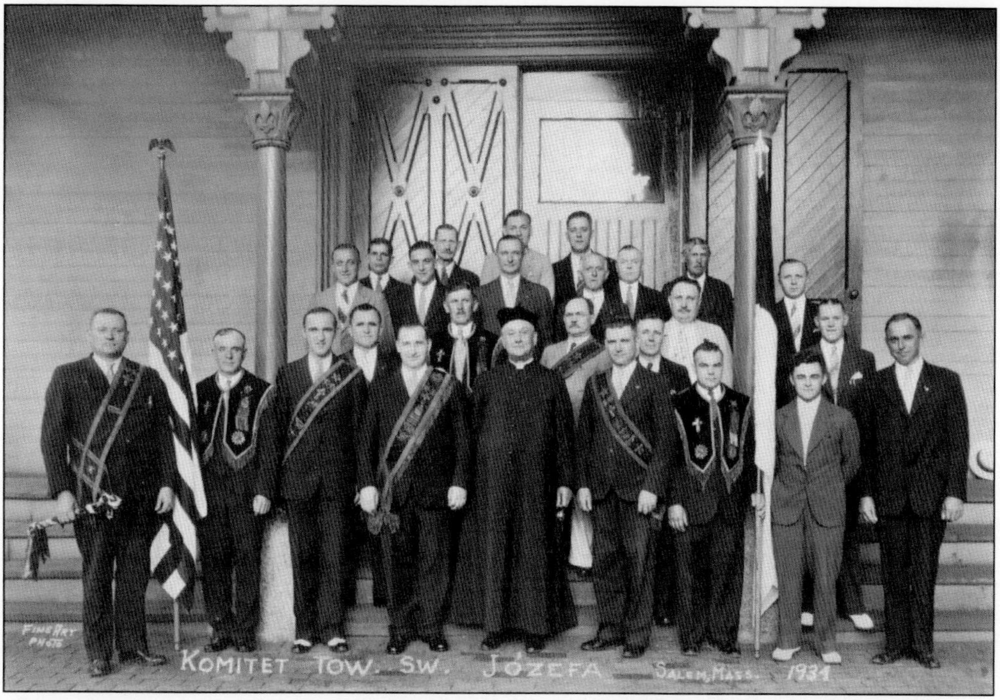

The St. Joseph's Society played a critical role in the lives of the Polish immigrants as they established their residence in Salem. The society welcomed new arrivals, reinforced Catholic religious affiliations, assisted with financial issues, provided housing, arranged for health care, enforced codes of moral conduct, and sponsored recreational activities. Election as an officer of the society was a great responsibility and high honor. Above, officers of the St. Joseph's Society in 1934 were photographed at their installation with Father Czubek, the pastor of St. John the Baptist Parish as well as the spiritual leader and trusted advisor for the group. Below, the next cohort of St. Joseph's Society members was installed as the executive committee in 1938. (Above, CG; below, LBM.)

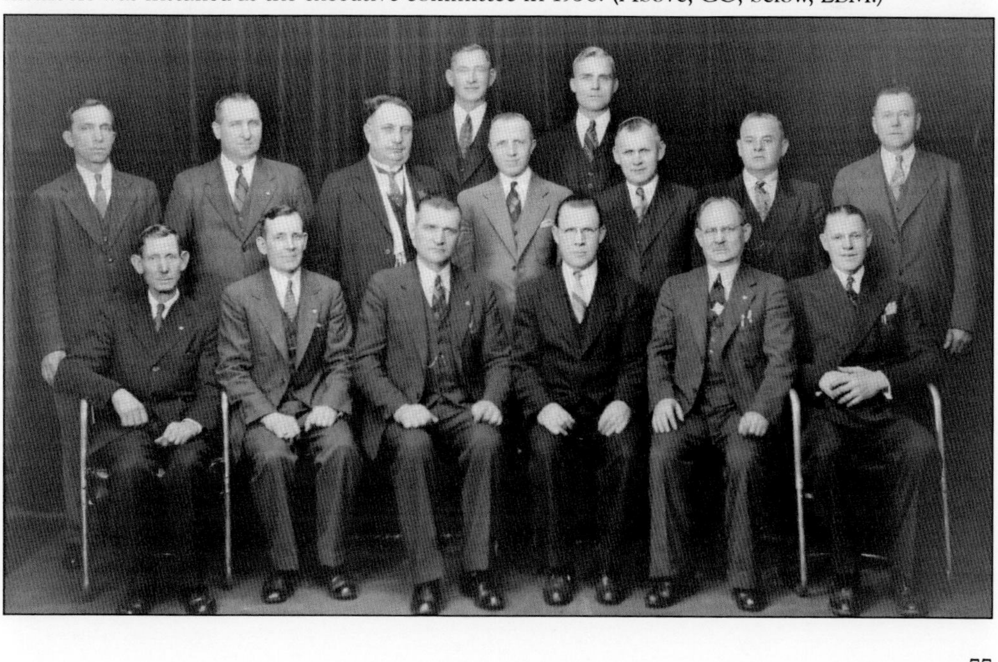

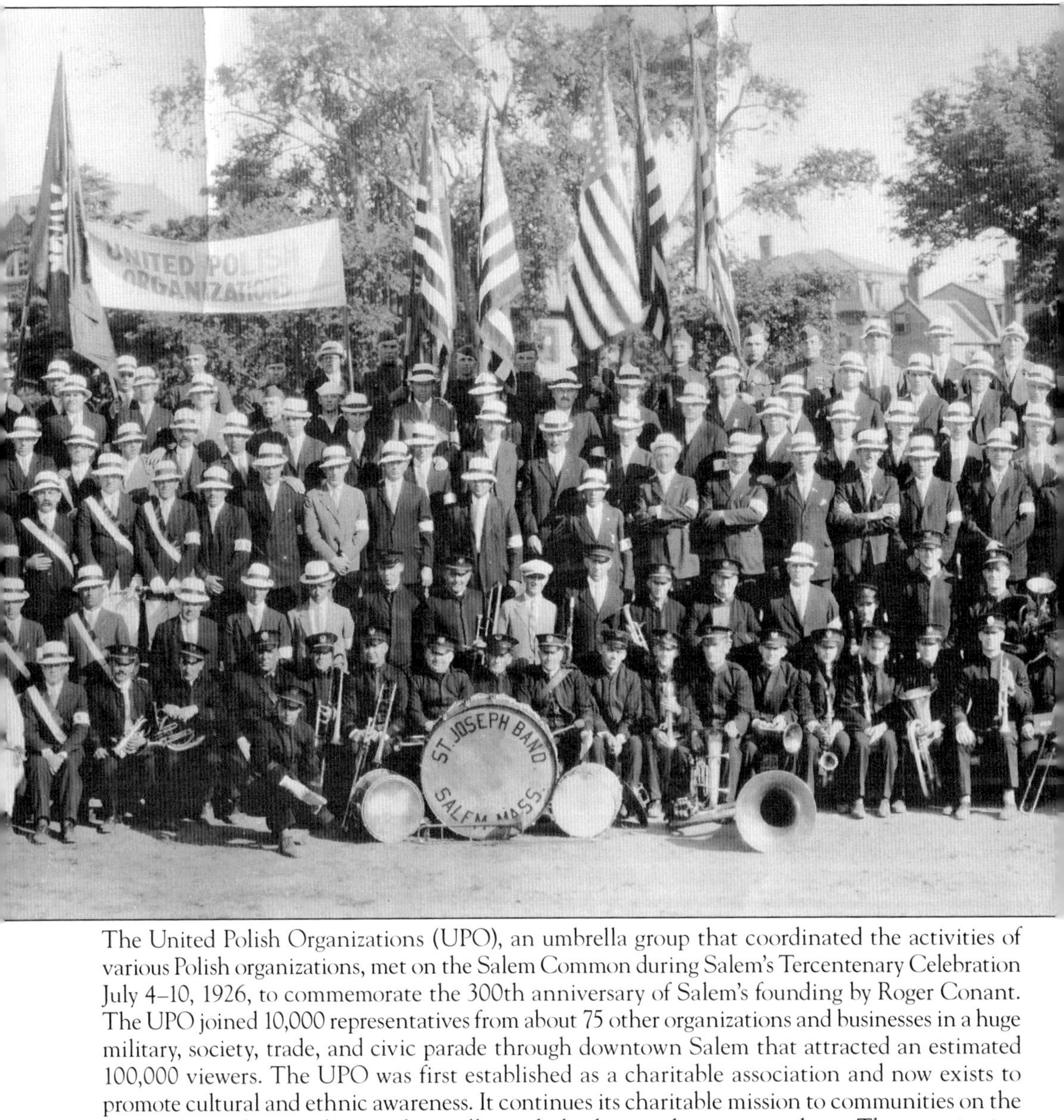

The United Polish Organizations (UPO), an umbrella group that coordinated the activities of various Polish organizations, met on the Salem Common during Salem's Tercentenary Celebration July 4–10, 1926, to commemorate the 300th anniversary of Salem's founding by Roger Conant. The UPO joined 10,000 representatives from about 75 other organizations and businesses in a huge military, society, trade, and civic parade through downtown Salem that attracted an estimated 100,000 viewers. The UPO was first established as a charitable association and now exists to promote cultural and ethnic awareness. It continues its charitable mission to communities on the North Shore of Boston by awarding college scholarships to deserving students. The organization also participates in local ethnic festivals and holds commemorative civic celebrations to recognize important Polish historical events, such as the annual recognition of Poland's Constitution Day. The Polish Constitution, signed on May 3, 1791, is the second-oldest written constitution in the world. (NPS.)

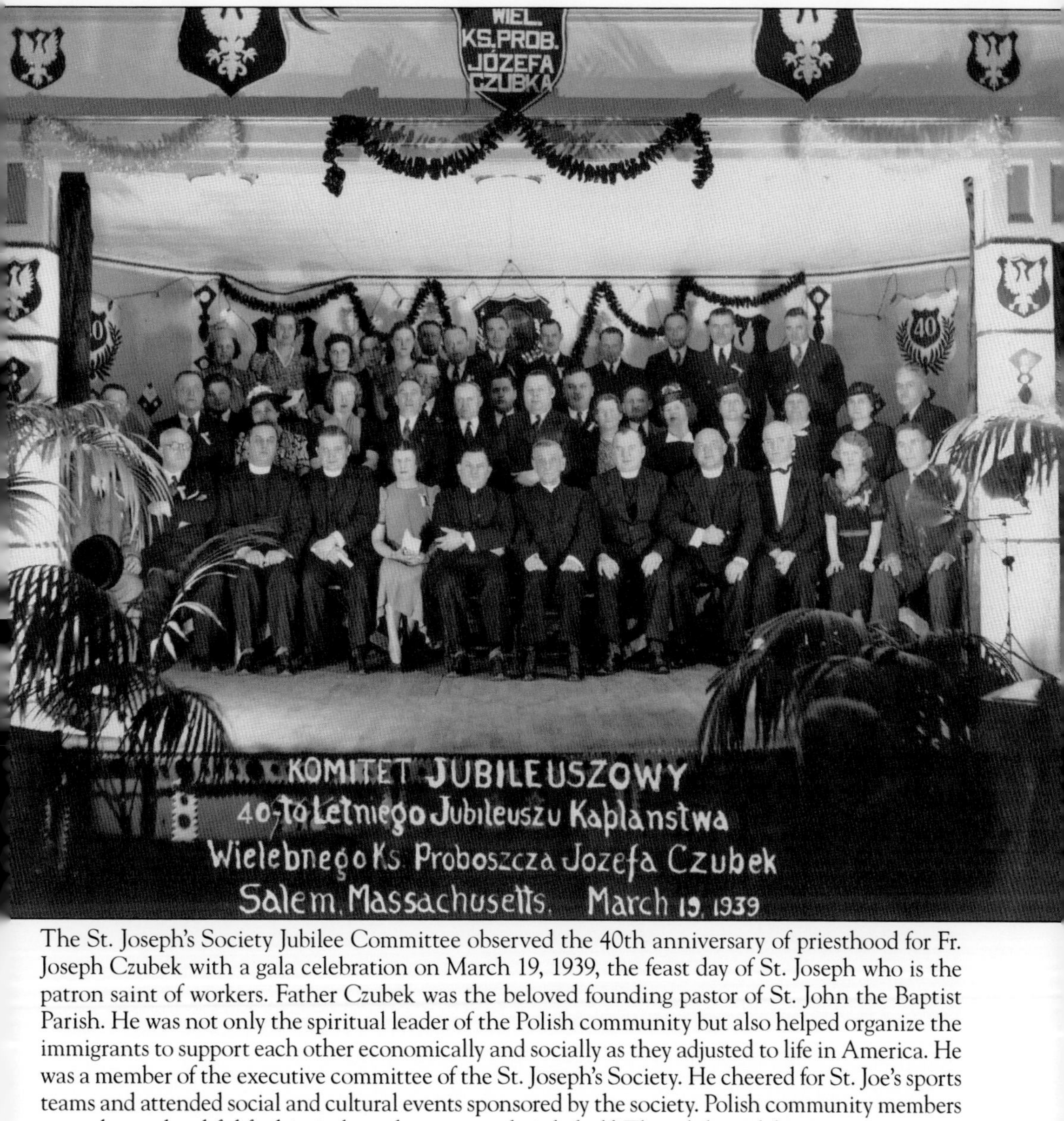

The St. Joseph's Society Jubilee Committee observed the 40th anniversary of priesthood for Fr. Joseph Czubek with a gala celebration on March 19, 1939, the feast day of St. Joseph who is the patron saint of workers. Father Czubek was the beloved founding pastor of St. John the Baptist Parish. He was not only the spiritual leader of the Polish community but also helped organize the immigrants to support each other economically and socially as they adjusted to life in America. He was a member of the executive committee of the St. Joseph's Society. He cheered for St. Joe's sports teams and attended social and cultural events sponsored by the society. Polish community members were always thankful for his tireless advocacy on their behalf. The jubilee celebration to recognize his pastoral milestone was an outpouring of the parishioners' gratitude and affection. (JK.)

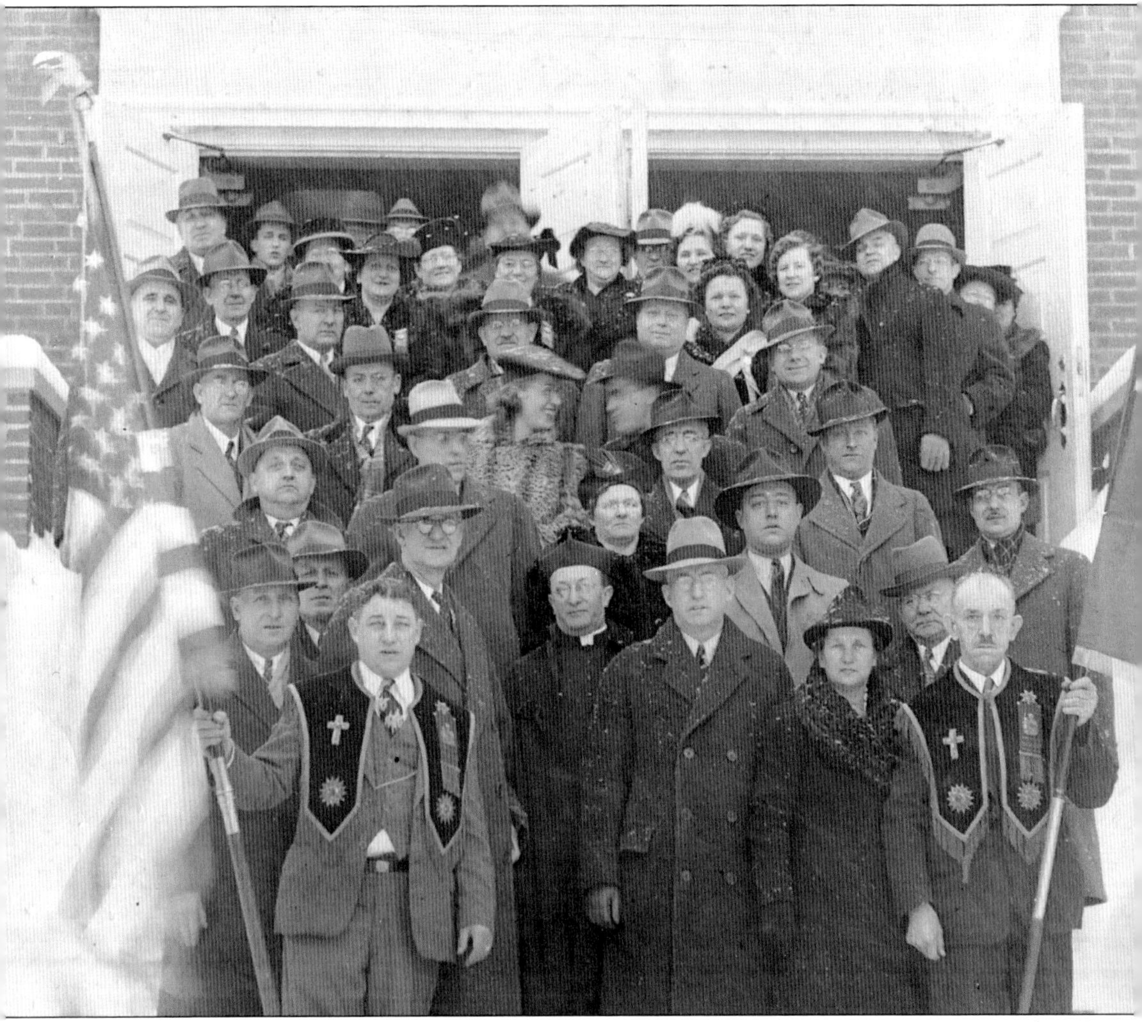

Officers of the Polish Roman Catholic Union (PRCU) of the St. Joseph's Society stand with Reverend Sikora and Salem mayor Edward Coffey (front, center) after mass at St. John the Baptist Church to celebrate the organization's 28th anniversary in the early 1940s. The PRCU was a politically active group in the Salem community. The local PRCU was a chapter of the Polish Roman Catholic Union of America (PRCUA), which was the first national Polish fraternal organization in the United States. Its motto "for God and country" reflected their loyalty and pride to live in America. The PRCUA was originally dedicated to ethnic unity, mutual benefit, and absolute fidelity to the Catholic Church. It now performs religious, charitable, educational, and civic work on behalf of its members and for the Polish American community. Members joined the PRCUA by purchasing its life insurance policies. (CG.)

GRAND NOVELTY PARTY

For the benefit of sick members

—Auspices of—

St. Joseph's Polish Society

Saturday eve., February 21st, 1948

7:30 p. m.

CLUB HALL

160 Derby St. -:- Salem, Mass.

Grand Variety of Prizes

Admission 50c Surprises for all!

Founded to provide mutual aid, the St. Joseph's Society of Brotherly Help often held fundraisers to assist their members. Minutes from the St. Joe's meetings showed that help for the sick was granted every month for one or two needy members. The awards were typically $5 or $10. (NPS.)

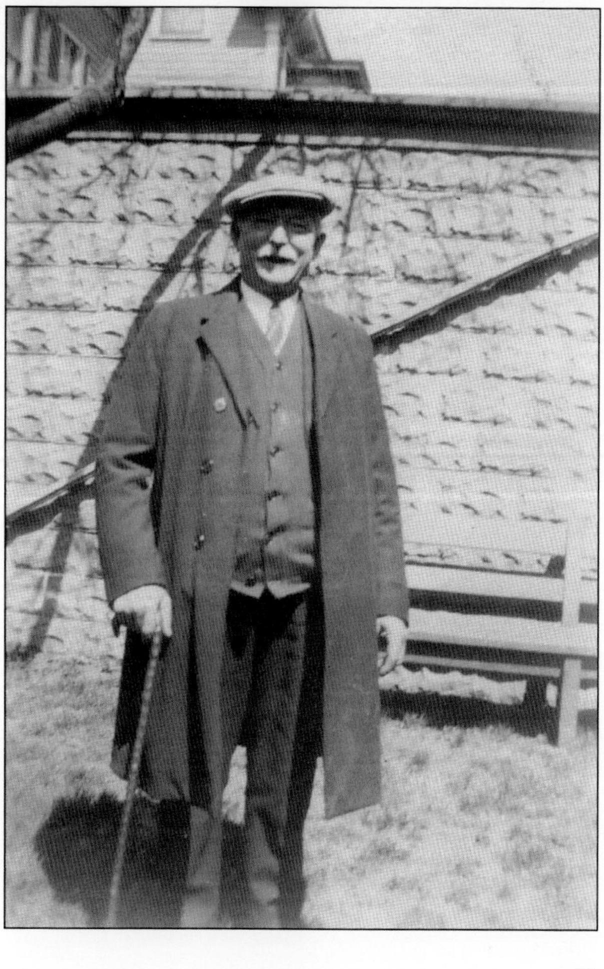

Wladyslaw Soboczinski is pictured in the yard of his family home at 40 Daniels Street in the mid-1940s. Soboczinski was a charter member of the St. Joseph's Society. He was seriously ill in May 1949 and died shortly after the St. Joseph's Society Golden Jubilee parade changed its route to pass by his house in a final tribute to him. (DSF.)

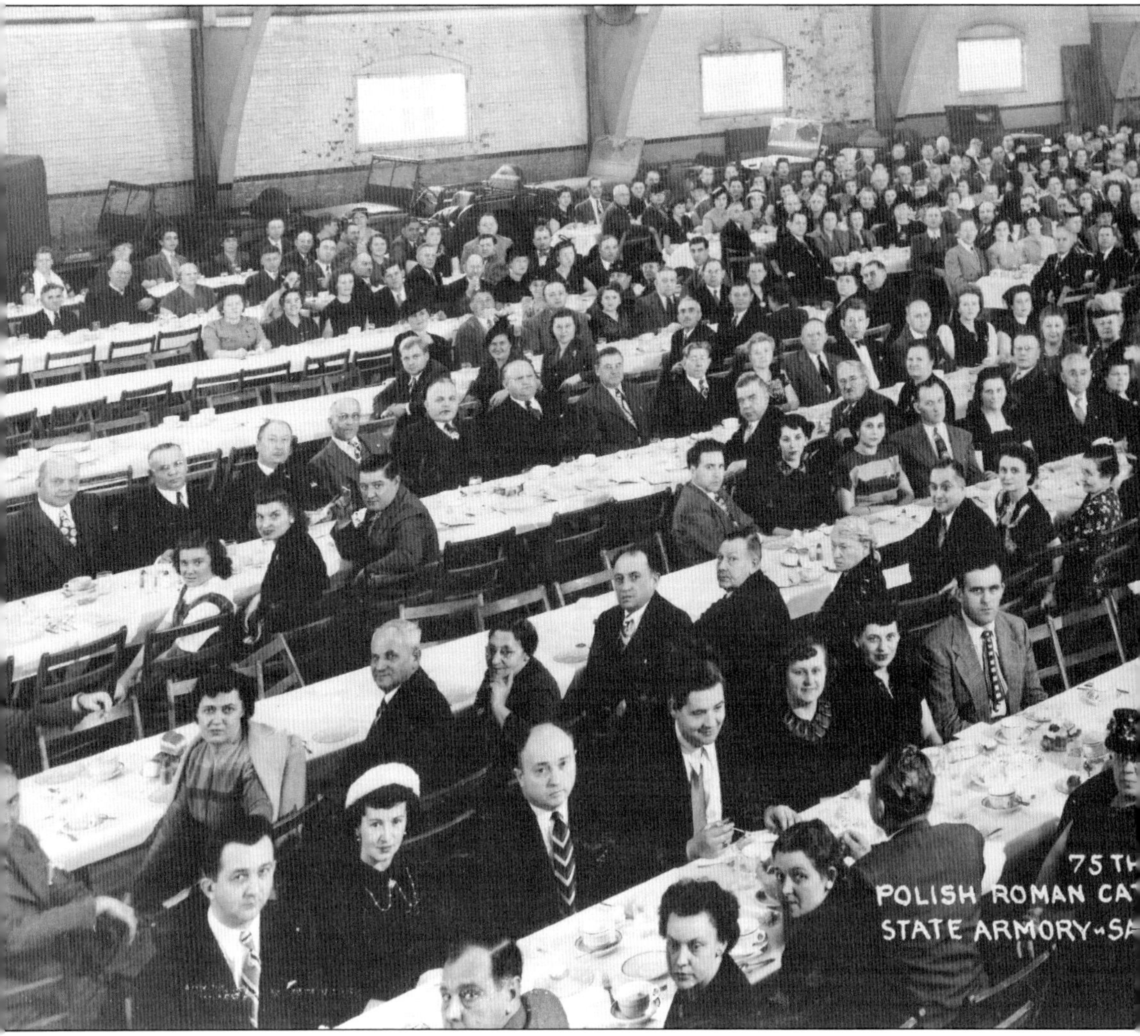

The Polish Roman Catholic Union of America, established in 1873, is the oldest Polish American fraternal benefit and Catholic loyalist organization in the United States. As an organization, the development of PRCUA spans the time frame starting with the earliest Polish immigrants to the United States to the current Polish American society. The *Narod Polski* is its official bimonthly

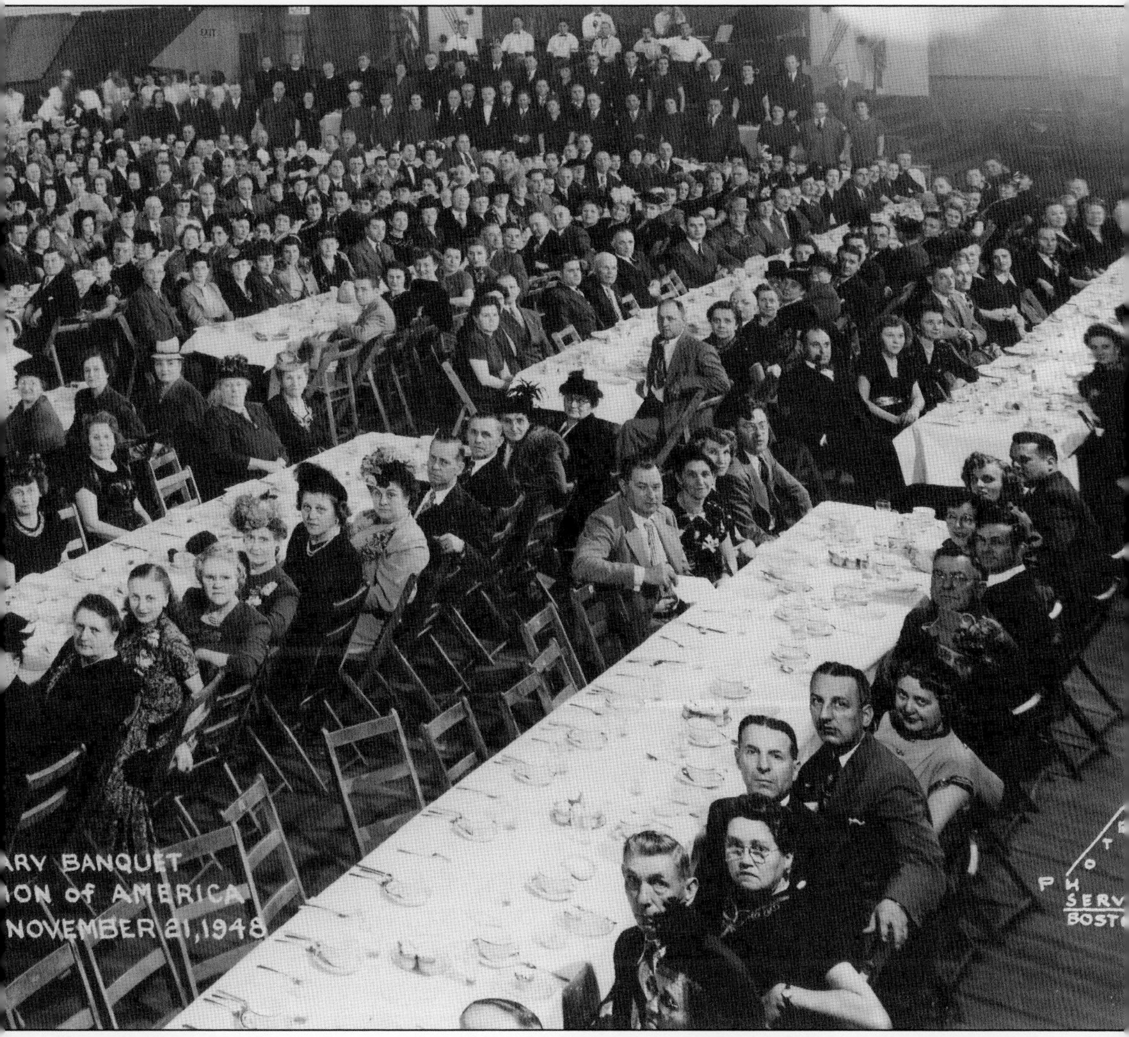

publication with articles written in English and Polish. The PRCUA held its 75th-anniversary banquet at the State Armory in Salem, Massachusetts, on November 21, 1948, with many members of the St. Joseph's Society and Polish representatives from outside of Salem in attendance. (LBM.)

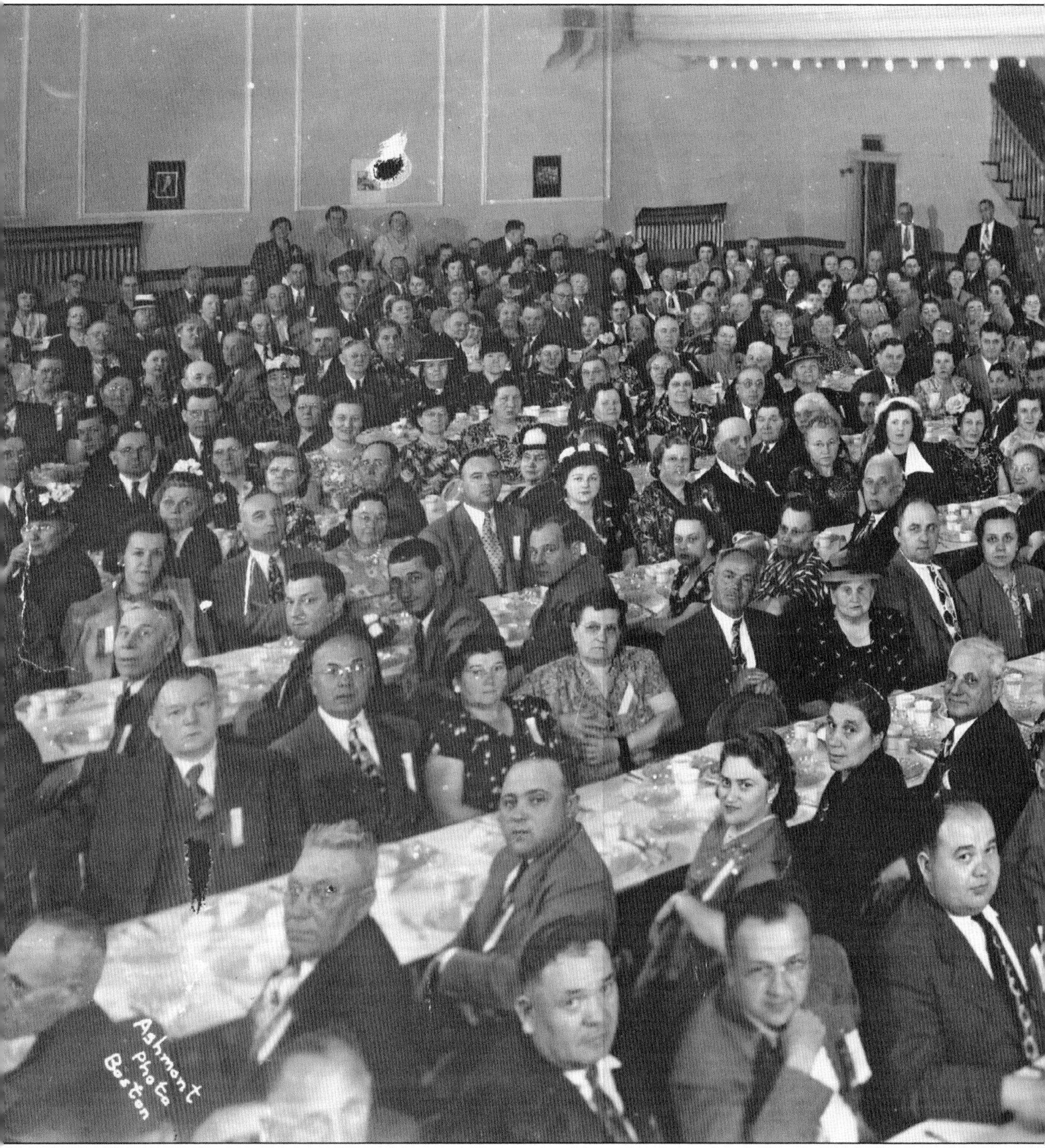

The St. Joseph's Society was the cornerstone of Polish community life in Salem. Founded as a mutual aid organization, most of the Polish residents of Ward One were members of the society. Throughout Memorial Day weekend in 1949, the St. Joseph's Society celebrated its 50th golden jubilee with a parade, mass, banquet, and a grand ball at the Now and Then Hall on May 28.

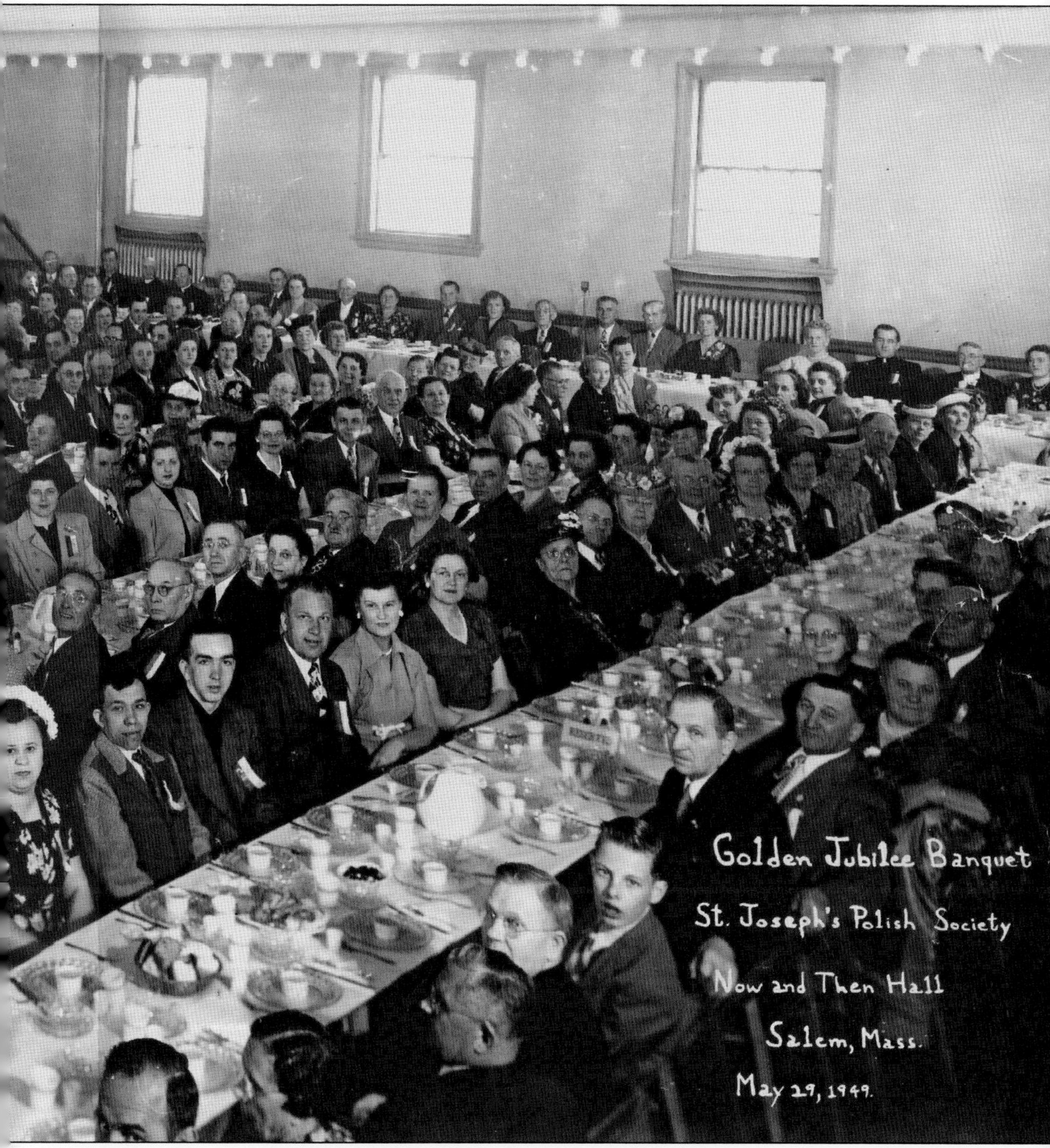

The Krakowiaki Orchestra played polkas and dance music throughout the evening. The hall was the scene of many cultural and social events for the Polish community. It was located at 36 Washington Square South with its entrance on 102 Essex Street. (SJB.)

145

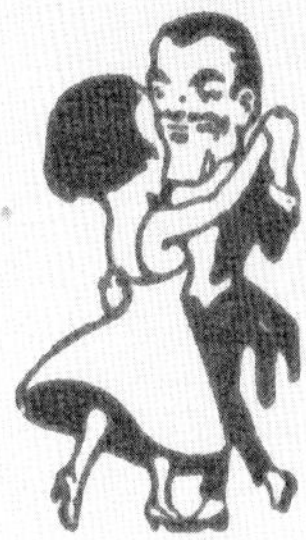

PIERWSZY 145

WIELKI BAL WIOSENNY

urządza

Towarzystwo Św. Józefa

w Salem, Mass.

w Sobotę, 16-go Kwietnia, 1932

Cena Biletu 35 Centów

Dances were important social events in the Polish community. This ticket was for "The First Big Ball of the Spring, sponsored by the St. Joseph's Society on Saturday, April 16, 1932." The price of admission was 35¢! (NPS.)

ST. JOSEPH'S DAY DANCE

160 Derby Street, Salem, Massachusetts

BUFFET 7-8 p.m.

SATURDAY, MARCH 19, 1983

DANCING 8:00 - 12:00 p.m.

JOEY SMOLA

VELVETONES ORCHESTRA

Donation:

No 143 **$6.50** per person

There is a story that St. Joseph's Day, which is two days after St. Patrick's Day, was observed by the Polish community to claim its own saint's holiday as a reaction to the dominant Irish Catholic influence in the United States. St. Joseph's Day, March 19, 1983, was celebrated with a dance at St. Joseph's Hall. (NPS.)

Seven

Sports

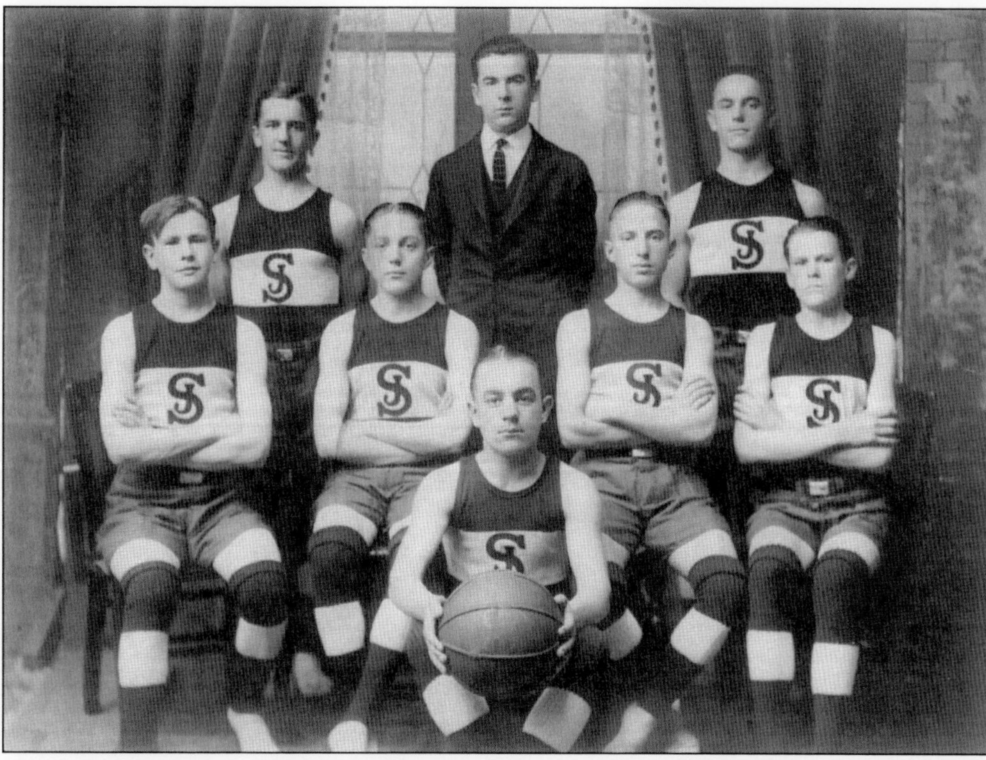

The St. Joseph's Society sponsored Polish Athletic Association sports teams that played other youth teams on the North Shore and Polish teams throughout the state. This 1924 basketball team included first-generation United States–born Polish youth. Pictured are, from left to right, (first row) team captain Joseph Bartula; (second row) Joseph Nowak, Frank Smolinski, Edward Olbrych, and Adam Stefanski; (third row) Louis Wilczenski, John Dumeracki, and Alex Tyburc. (RNC.)

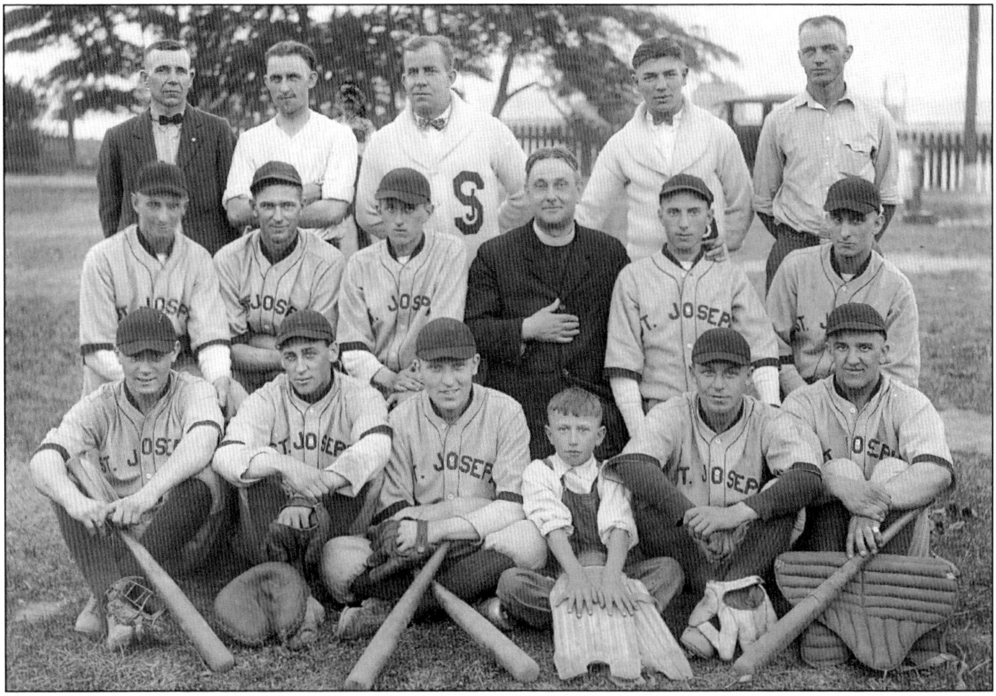

St. Joseph's Society baseball teams played other Polish teams in the Boston area and occasionally traveled outside Massachusetts to compete in national games sponsored by Polish organizations. Pictured in the mid-1920s are, from left to right, (first row) F. Kohn, S. Kozlowski, J. Jankowski, S. Olbrych (bat boy), J. Kusek, and L. Wilczenski; (second row) P. Philip, F. Sobocinski, M. Kowalski, Fr. J. Czubek, E. Olbrych, and P. Castanguay; (third row) W. Dolmat, S. Maga, E. Cody, P. Bartula, and B. Maga. (NPS.)

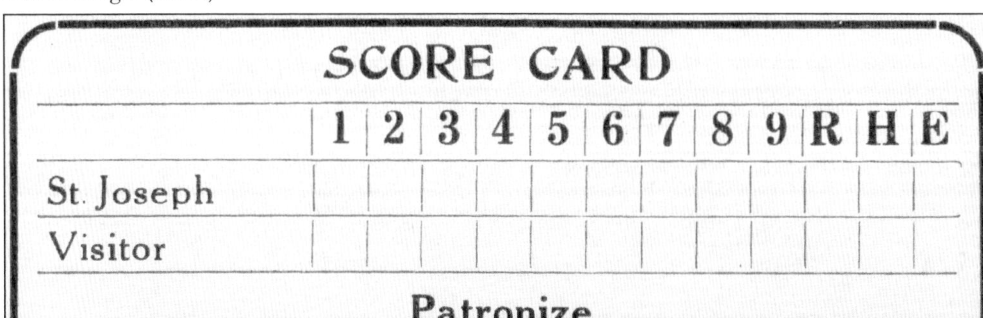

SCORE CARD

	1	2	3	4	5	6	7	8	9	R	H	E
St. Joseph												
Visitor												

Patronize

JOHN KARBOWNICZAK

Furniture and Coal

155 Derby St. Tel. 1198 Salem, Mass.

Polish businesses sponsored the St. Joseph's Society's baseball teams. Local merchant John Karbowniczak, whose furniture store was across the street from St. Joseph's Hall, provided score cards for home games. Baseball games were played at Rowell's Field, located near Salem Willows, at the current site of the New England Power Plant on Fort Avenue. (NPS.)

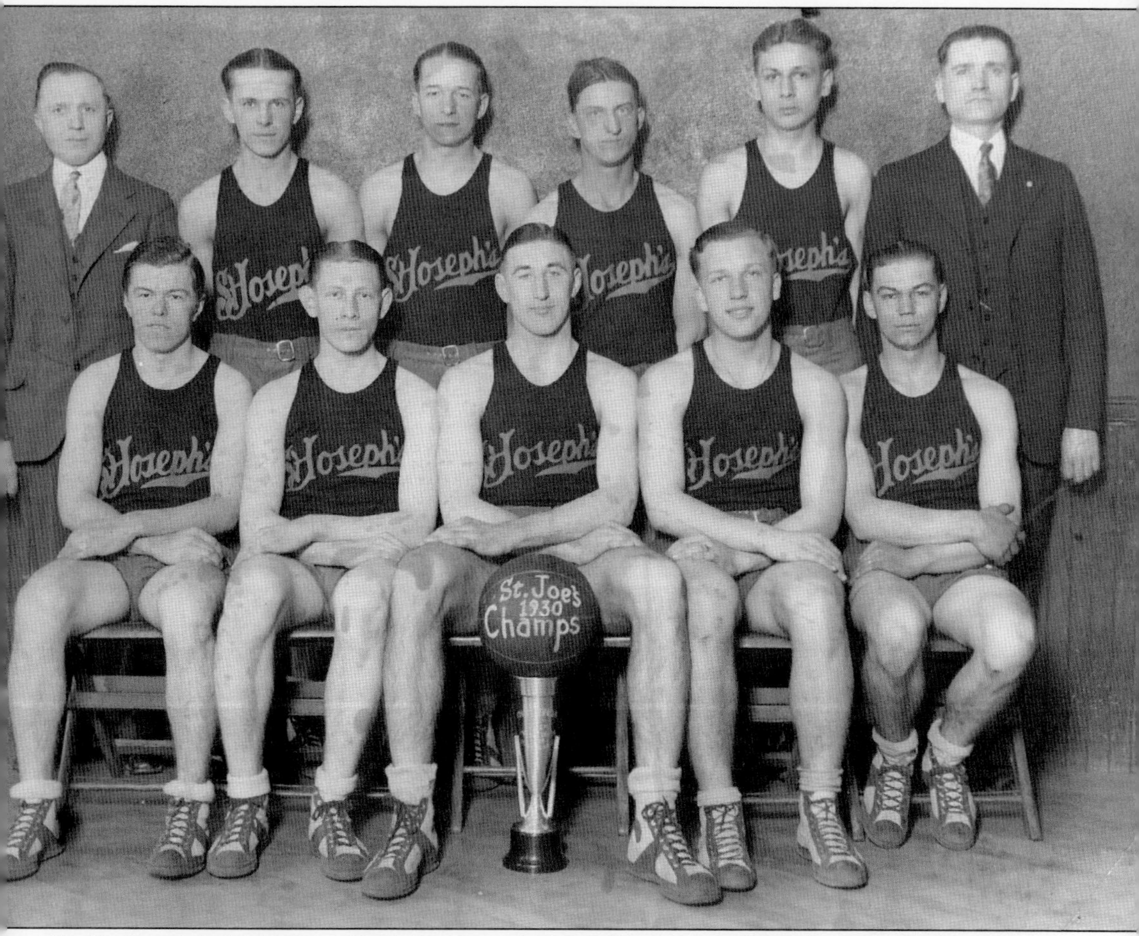

The St. Joseph Polish Roman Catholic Union basketball team won the Salem Basketball League Championship in 1930. In the photograph are, from left to right, (seated) R. "Sparky" Dombrowski, J. "Sparrow" Wroblewski, A. Ezmunt, E. Graczyk, and J. Trojanowski; (standing) club officer B. Kobuszewski, B. "Shimmy" Siemiontowski, X. "Subsy" Hincman, L. "Slash" Gorski, A. Sowinski, club officer J. Olszewski. Al Ezmunt and Ed Graczyk were also outstanding athletes at Salem High School. The St. Joseph's Society charged admission to the games to help support the teams. Even in the Depression years of the 1930s, the price of admission was an affordable 25¢ for a Monday night's entertainment of two games of basketball and a musical performance. Music was part of most Polish gatherings, which included sporting events. Ben Hacker's Orchestra band was sometimes featured during breaks in the action at the games at St. Joe's Hall. (NPS.)

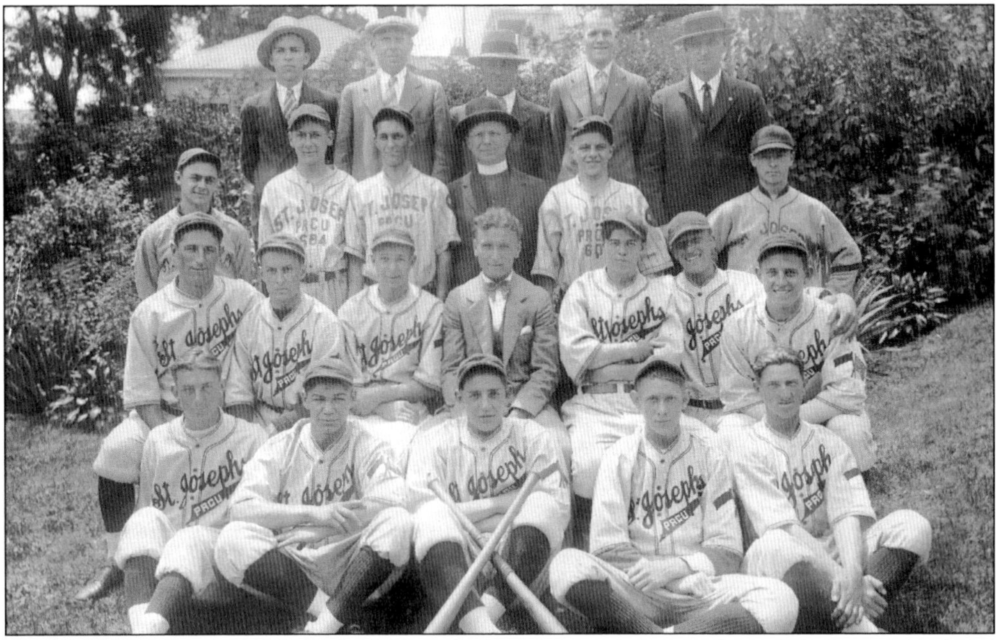

Semiprofessional baseball flourished through the Depression years. The Polish Roman Catholic Union sponsored this 1930 St. Joseph's team that won the city championship. Pictured are, from left to right, (first row) S. Lesczynski, J. Trojanowski, L. Brudzynski, J. Wroblewski, and L. Gorski; (second row) A. Hincman, J. Swiniarski, X. Hincman, J. Filip, R. Dombrowski, E. Graczyk, and P. Piecewicz; (third row) C. Bartnicki, A. Sowinski, L. Hincman, Rev. J. Piszczalka (spiritual advisor), F. Kocialka, and E. Bartnicki; (fourth row) club officers A. Dzierzanowski, F. Wroblewski, M. Sumski, H. Kobuszewski, and S. Graczyk. (LBM.)

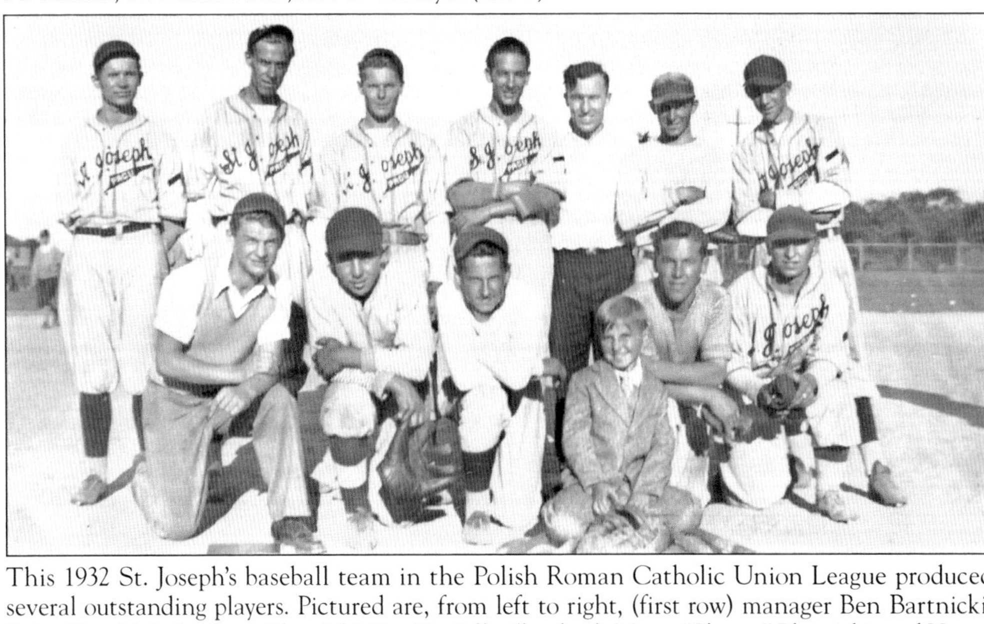

This 1932 St. Joseph's baseball team in the Polish Roman Catholic Union League produced several outstanding players. Pictured are, from left to right, (first row) manager Ben Bartnicki, Boley Przydzial, Anthony Plutnicki, Kaz Kocialka (bat boy), Matty "Shorty" Plutnicki, and Henry "Sam" Symbarski; (second row) Stash Gorczyka, Vic Pszenny, Joe Marchinkowski, Larry Gelineau, coach Joe Jankowski, Ted Hincman, and Ben Zielski. (RP.)

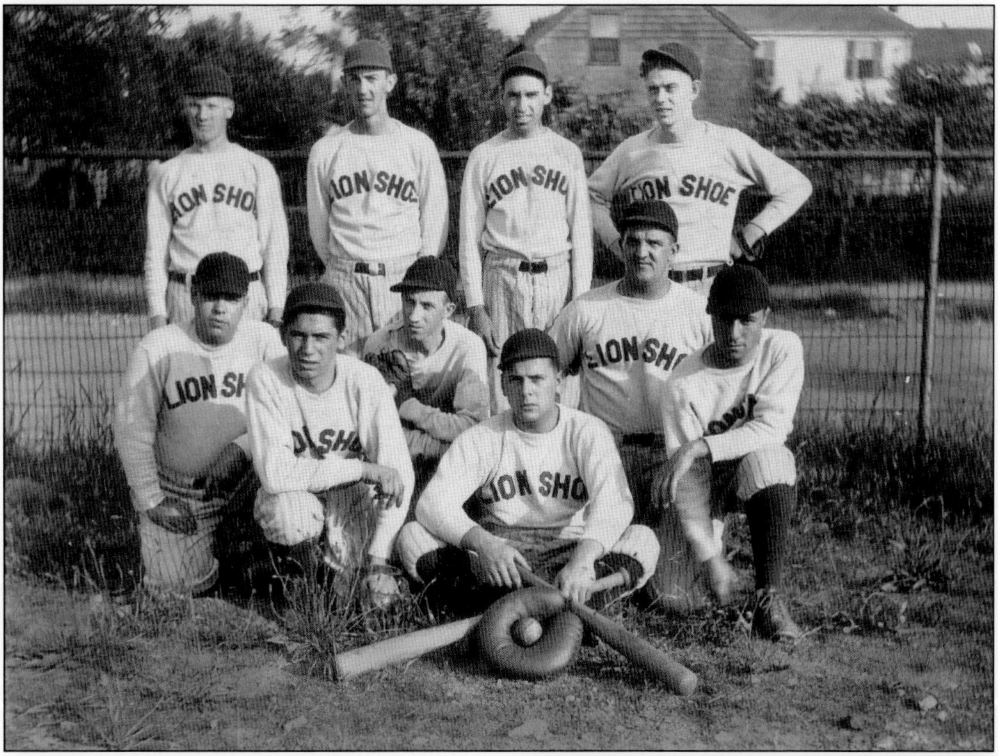

Factories often sponsored social or recreational outlets, such as picnics and baseball teams. The 1930 Lion Shoe baseball team fielded members of the Salem Polish community. Catcher Louis Wilczenski is pictured kneeling in the second row, second from the right. (FLW.)

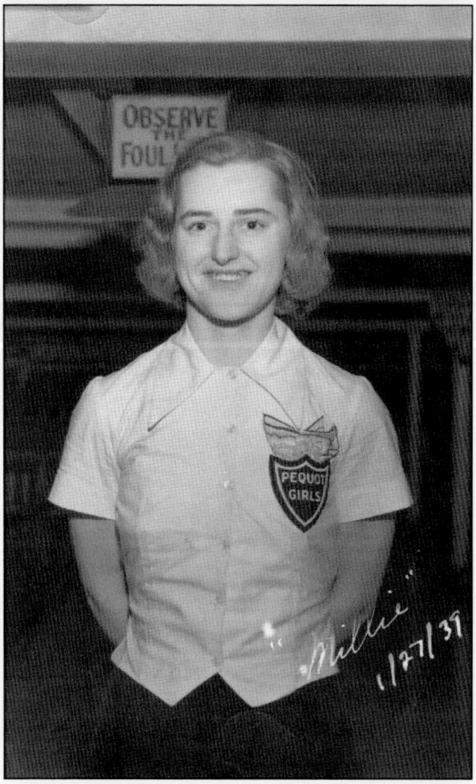

There were fewer organized sports teams for women than men in Salem. Candlepin bowling leagues were popular, and various businesses and clubs sponsored competitive teams. Millie Pszenny Szybiak, shown here in her early twenties, was a star bowler for the Pequot Mills girls' team in 1939. (CSB.)

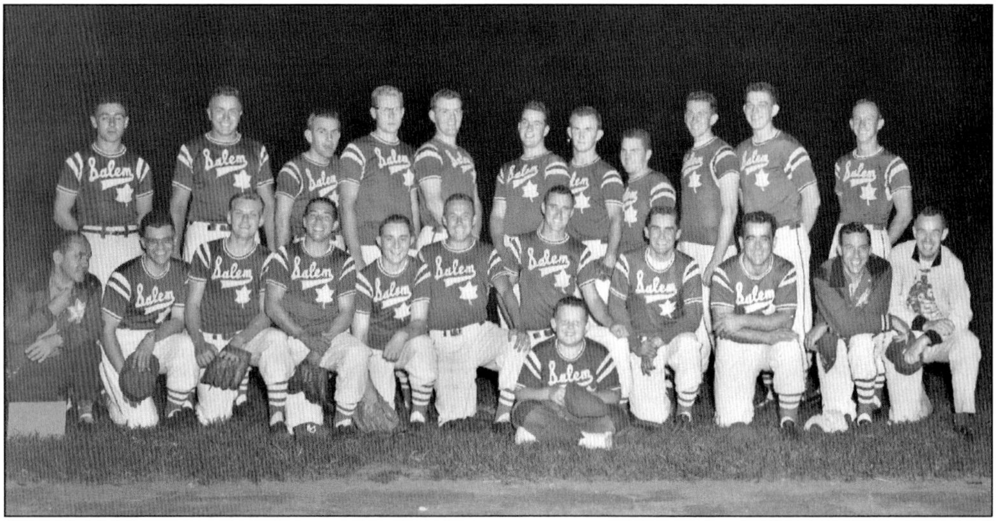

In 1958, the Maple Leafs were the Salem Chamber of Commerce Softball League champions by edging the Leather Workers, 3-2, in front of a record crowd at Mack Park. Team members are, from left to right, (first row) coach Matthew "Shorty" Plutnicki, Bob Cummings, Jim Grocki, Roger Dalton, Dick Morin, Jack Birmingham, Charlie Carroll, Ron Plutnicki, Buster Viselli, and manager Cass Knight; (second row) unidentified player, Bob Gibley, Don Brennan, Jim Smerczynski, Don Kowalski, Lee Webster, Mike Harrington, Mike Maguire, Joe Arundel, Bob Piecewicz, and Jim Moroney. Team sponsor Steve Davidowicz expected his players to be good role models and citizens. At Thanksgiving, the team members would locate needy Salem families who then received a dinner donated through Steve's company, Maple Leaf Meat Products. Members of the team and their dates celebrated the winning season at Blinstrub's Village in Boston (Above, RP; below, JBM.)

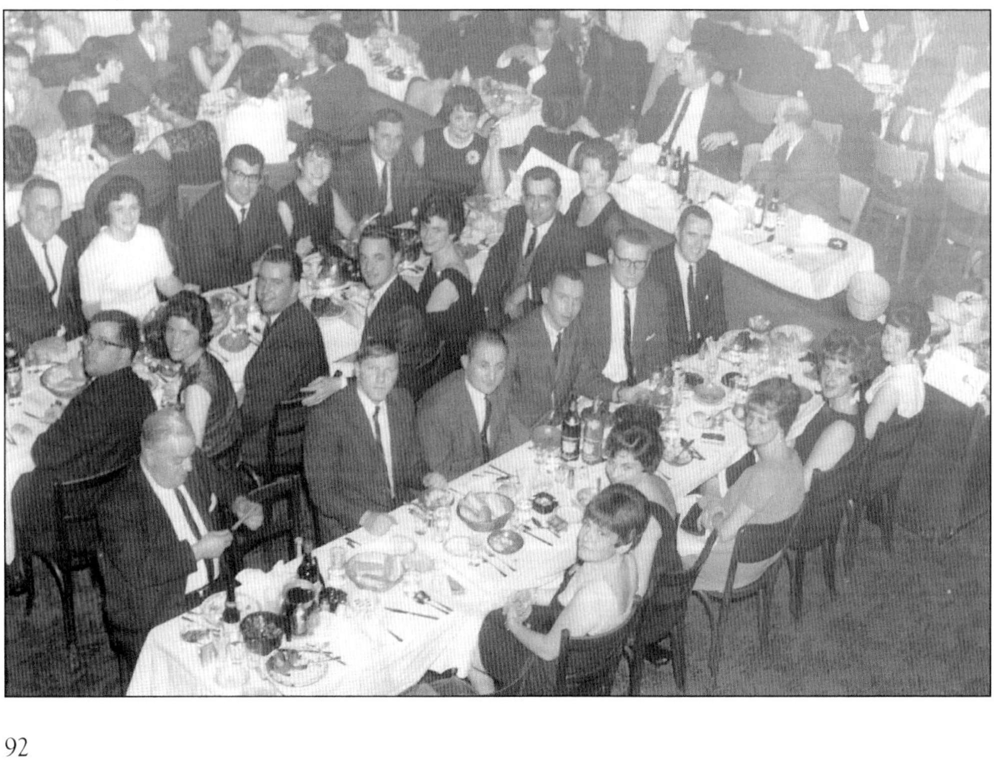

Candlepin bowling was first played in Worcester, Massachusetts, in 1880. It quickly caught on as an individual and team sport throughout New England. The game is similar to 10-pin and duckpin bowling with a few differences in rules. The pins are "candle shaped," and the ball only weighs two pounds, seven ounces. It was a sport popular for women's teams. Here, Millie Szybiak lined up for a strike. (CSB.)

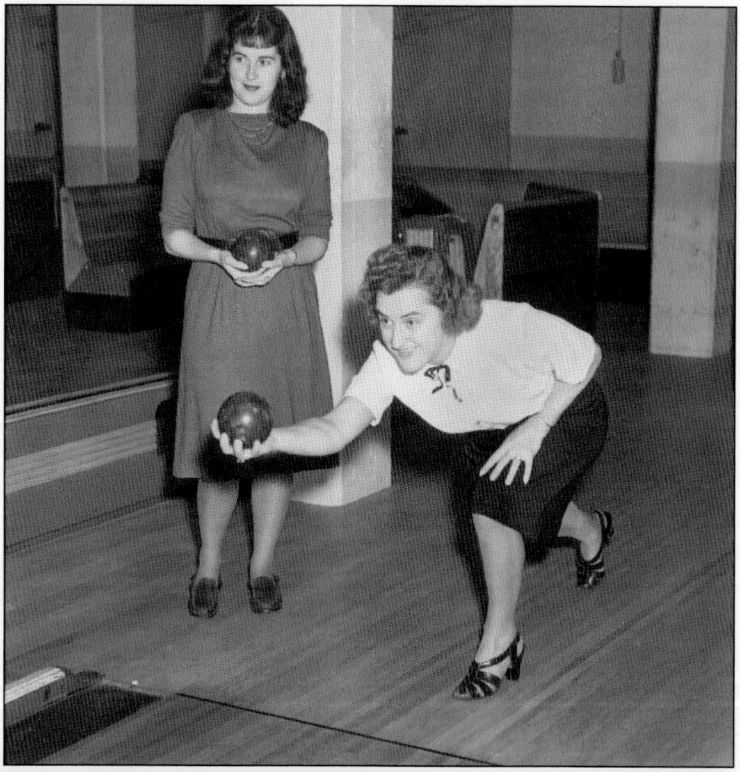

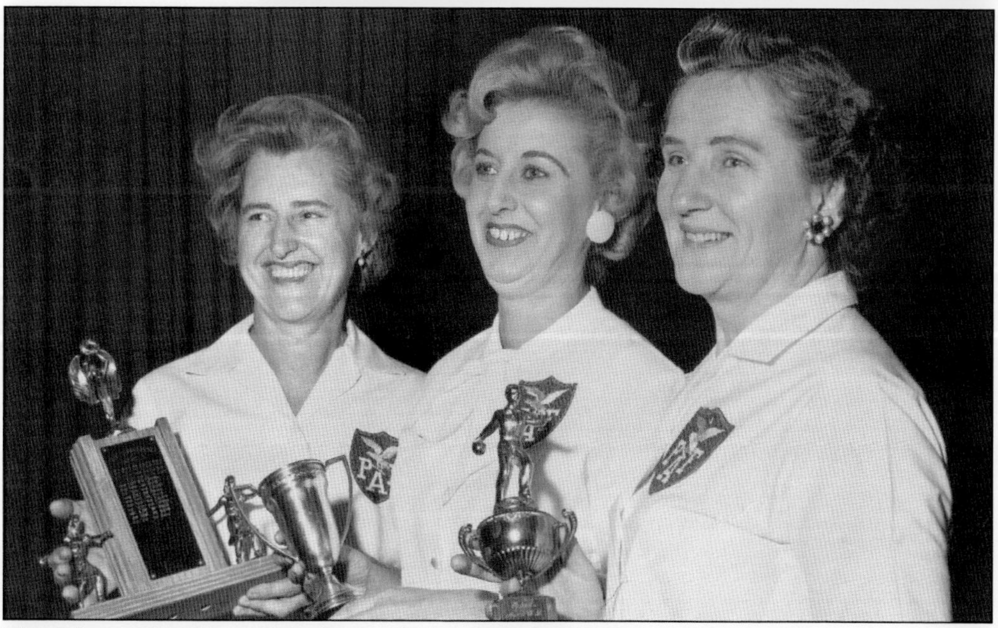

The Falcons Nest No. 188 had a candlepin team that bowled weekly at Heff's under the A&P grocery market on Federal Street in Salem in the 1950s. On Palm Sunday, the Falcons competed against other nests in the area, and trophies were awarded. Pictured are the Salem Polish Falcons Candlepin Bowling champions. Millie Szybiak (left) holds the first-place trophy. Bea Karpowicz (center) and Genia Day also placed among the winners. (CSB.)

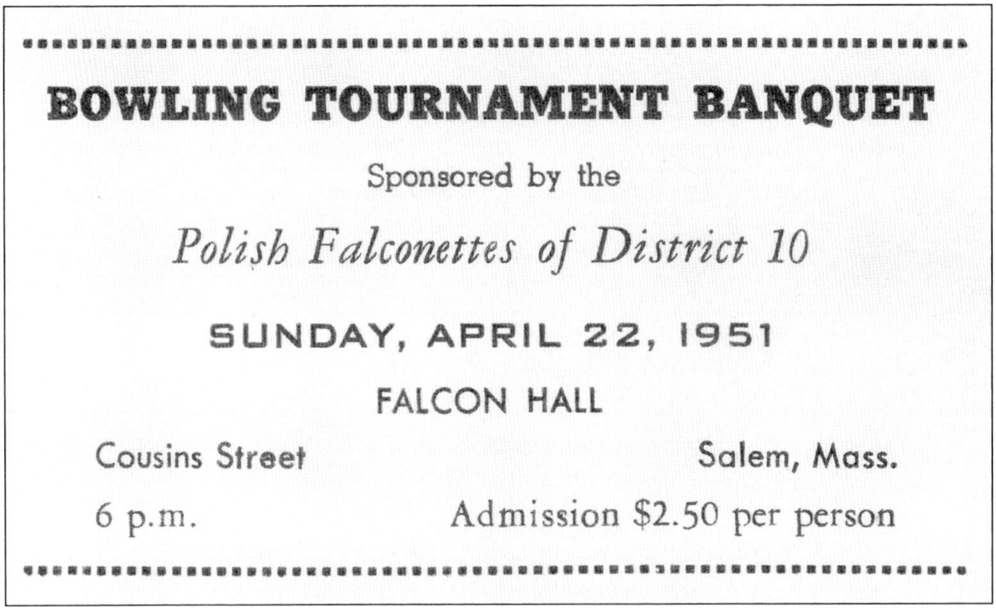

BOWLING TOURNAMENT BANQUET

Sponsored by the

Polish Falconettes of District 10

SUNDAY, APRIL 22, 1951

FALCON HALL

Cousins Street Salem, Mass.

6 p.m. Admission $2.50 per person

The Falcons' motto "*w zdrowym ciele zdrowy duch*" echoed a Latin saying, "a healthy spirit in a healthy body." The organization had a philosophy of physical fitness, exercise, and sport as a way to build camaraderie. Falcons-sponsored bowling team members found ways to socialize with each other and to celebrate their triumphs. Salem's Polish Sokolica, translated Falconettes, sold tickets to fund their end-of-the-season bowling banquet in 1951. (APW.)

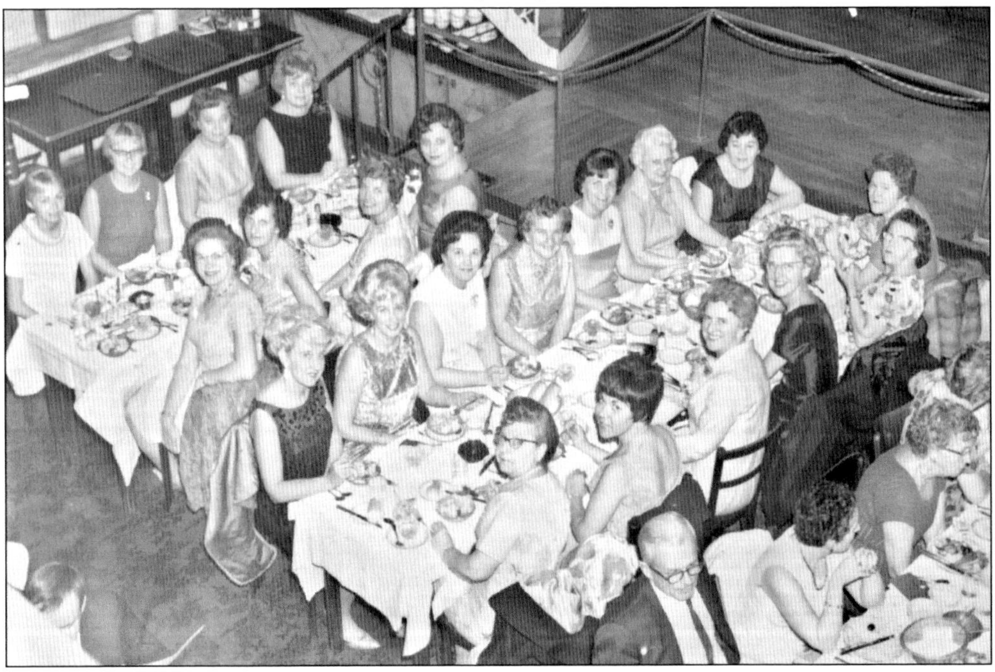

Members of Salem's Polish community of a certain age will remember Blinstrub's Village in South Boston around 1960. It was a leader in Boston entertainment and the place to go to see big-name performers through the 1950s and 1960s. No wonder the Salem Falconettes picked Blinstrub's for their end-of-bowling-season party! (LBM.)

Eight

WORK

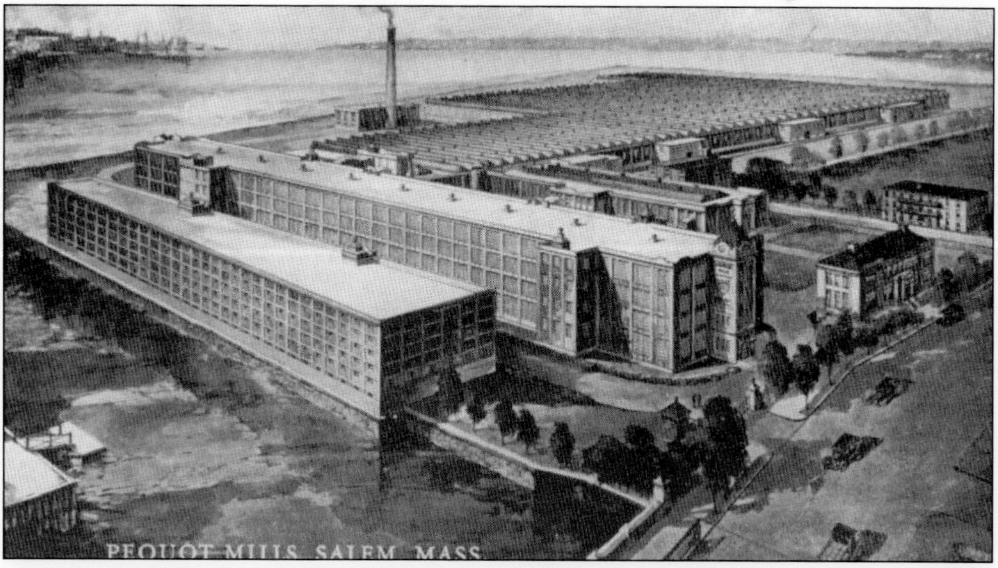

This vintage 1910 postcard shows the original Naumkeag Steam Cotton Company. As the manufacturer of Pequot sheets and pillowcases, it became known as "Pequot Mills." The mill burned in the 1914 Salem fire but was quickly rebuilt and updated. Many Polish women were employed at the mill from the late 1800s until it moved to South Carolina in 1953. (FLW.)

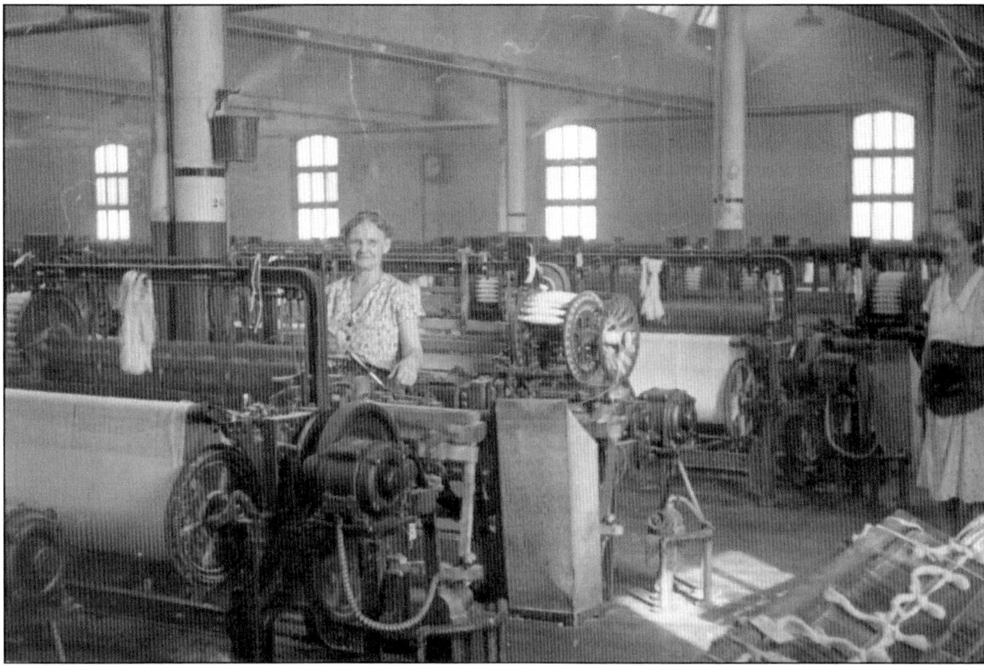

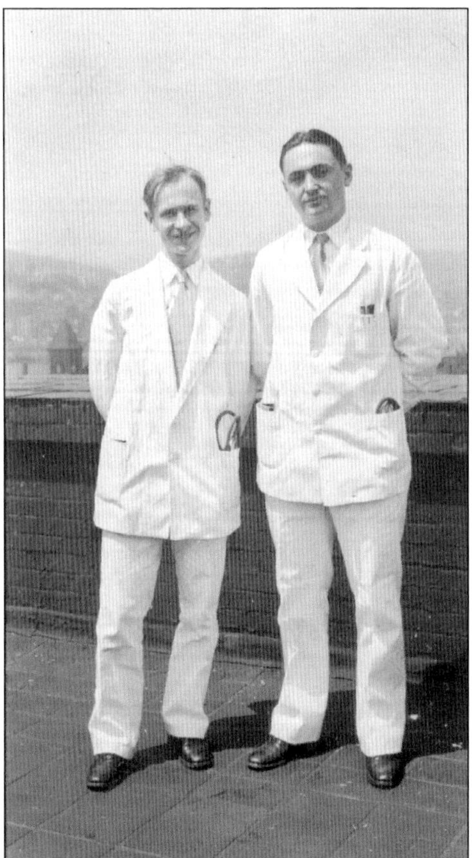

Tekla Nowak is pictured around 1930 working in the weaving shed of the Pequot Mills. Her income helped fund her son Joseph's medical education. The Polish Students' Club of Salem, organized in 1925, also supported talented youth in acquiring advanced education. Dr. Joseph Nowak (left), a first-generation Polish American, received the club's scholarship in obtaining a medical degree. His whole family worked to finance his education. Joseph graduated from Salem High School, majored in premedical studies at the University of Massachusetts/Middlesex College of Medicine and Surgery, and received a medical degree in 1933 from the College of Physicians and Surgeons in Boston. Middlesex College was unusual in accepting students based on merit rather than social status. At the time, medicine was a prestigious, if not lucrative, profession. Doctor Nowak was often paid for his services with food. (Both, RNC.)

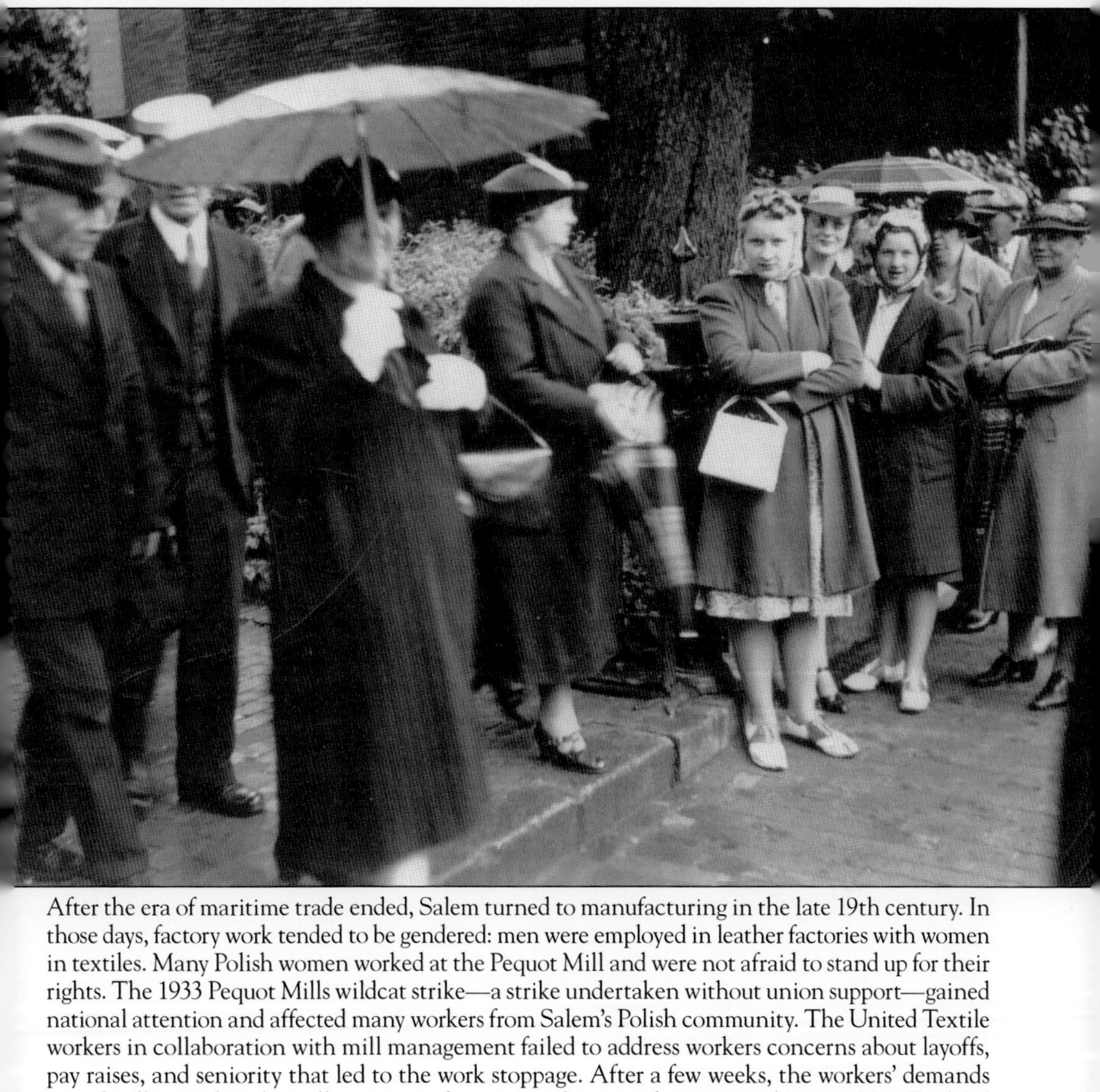

After the era of maritime trade ended, Salem turned to manufacturing in the late 19th century. In those days, factory work tended to be gendered: men were employed in leather factories with women in textiles. Many Polish women worked at the Pequot Mill and were not afraid to stand up for their rights. The 1933 Pequot Mills wildcat strike—a strike undertaken without union support—gained national attention and affected many workers from Salem's Polish community. The United Textile workers in collaboration with mill management failed to address workers concerns about layoffs, pay raises, and seniority that led to the work stoppage. After a few weeks, the workers' demands were finally met, but the mill was never the same as the manufacturing industry in New England was already in decline. Pequot Mill finally closed in the early 1950s. (LBM.)

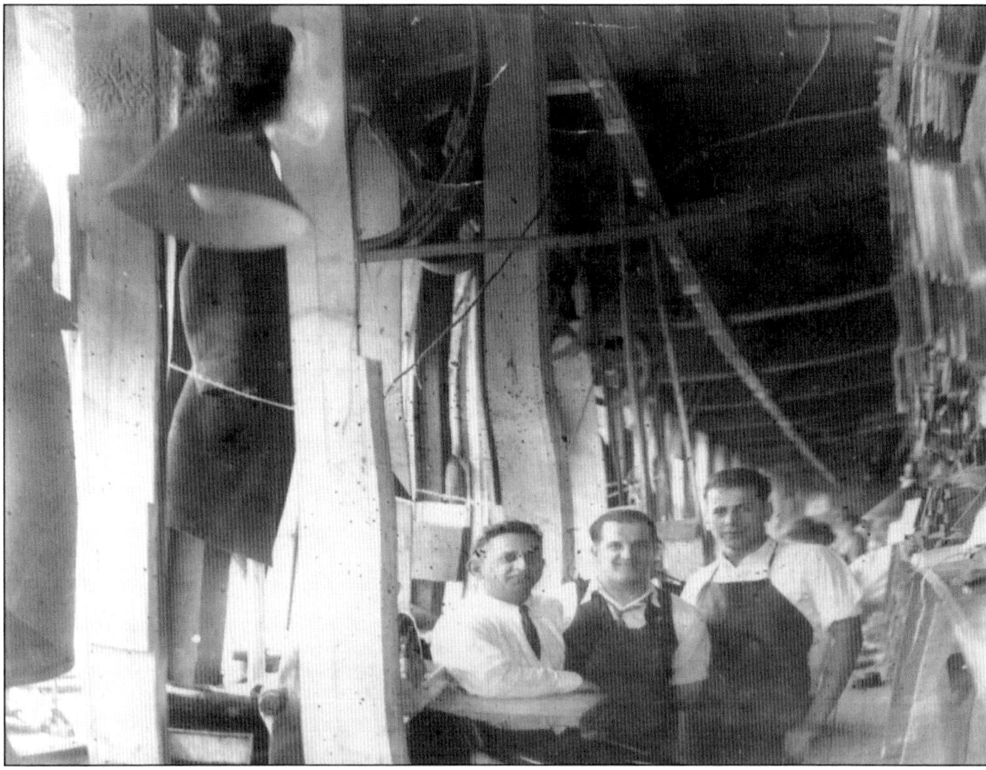

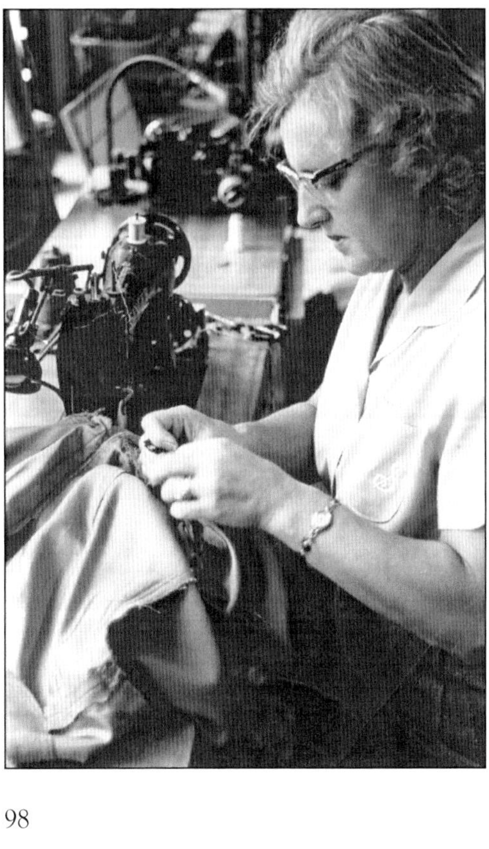

There were many factories producing leather goods in the Derby Street area and around the North Shore. Immigrants and first-generation, United States–born Poles often worked difficult and sometimes dangerous jobs in leather factories. Louis Wilczenski is in the center of this photograph taken at Carr Leather Company in Peabody, Massachusetts, in the mid-1940s. (FLW.)

Textiles were important to Salem's economy from the mid–19th to mid–20th century. Many Poles relied on the Pequot Mills for their livelihood. In its heyday, the mill was Salem's largest employer with over 2,000 workers, many of whom lived in the Derby Street area. Emilia Pszenny Szybiak was photographed while working at her sewing machine. (NPS.)

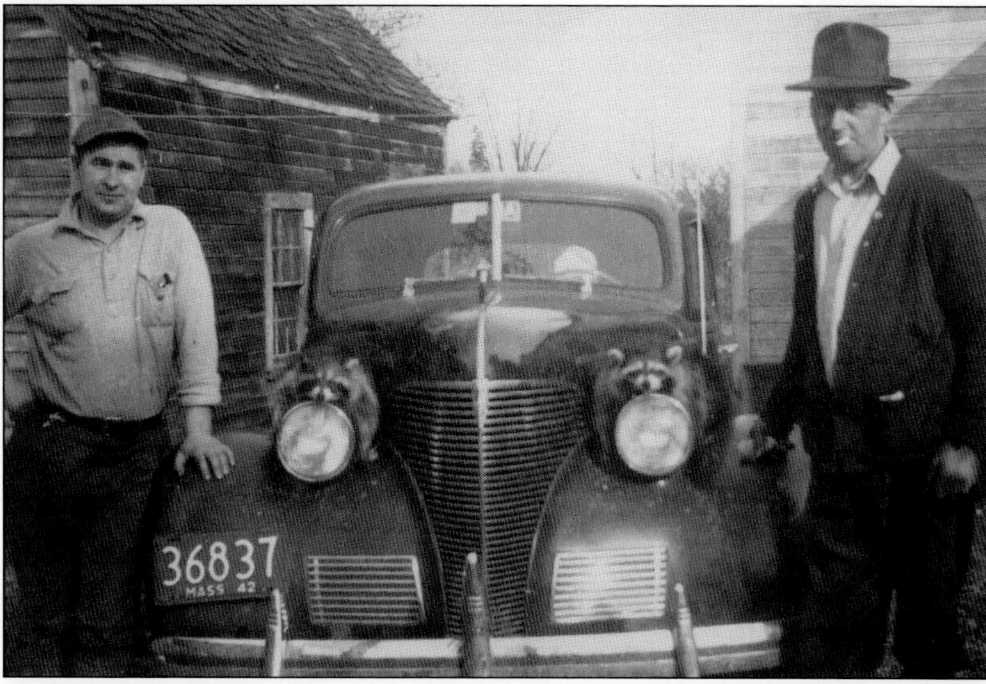

Hunting raccoons helped solve a meat shortage during World War II. An article in the *Salem Evening News* (October 22, 1943) reported that raccoon meat tastes like calves' liver and some parts resemble turkey. The hunters sold the pelts to fur markets. (RNC.)

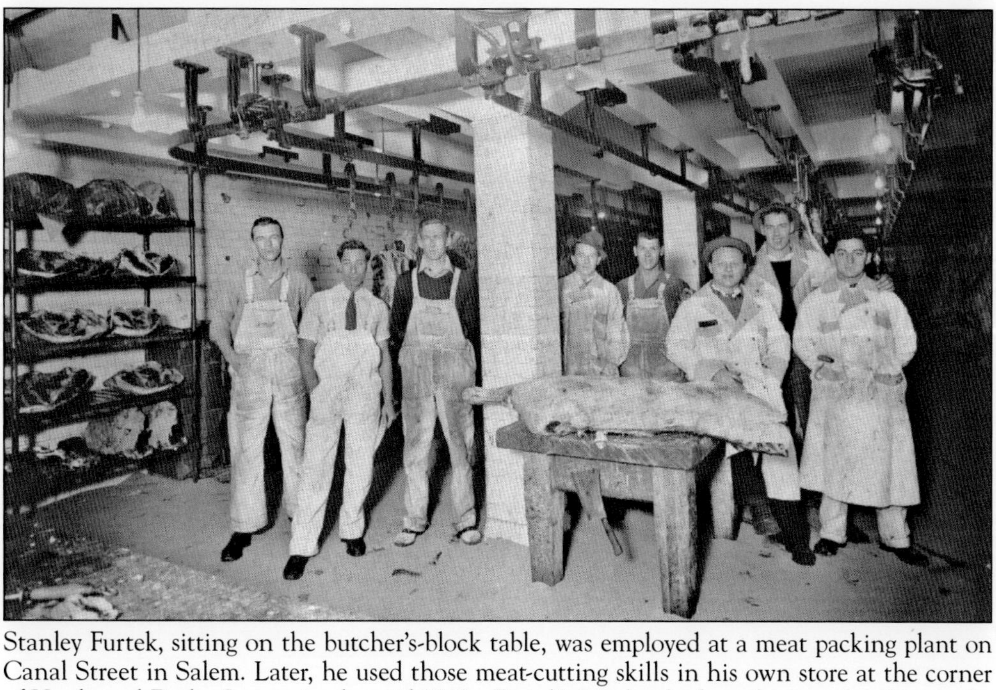

Stanley Furtek, sitting on the butcher's-block table, was employed at a meat packing plant on Canal Street in Salem. Later, he used those meat-cutting skills in his own store at the corner of Hardy and Derby Streets in the mid-1940s. Furtek's Market had sawdust on the floor and a walk-in meat cooler. Stanley used a pencil to add up the customer's bill on brown-paper grocery bags. (RNC.)

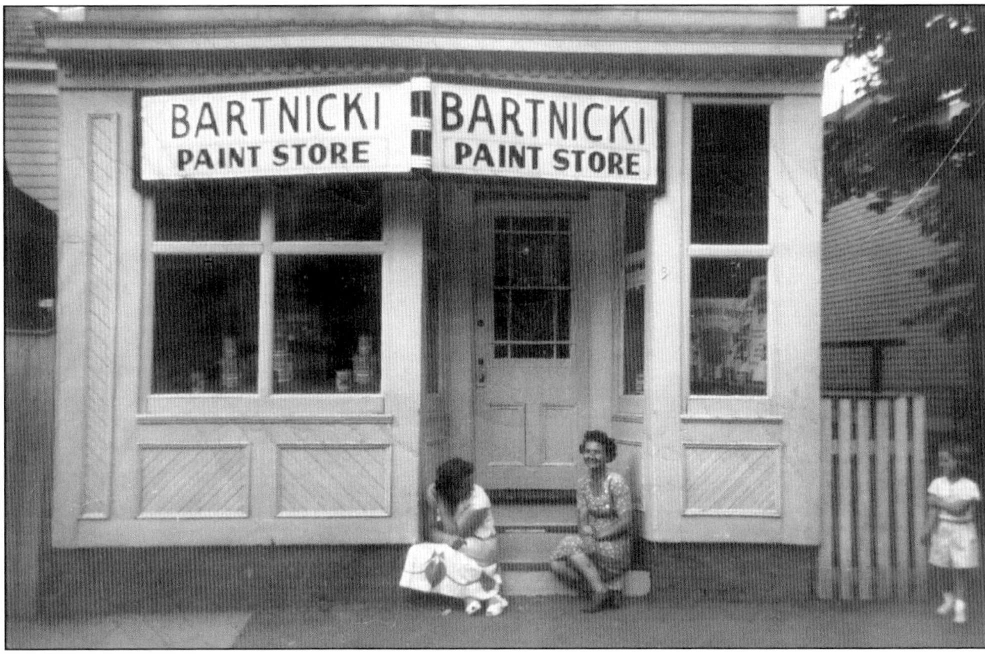

Teofil Bartnicki opened his paint store on Bentley Street in the early 1900s and, with the help of his son Edmund, remained in business until the 1940s. Teofil also sold candles and religious articles in the store to attract customers and supplement his income. Sophie (Lesczynski) Ouellette (right) and a friend were photographed sitting on the steps. (LBM.)

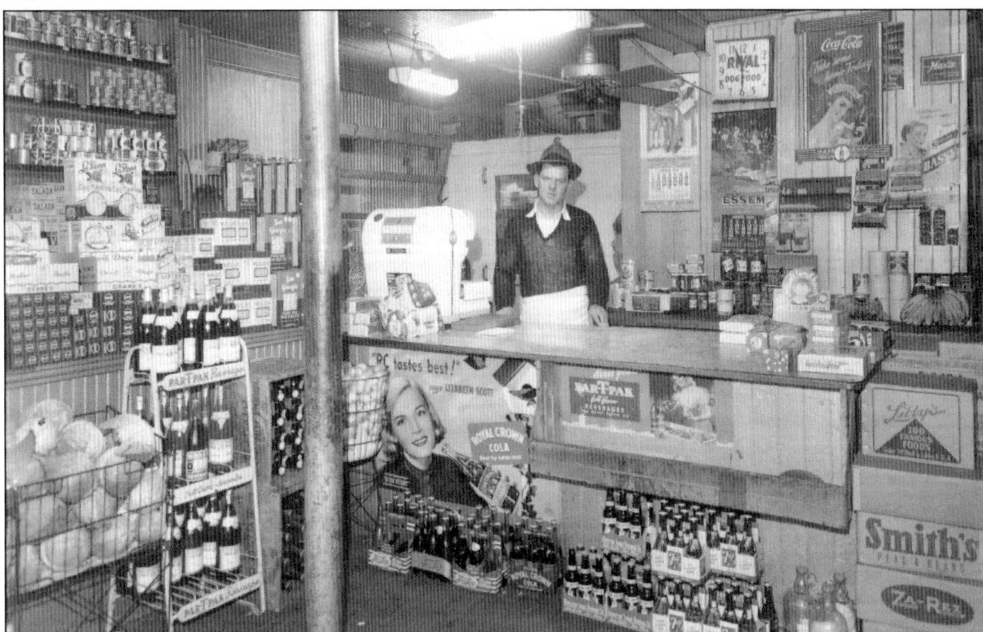

John Witkos is photographed behind the counter in his Witkos's Market, located 126 Derby Street, in 1951. John was widely known in Salem by the nickname "Mike Hogan." Even though his Polish name was not too difficult to pronounce, people often Anglicized immigrant names. It was rumored that banks would even cash checks for him that were made out to Mike Hogan. (NPS.)

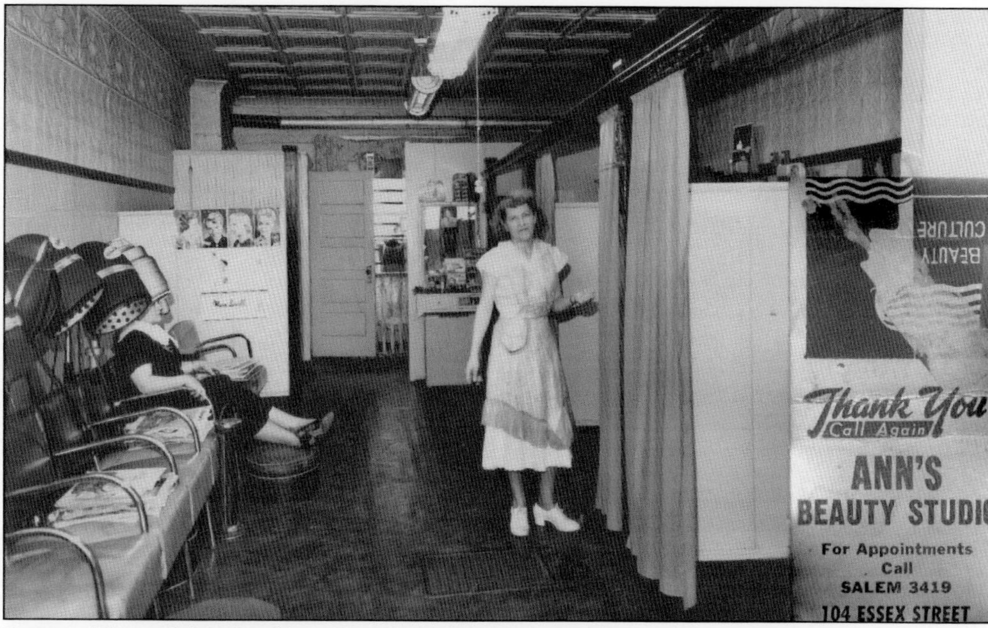

Regina (Plutnicki) Wharff, owner of Ann's Beauty Studio, was a hairdresser for many Polish ladies. She bought the shop after World War II and operated it on Essex Street until the building was razed to make room for the Hawthorne Hotel parking lot. Regina then moved her shop to the second floor of a building on Central Street and renamed it "OMI" until she retired in the 1970s. (RPW.)

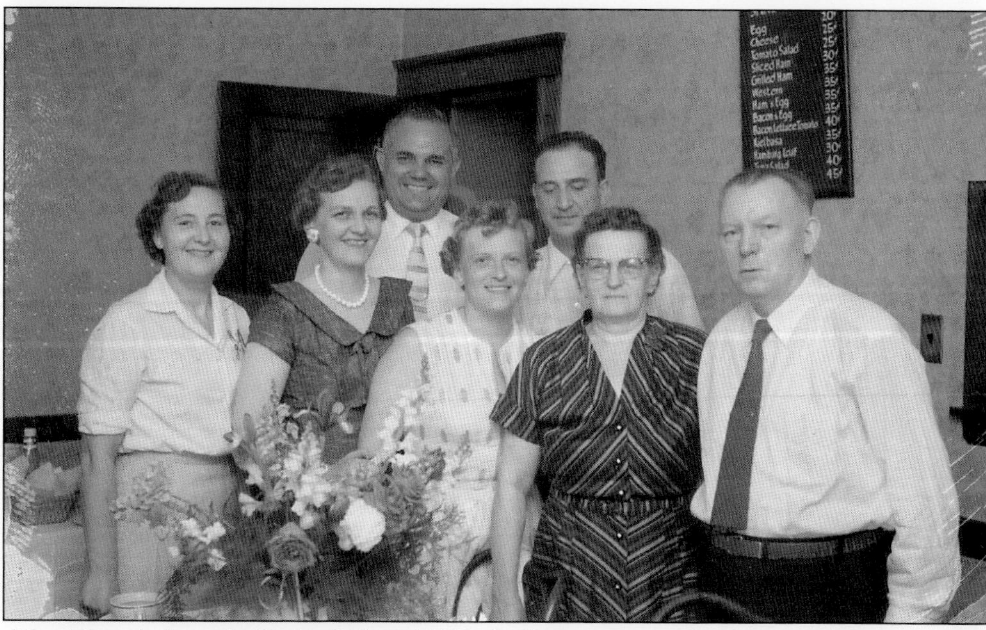

Adam's Lunch, later the Derby Café at 156 Derby Street, remained in business from about 1940 to 1967. Note the sandwich prices in 1950! Alfred Dobrosielski snapped this picture at a family birthday celebration in the back dining room. Pictured are, from left to right, Hyacinth (Pszenny) Dobrosielska, Frieda (Dobrosielska) Kobos, Joseph Kobos, Isabel (Dobrosielska) Mazurkiewicz, Henry Mazurkiewicz, Constance (Blaszkiewicz) Dobrosielska, and Adam Dobrosielski. (PD.)

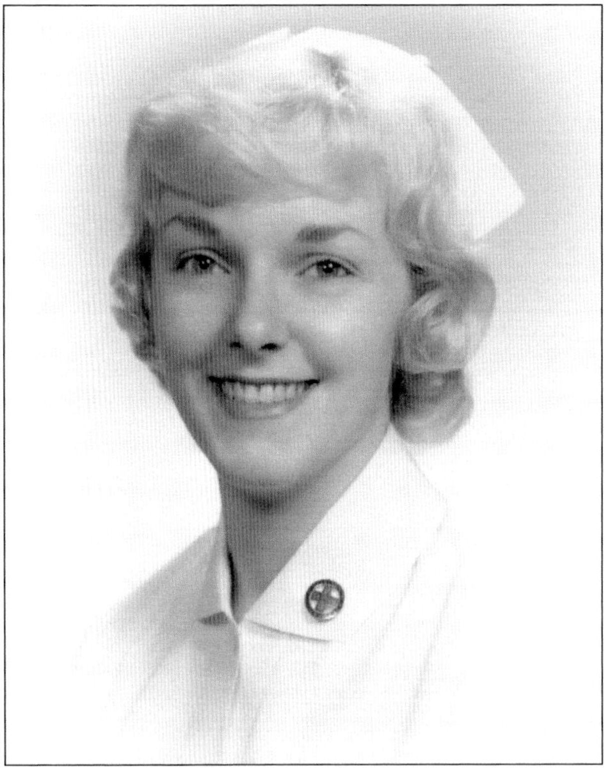

Linda Baldwin (Moustakis) grew up in the Polish neighborhood and, after moving to various locations around the city, returned to live in her childhood home. She graduated from St. John the Baptist School, Salem High School, and the Salem Hospital School of Nursing. Throughout her 39-year career at Salem Hospital/North Shore Medical Center, she was employed in the operating room. (LBM.)

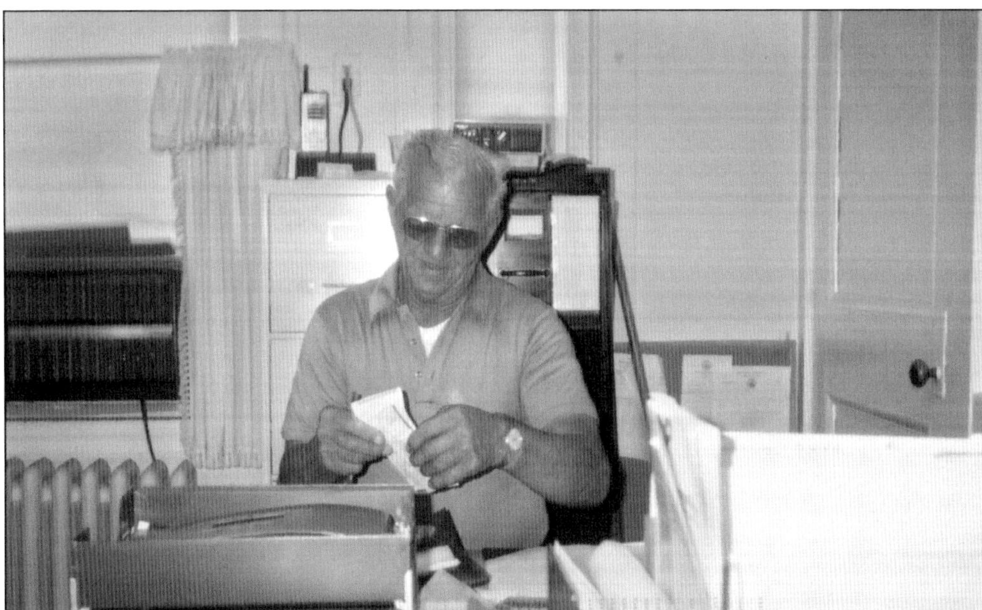

Working at his desk, Steve Pydynkowski was assistant Salem harbormaster from 1960 to 2005. The waters surrounding Salem are patrolled by harbormasters who are trained in both marine and law enforcement skills. The harbormasters work in close relationship with the Salem Police Department and the US Department of Homeland Security and are available to respond to emergencies 24 hours a day, seven days a week. (RNC.)

Nine

COMMUNITY

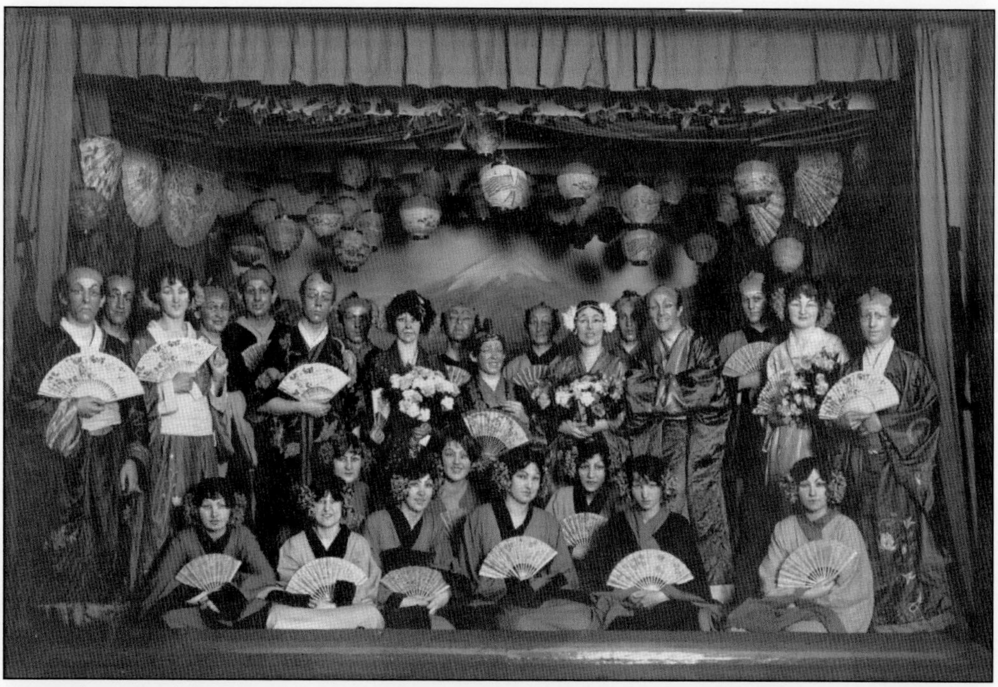

Located in Ward One in Salem, the House of Seven Gables sponsored a number of Gilbert and Sullivan musical productions at Turner Hall that involved members of the Polish community. Here, the cast of *The Mikado* lined up for a curtain call around 1930. (MHN.)

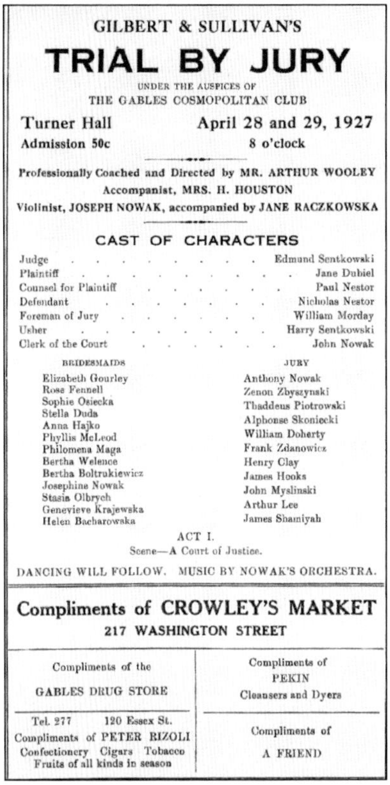

GILBERT & SULLIVAN'S

TRIAL BY JURY

UNDER THE AUSPICES OF
THE GABLES COSMOPOLITAN CLUB

Turner Hall **April 28 and 29, 1927**
Admission 50c **8 o'clock**

Professionally Coached and Directed by MR. ARTHUR WOOLEY
Accompanist, MRS. H. HOUSTON
Violinist, JOSEPH NOWAK, accompanied by JANE RACZKOWSKA

CAST OF CHARACTERS

Judge	Edmund Sentkowski
Plaintiff	Jane Dubiel
Counsel for Plaintiff	Paul Nestor
Defendant	Nicholas Nestor
Foreman of Jury	William Morday
Usher	Harry Sentkowski
Clerk of the Court	John Nowak

BRIDESMAIDS	JURY
Elizabeth Gourley	Anthony Nowak
Rose Fennell	Zenon Zbyszynski
Sophie Osiecka	Thaddeus Piotrowski
Stella Duda	Alphonse Skoniecki
Anna Hajko	William Doherty
Phyllis McLeod	Frank Zdanowicz
Philomena Maga	Henry Clay
Bertha Welence	James Hooks
Bertha Boltrukiewicz	John Myslinski
Josephine Nowak	Arthur Lee
Stasia Olbrych	James Shamiyah
Genevieve Krajewska	
Helen Bacharowska	

ACT I.
Scene—A Court of Justice.

DANCING WILL FOLLOW. MUSIC BY NOWAK'S ORCHESTRA.

Compliments of CROWLEY'S MARKET
217 WASHINGTON STREET

Compliments of the
GABLES DRUG STORE

Compliments of
PEKIN
Cleansers and Dyers

Tel. 277 120 Essex St.
Compliments of PETER RIZOLI
Confectionery Cigars Tobacco
Fruits of all kinds in season

Compliments of
A FRIEND

Caroline Emerton, a wealthy Salemite, established the House of Seven Gables Settlement Association in 1908. As part of a national social reform movement at the time, one of the missions of the Gables Association was to Americanize the Polish immigrants and assimilate them into the cultural life of the city, state, and nation. The Gables Cosmopolitan Club produced the Gilbert and Sullivan spoof *Trial by Jury* in April 1927, which featured many Poles as actors. The cast members of *Trial by Jury* took a bow after their performance in front of an audience largely filled with members of the Polish community. (Both, MHN.)

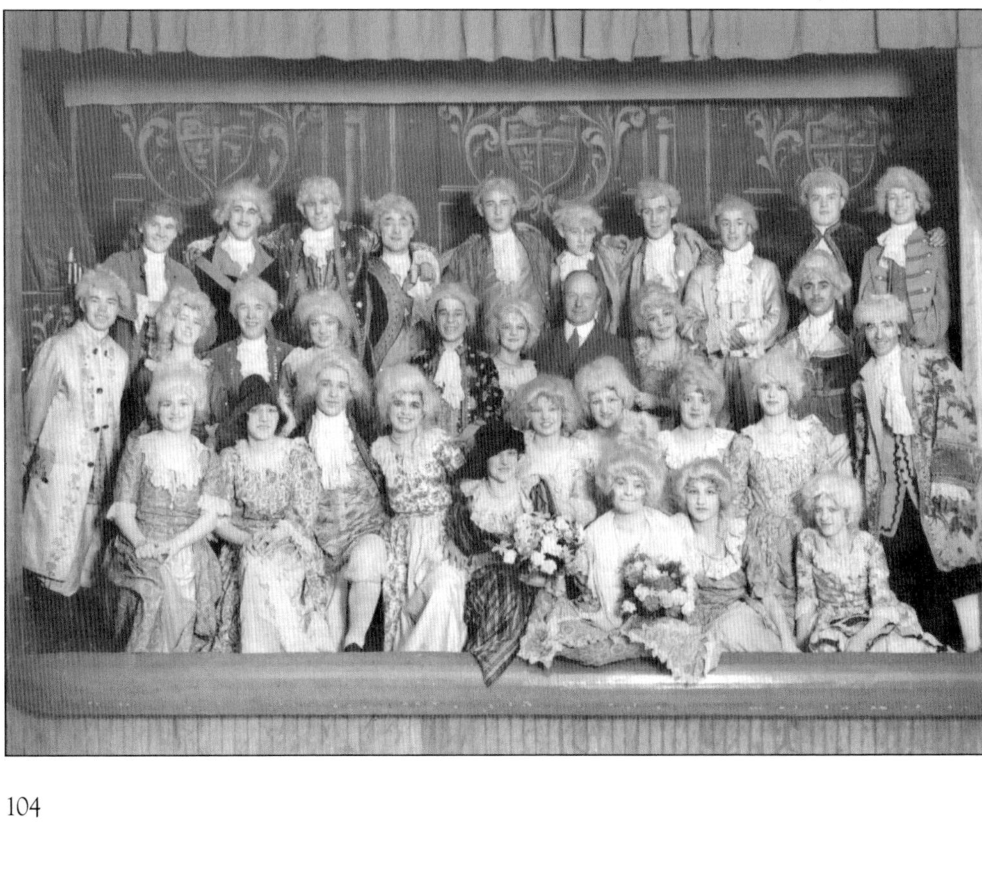

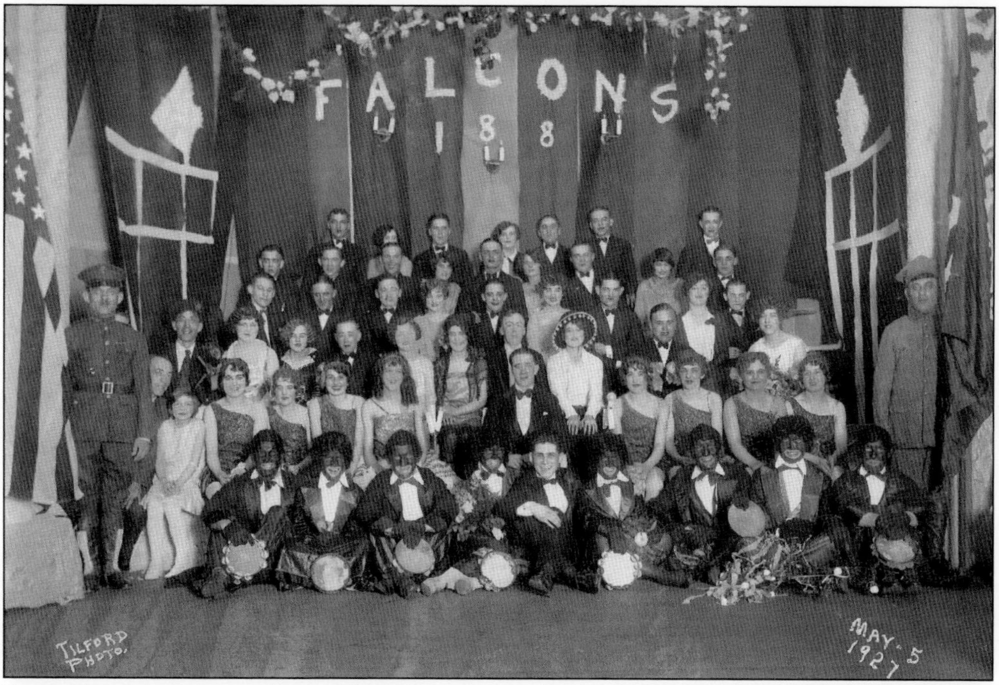

Pictured are the cast members of the Falcons' second annual Minstrel Show. The event was very popular within and outside the Polish community. The *Salem Evening News* reported that over 750 people attended the performance at the Now and Then Hall on May 5, 1927. (ND.)

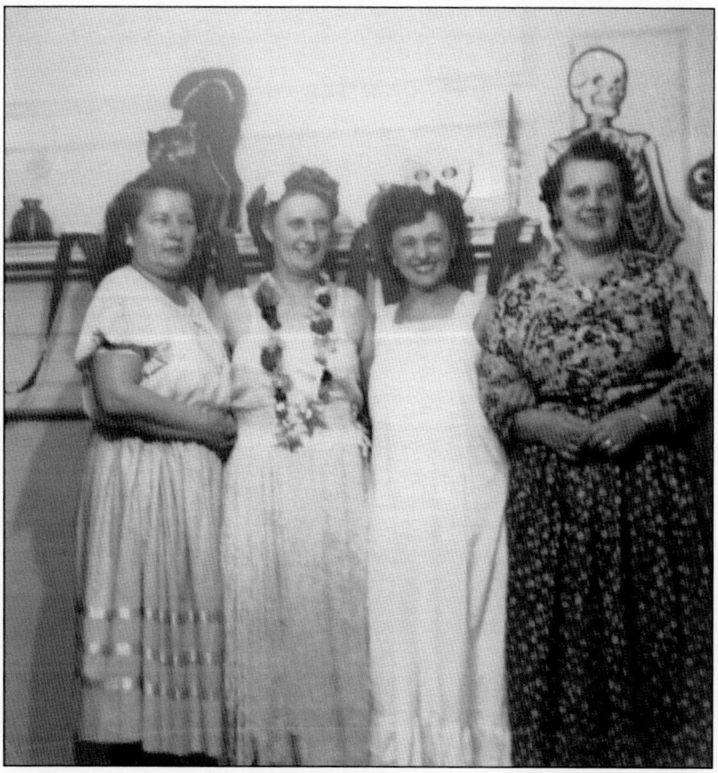

Nowadays, Halloween is a major celebration in Salem. Even in the 1940s, members of the Polish Women's Club gathered to celebrate Halloween with a costume party at the House of Seven Gables. Pictured are, from left to right, Stella Bik Pasquinelli, Helen Olbrych, Jane Bartnicki, and Julia Wilczenski Piasecki. (LBM.)

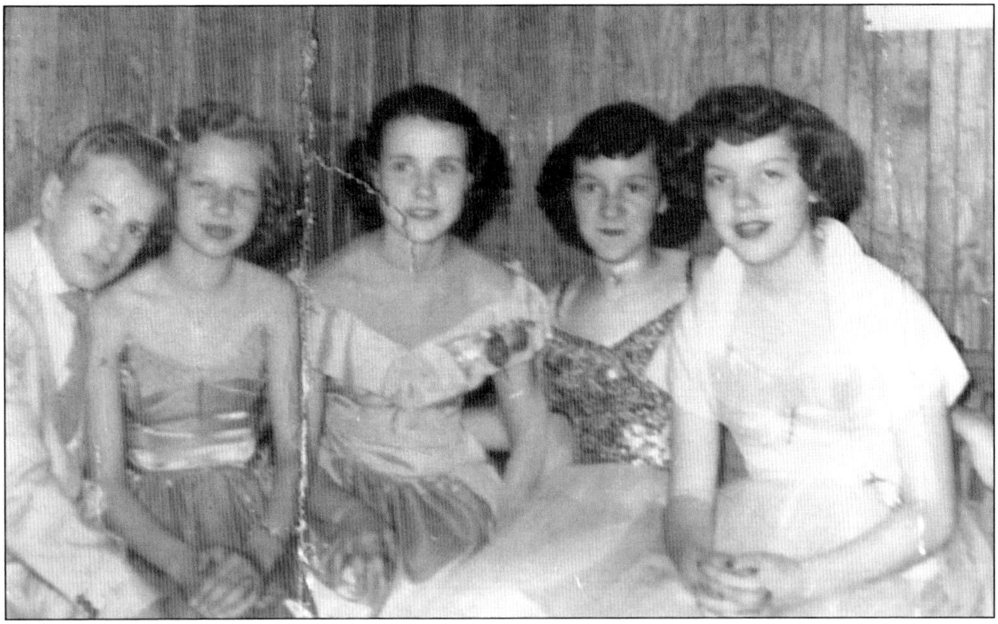

The House of Seven Gables was a neighborhood institution where the Poles met with the Yankees of Salem. It was established as part of a national movement to assist immigrants become good United States' citizens. The Gables sponsored various recreational and educational activities for teenagers, including dance lessons. Attending a Friday night dance in 1953 were, from left to right, Bobby Dombrowski, Joan Carson, Helen Jaskiel, Helen Zendarski, and Pauline Pelletier. (PP1.)

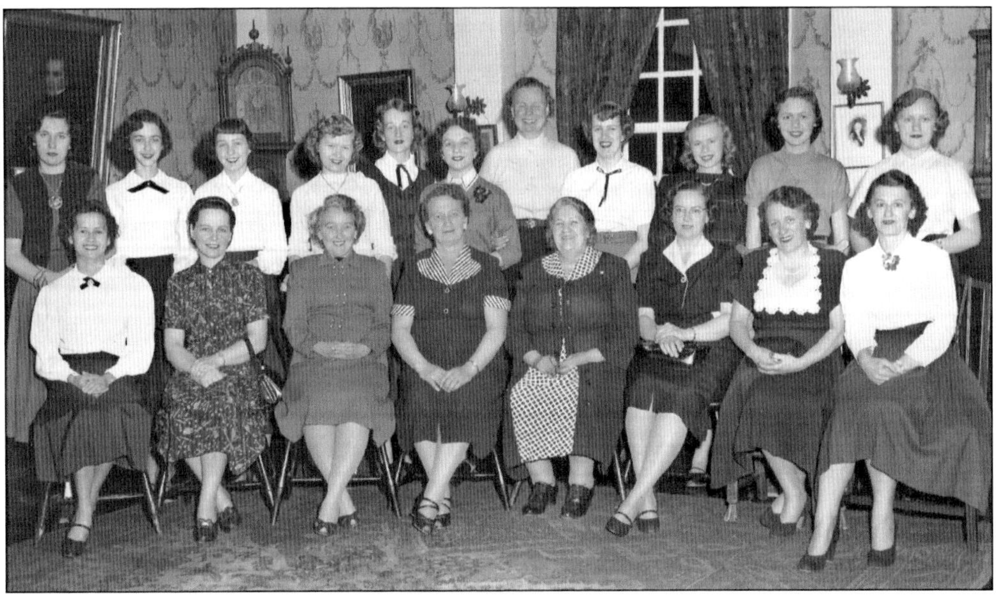

Polish community members attended banquets for mothers and daughters at the House of Seven Gables in 1953. Mothers are, from left to right, (seated) Josephine Foye, Mary Hincman, Anna Dombrowski, Theresa Lach, Laurie Labelle, Alice Raymond, Alice St. Pierre, and Genevieve Zinkovich. Daughters are, from left to right, (standing) Virginia Lorenz, Christine Foye, Dorothy Hincman, Dorothy Dombrowski, Dorothy Lach, Sylvia LaBelle, Nancy Raymond, Carol St. Pierre, and Ann Zinkovich. In the center back are Joan Batting and Helen Chapin. (DHS.)

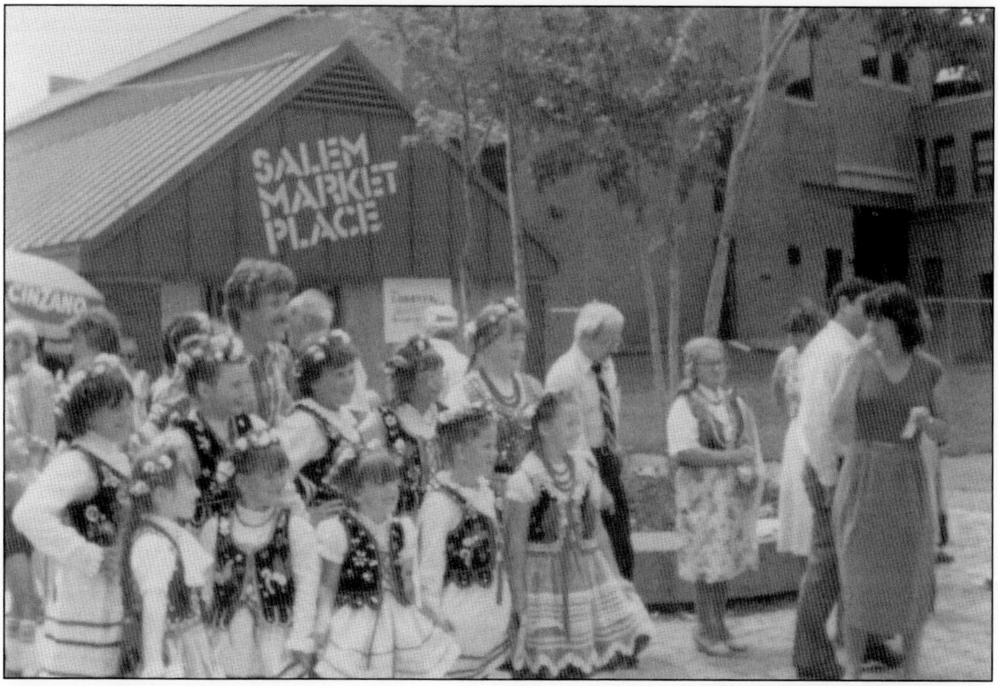

Girls in traditional costumes posed for pictures during Salem's Polish Festival in 1983. Salem hosted this cultural festival to recognize its Polish citizens, to celebrate the city's diversity, and to attract tourists during the summer months. Local residents and out-of-town visitors enjoyed polka music, dancing, and Polish food. (LBM.)

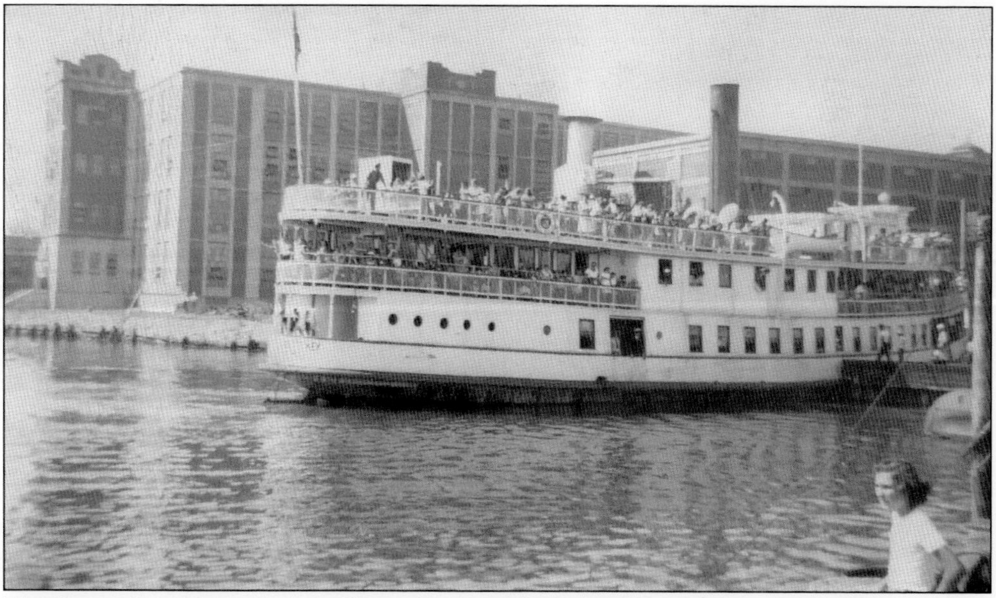

The *Francis Scott Key* steamboat (formerly named the *Susquehanna*) leaves Salem Harbor in 1950 taking residents of the city on an excursion to Nantasket Beach in Hull, Massachusetts. A few Polish community members who were onboard remembered that the boat was barely seaworthy, making for a rough ferry ride. The boat was built in 1898 and sold for scrap metal the year after that Nantasket trip. (LBM.)

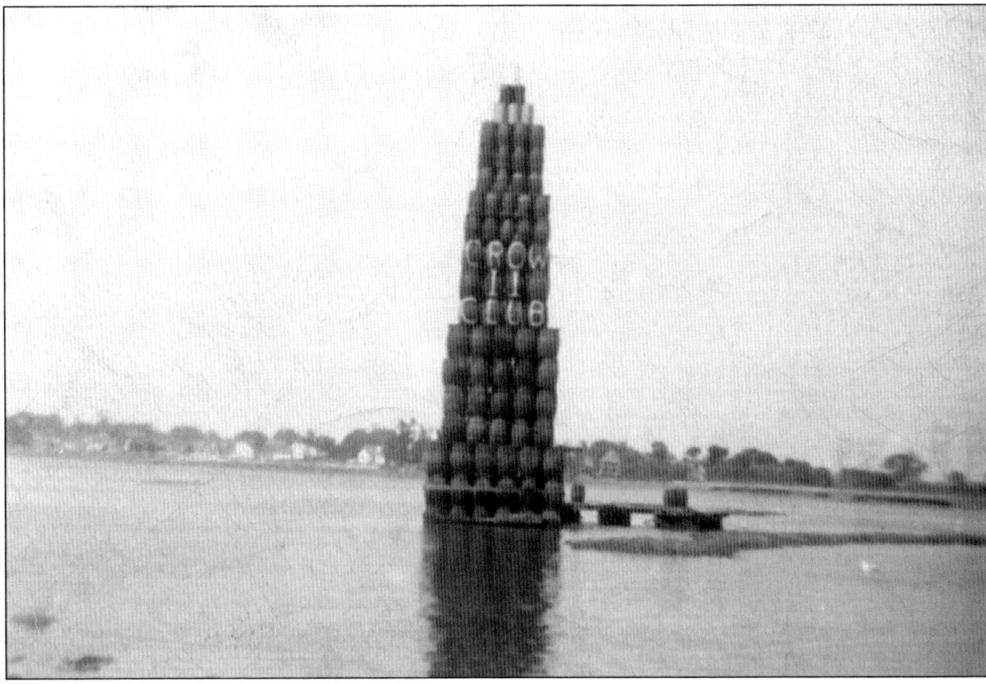

Although not a Polish organization, many Ward One Poles were members of the Crow II Club. In the summer, empty barrels from local tanneries were stacked for a Fourth of July bonfire. Leo Szybiak would climb to the top to ignite the blaze. (CSB.)

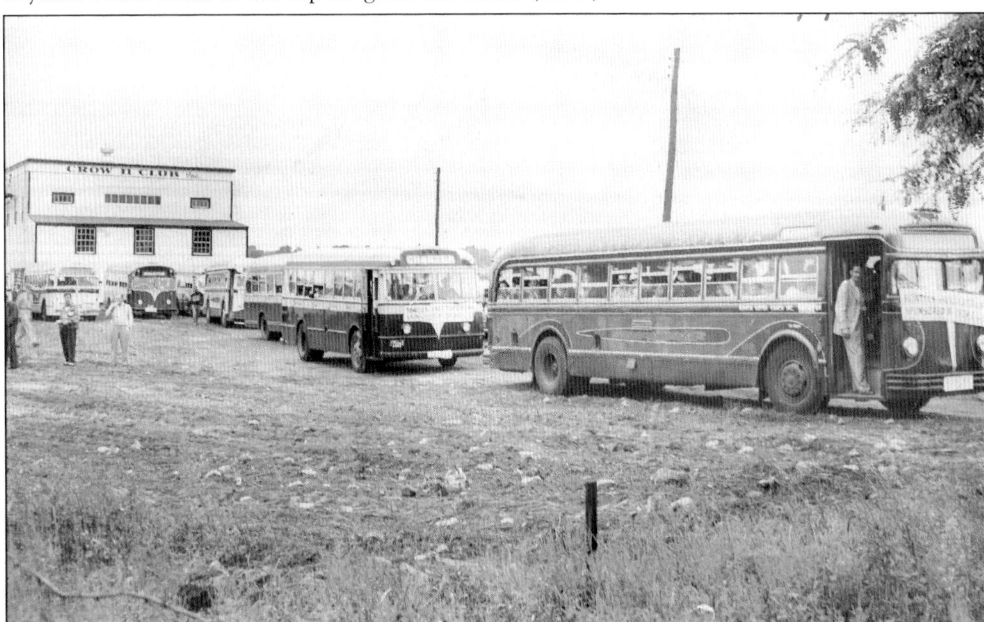

With proceeds from its Fourth of July lawn parties, Crow II Club was able to afford bus trips to Canobie Lake Park in Salem, New Hampshire, for the members' children. The park had a pool, roller coaster, and other rides, and games of skill or chance to play for prizes. For many children, this trip was a highlight of their 1951 summer vacation. (FZ.)

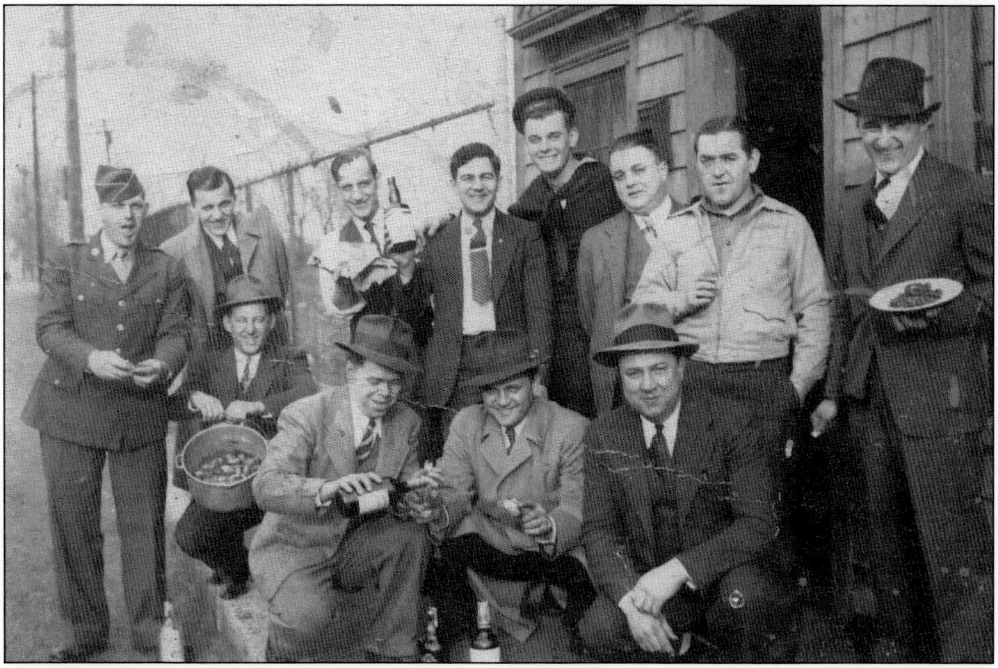

Frank Zdanowicz (kneeling with a pot of clams) and his Ward One buddies enjoyed a clambake at the Crow II Club. The photograph was taken around 1950. Pictured are, from left to right, (first row) Sparky Dombrowski, Mickey Gromeko, and Mike Kliss; (second row) Ben Swiniarski, Paul "Lucky" Paskowski, Zeno Zbysynski, Jim Vardalakis, John Palmer, Councilman Julien Szetela, Zig Grocki, and Dory Hincman. (FZ.)

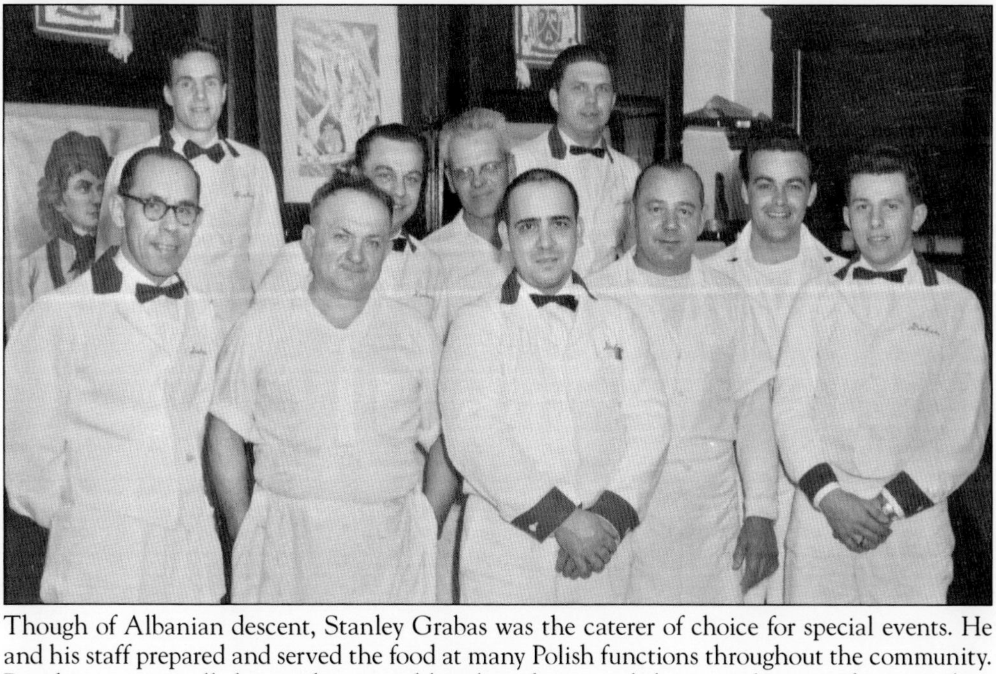

Though of Albanian descent, Stanley Grabas was the caterer of choice for special events. He and his staff prepared and served the food at many Polish functions throughout the community. Residents can recall the candy-covered hazelnut favors and the typical menu of roast turkey, stuffing, gravy, mashed potatoes, and peas. (PLAV.)

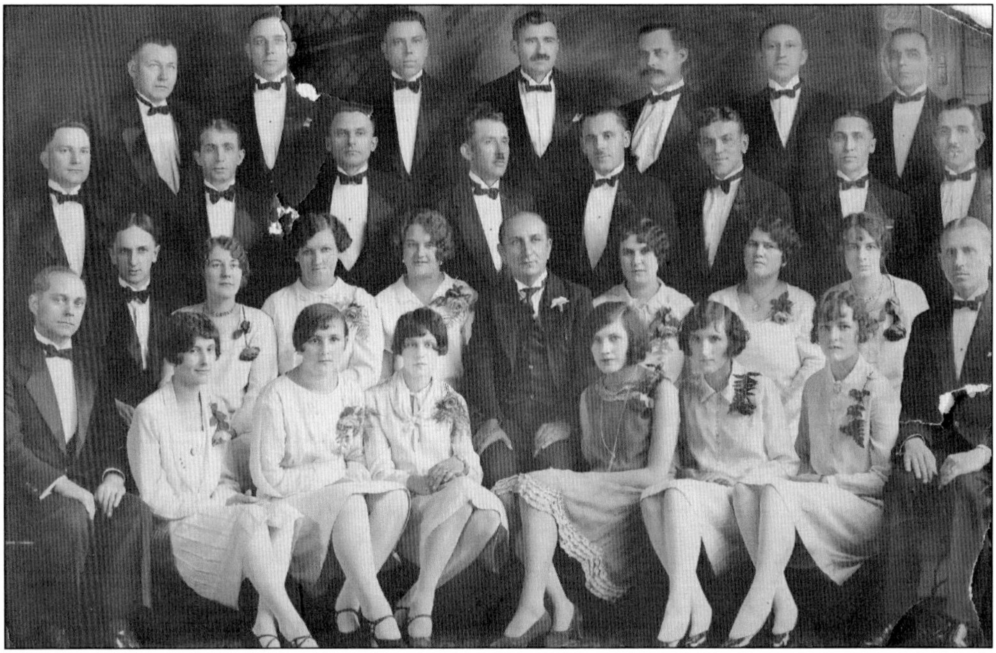

The Polish Chopin Choral Society practiced in a hall on Derby Street that is now Swiniuch Park. Their repertoire was Polish and patriotic, usually opening with the Polish national anthem "Boze cos Polske" and highlighting the works of Polish composer Frederic Chopin. Conductor Nurczynski is seated in the center of the second row in the photograph, taken about 1930. The group performed throughout the North Shore and Boston. (MHN.)

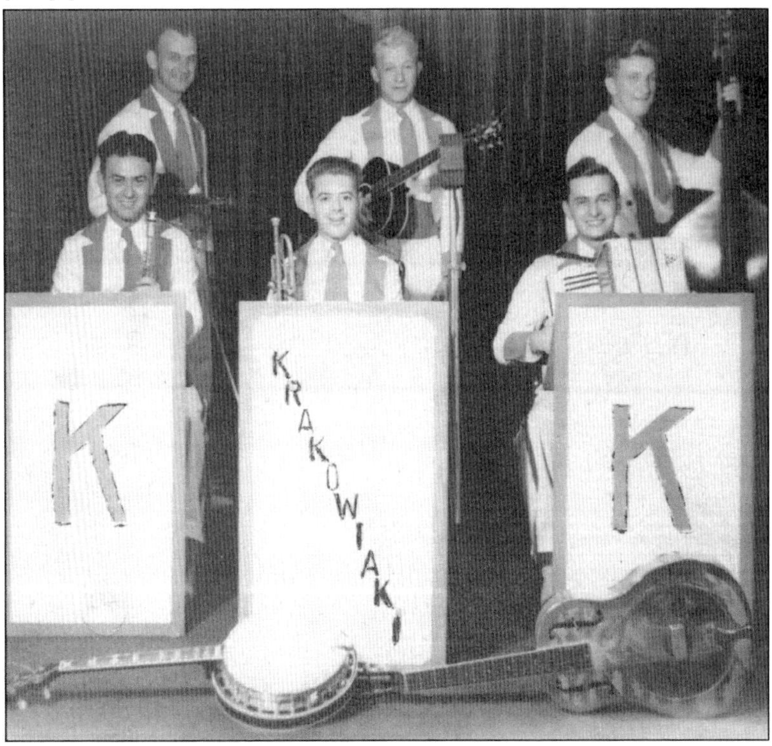

The Krakowiaki Orchestra was the main attraction at many Polish events and was featured at the St. Joseph's Jubilee Ball the evening of May 28, 1949. The orchestra's name is associated with the formal royal capital city of Krakow and the Krakowiak, which is considered Poland's national dance. (LBM.)

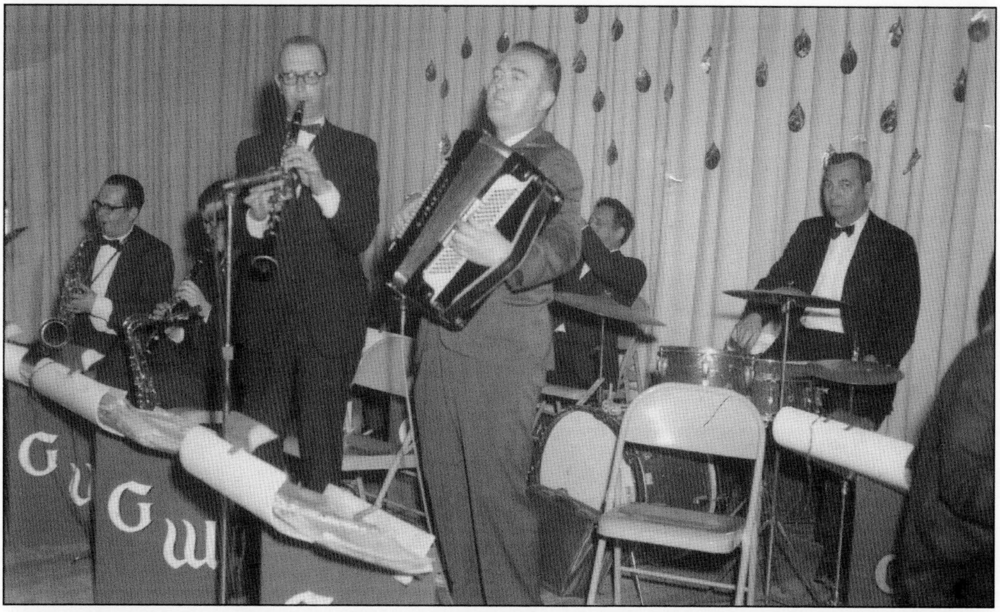

Stanley Semenchuk initiated the Social Activity Club at St. John the Baptist Parish that sponsored dances with Gene Wisniewski's Polka Band in the school auditorium in the 1960s and 1970s. Attending a Social Activity Club function were, from left to right, Kay Solodiuk, Gene Wisniewski, Monsignor Sikora, and Steve Czarnecki. Kay and Steve were honored for promoting the St. John dances on their WESX (1230 on the AM dial) radio show, the *Steve & Kay Polka Review*. Salem's Polish community members tuned into the *Polka Review* that aired every Sunday afternoon. In 1967, Frank Litwin and, later, his son Bob took over the broadcast as *Litwin's Polka Variety* and operated for over 30 years until the station was sold and changed its programming. (Both, DHS.)

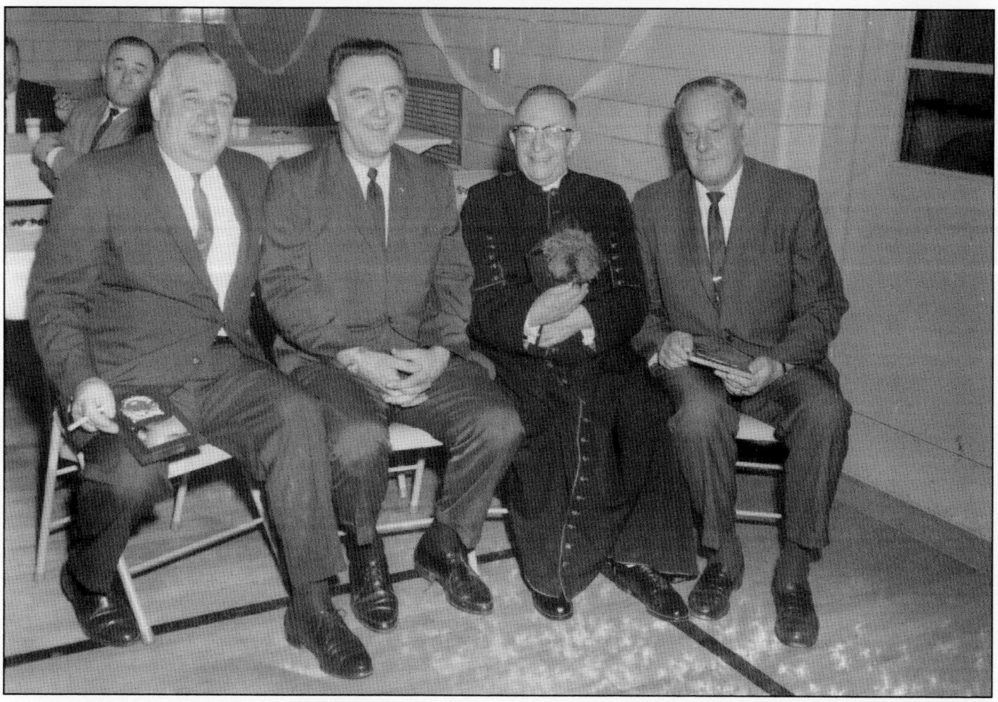

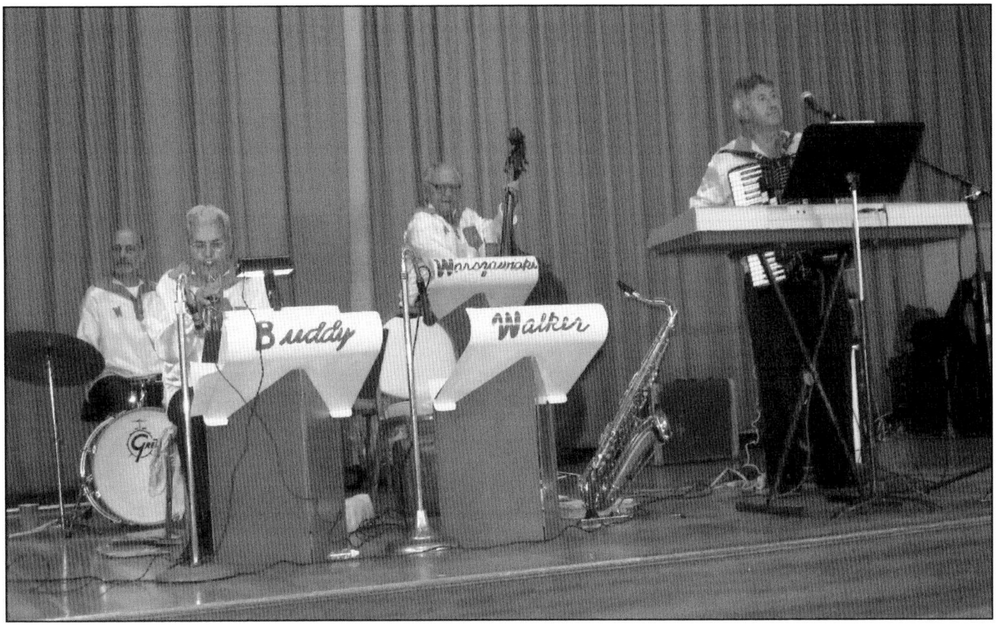

Buddy Walker's Warszawicki Orchestra played at the 2010 St. John the Baptist Polish picnic. The group has been playing at dances, festivals, weddings, and other Polish events on the North Shore since 1949. "Genevieve's Waltz," written by Tony Malionek in memory of Buddy's mother, is always in the repertoire, and the orchestra always takes requests for sentimental favorites from the audience. (RNC.)

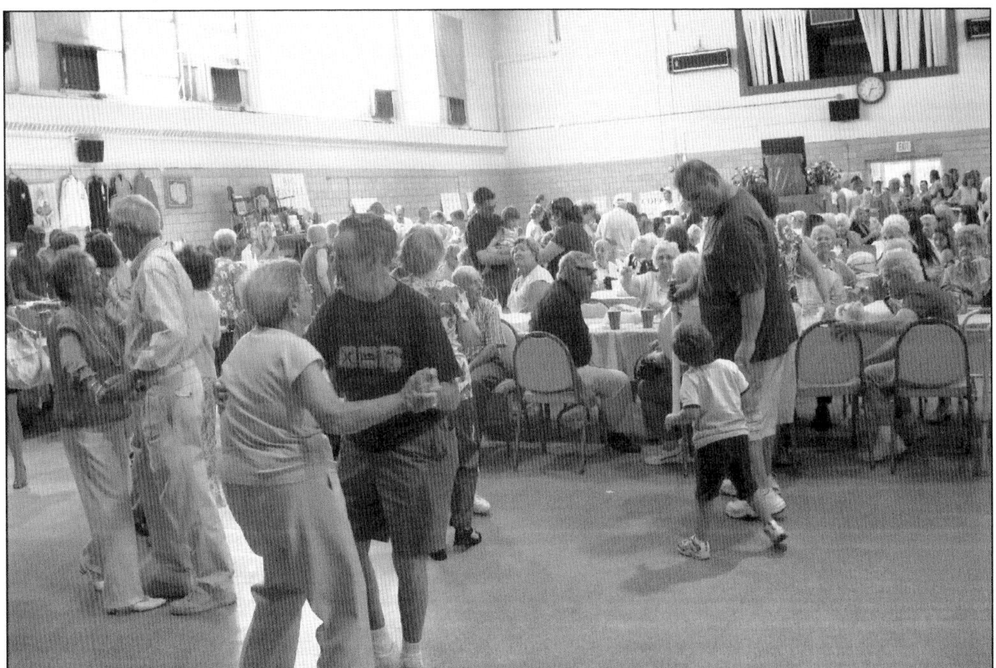

Friends and family gather every year for Polish food and music at the St. John the Baptist picnic. It is a major fundraiser for the parish. Couples enjoyed dancing to Buddy Walker's polka music in 2010. The 2/4 rhythm of the polka is a very lively, upbeat tempo—great for dancing! (RNC.)

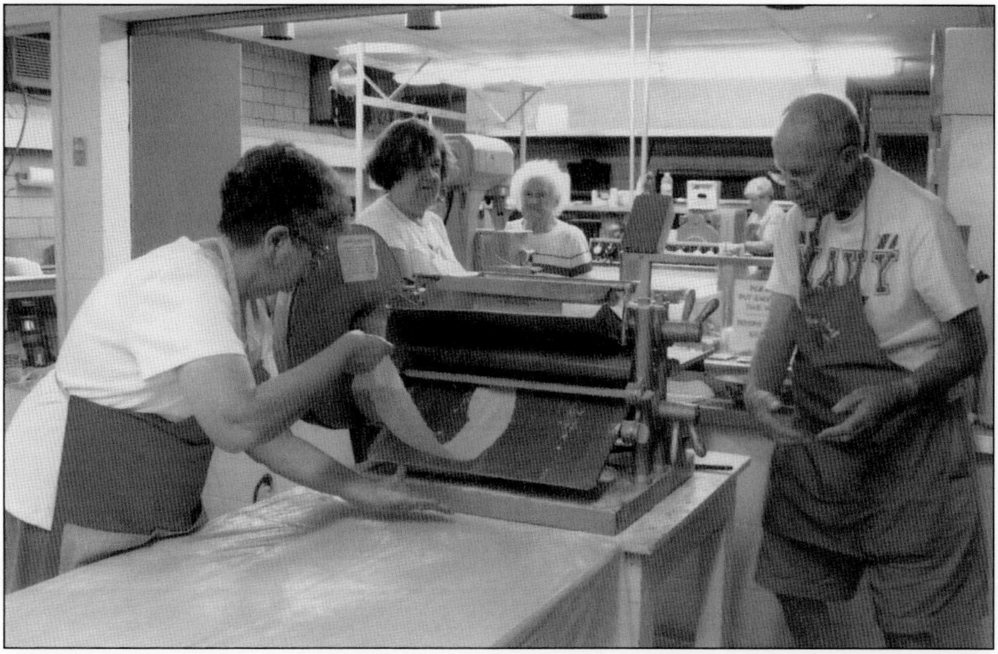

Parishioners worked hard weeks before the 2010 picnic to make sure that the supply of Polish food and sweet treats would meet the demands of picnickers. Here, Paula and Louis Malionek stretched the dough that other helpers cut and shaped to make *chrusciki*, a bow tie–shaped deep-fried dough sprinkled with powdered sugar. (RNC.)

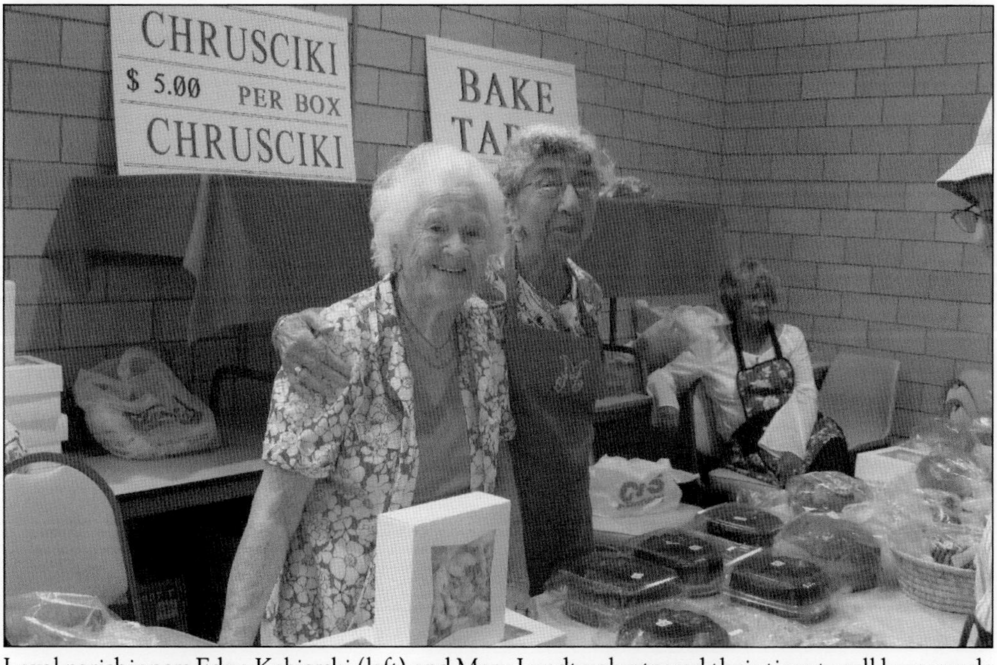

Loyal parishioners Edna Kobierski (left) and Mary Lyndt volunteered their time to sell homemade baked goods and chrusciki (loosely translated as cookie) at the 2010 parish picnic. Hundreds of boxes of the sugar-dusted chrusciki are sold each year with the profit donated to support the church. (RNC.)

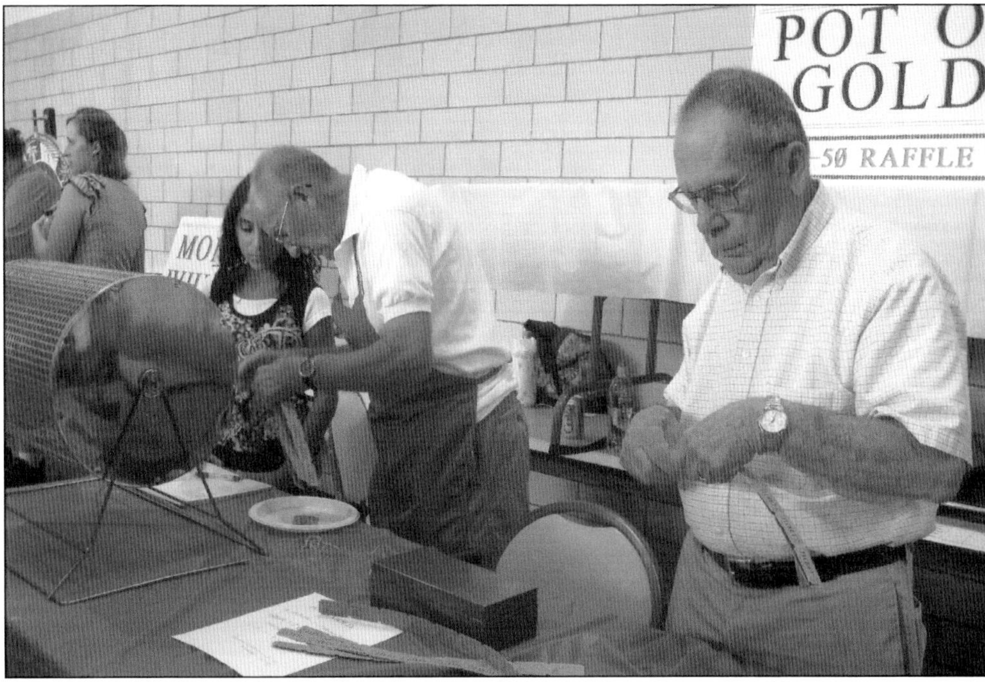

Louis Malionek (left) and Paul Orlando (right) sold "Pot of Gold" 50/50 raffle tickets at the 2010 Parish picnic. Drawings were held every hour. Guests bought tickets in hopes of winning half the pot with the church keeping the other half of the proceeds. (RNC.)

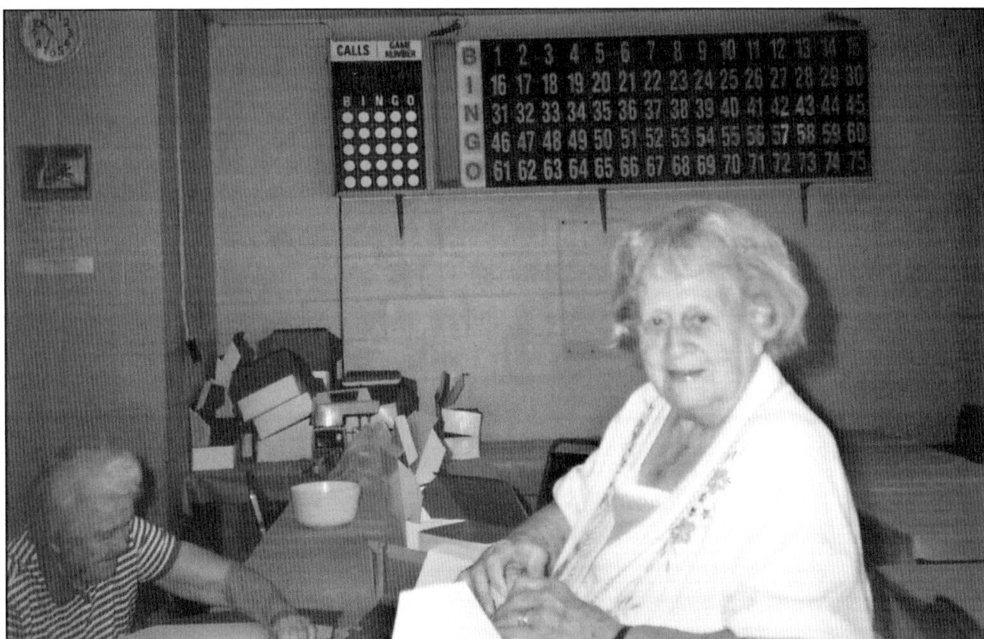

Regina Martin, pictured here in 2000, volunteered at St. John the Baptist bingo for many years. The weekly bingo games are a much-needed source of income for the church. Regina was a prominent member of St. John's. She participated in all aspects of Parish life and worked tirelessly for its benefit. (NM.)

Ten

CITIZENSHIP

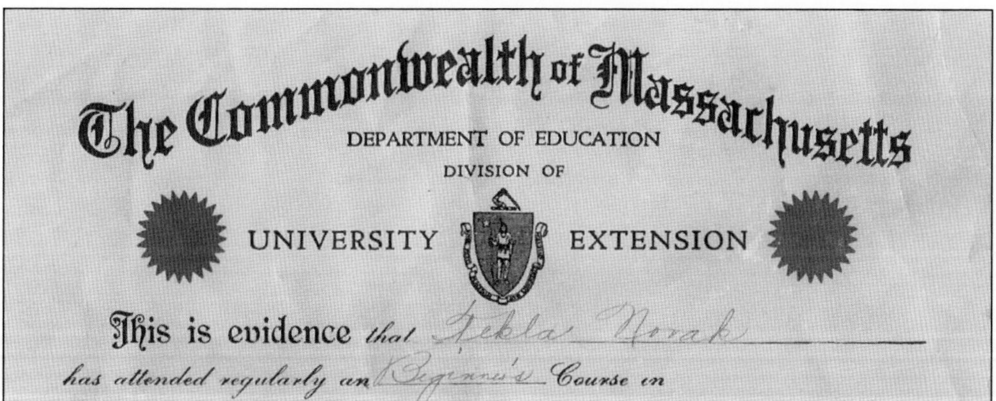

The Commonwealth of Massachusetts
DEPARTMENT OF EDUCATION
DIVISION OF
UNIVERSITY EXTENSION

This is evidence that Tekla Novak
has attended regularly an Beginner's Course in
English for American Citizenship
conducted at Naumkeag Mill under authority of Secs. 9 and 10,
Chap. 69, General Laws. Attendance 42 hours, from Nov 2 to March 31
Date MAR 18 1926

Superintendent of Schools

State Supervisor of Adult Alien Education

In Charge of Adult Alien Education

Becoming an American citizen was a major goal and significant achievement for many Polish immigrants. The Seven Gables Settlement House offered English language lessons as part of its progressive education mission to help the Polish-speaking residents assimilate in American society. This certificate documented Tekla Nowak's completion of an English course for citizenship in 1926. (JKW.)

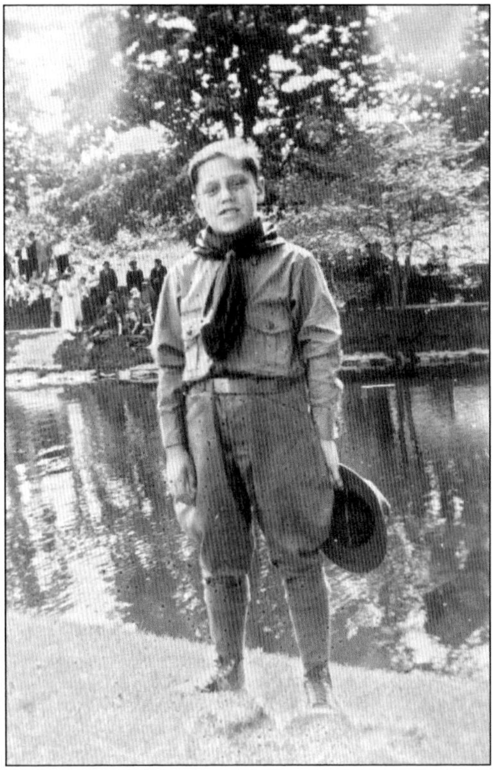

First-generation, United States–born Polish children were assimilating into American society by participating in youth scouting programs. Frank Plutnicki is pictured here at Boy Scout camp in the early 1930s. Parents and the St. Joseph's Society each contributed half the cost to send boys to summer camp in New Hampshire. (RPW.)

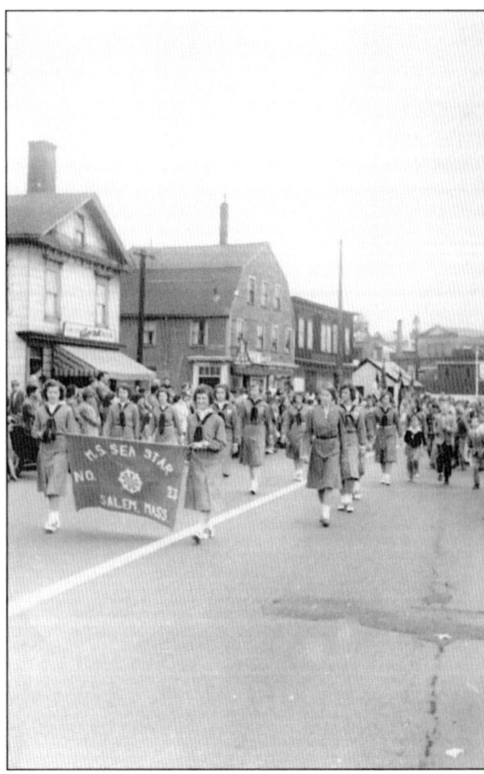

Alice Pronska (Wojciehowski) carrying the banner on the left and other girls from the Polish community were among the members of the House of Seven Gables Mariners' Troop marching on North Street to Greenlawn Cemetery for Memorial Day services around 1950. (APW.)

Members of the Polish community served in the military during peacetime. Louis Wilczenski joined the Massachusetts National Guard in 1928 as a member of the 102nd Field Artillery. He obtained competency as a sharpshooter and was honorably discharged in 1932. (FLW.)

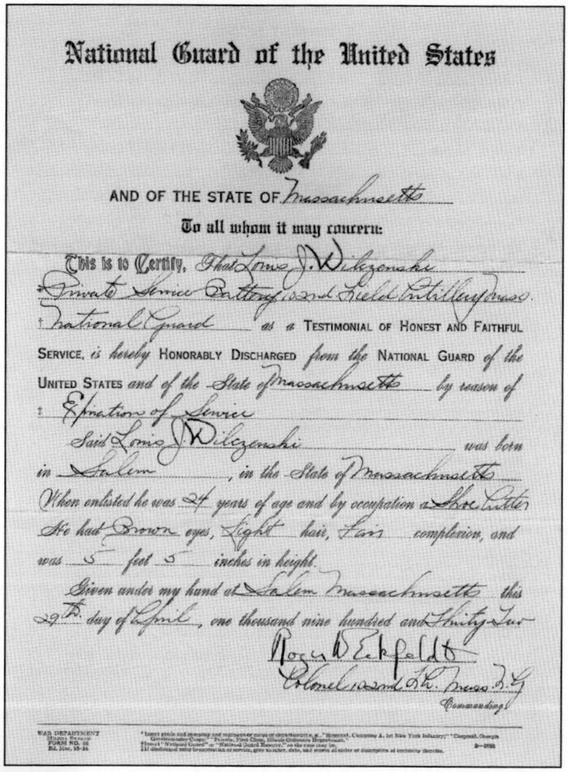

National Guard of the United States

AND OF THE STATE OF Massachusetts

To all whom it may concern:

This is to Certify, That Louis J. Wilczenski Private Service Battery 102nd Field Artillery Mass. National Guard as a TESTIMONIAL OF HONEST AND FAITHFUL SERVICE, is hereby HONORABLY DISCHARGED from the NATIONAL GUARD of the UNITED STATES and of the State of Massachusetts by reason of Expiration of Service

Said Louis J. Wilczenski was born in Salem, in the State of Massachusetts

When enlisted he was 24 years of age and by occupation a Shoe Cutter

He had Brown eyes, Light hair, Fair complexion, and was 5 feet 5 inches in height.

Given under my hand at Salem Massachusetts this 29th day of April, one thousand nine hundred and Thirty-Two

Roger W. Eckfeldt
Colonel 102nd F.A. Mass. N.G.
Commanding

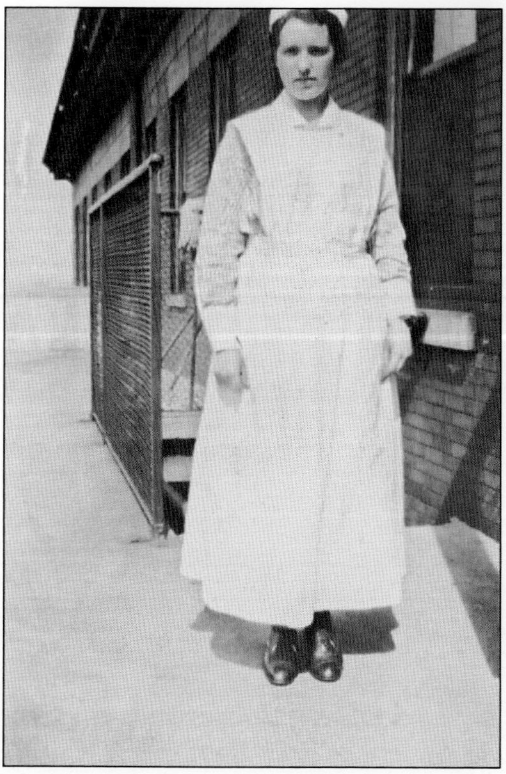

Salem native Victoria Kowalski grew up on Bentley Street, obtained her nursing credentials at St. Mary's School in Chicago, and then enlisted as a US Army nurse. She cared for the allied soldiers wounded at the Battle of Monte Cassino (also known as the Battle for Rome), near Sorrento, Italy, during World War II. (RNC.)

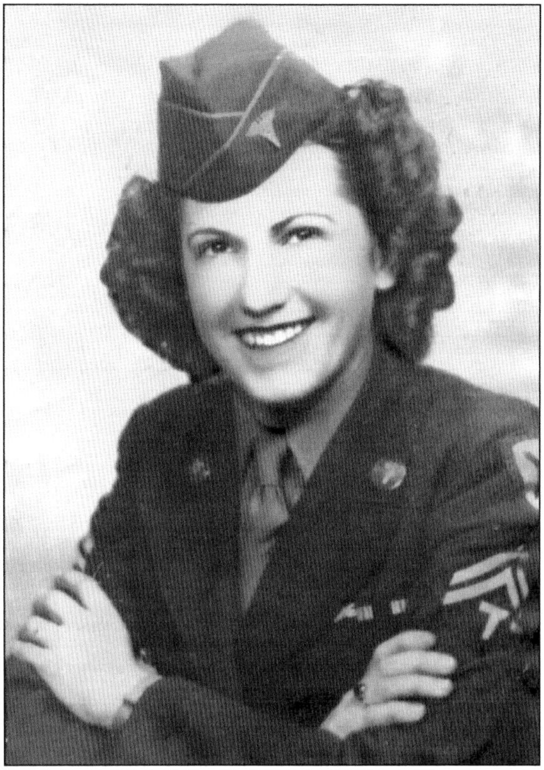

Many Polish families of Salem supported the war effort by sending their daughters and sons to serve in the US military. Sister and brother Regina and Frank Plutnicki enlisted in the Army and Navy, respectively, during World War II. Regina joined the Women's Army Corps (WACs) where she served as a medical technician at Fort Dix/McGuire Air Force Base, treating soldiers returning from combat with injuries sustained in the war. Pictured in his Navy uniform, Frank Plutnicki served on a naval destroyer ship in the Pacific theater during World War II. (Both, RPW.)

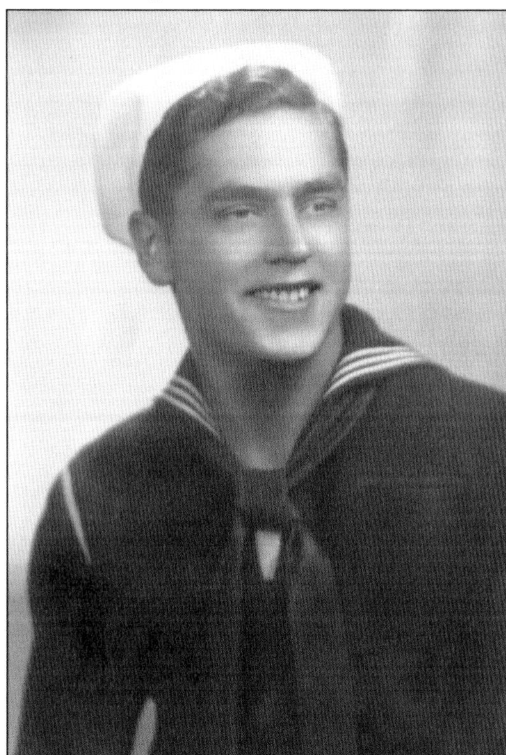

Trained as a medical technician in the US Army, William Kowalski assisted medical officers in caring for soldiers wounded in World War II. He served in the Aleutians and the European theater as a member of the 20th Field Hospital from 1942 until he was honorably discharged in 1945. (JKW.)

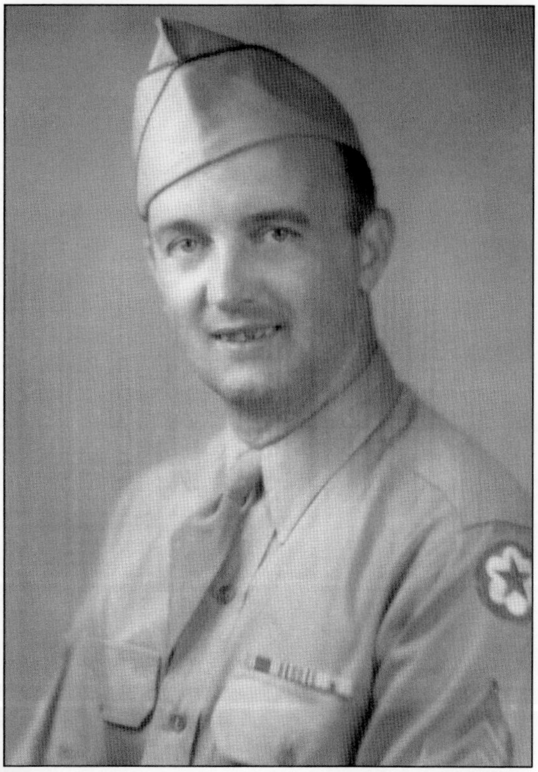

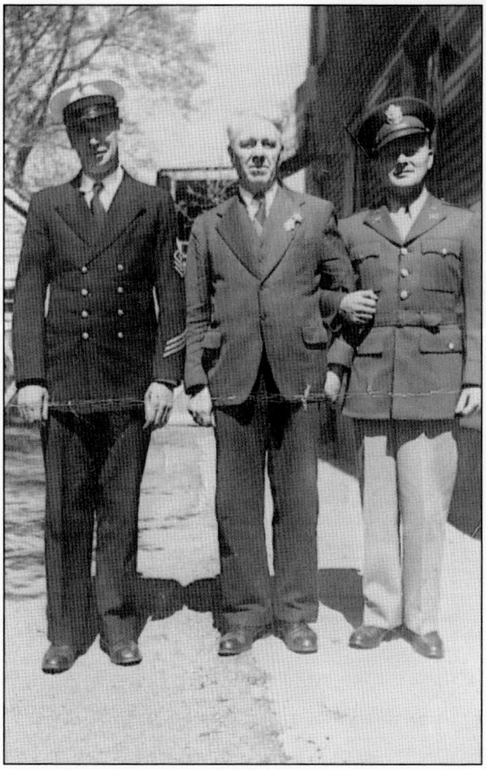

This picture, taken in the mid-1940s, shows a proud John Furtek of Hardy Street standing between his son-in-law Roy Carter (left), chief machinist mate in the US Coast Guard, and son Stanley Furtek of the US Army. Stanley also served in the Navy before enlisting in the Army for a second stint in the military. (RNC.)

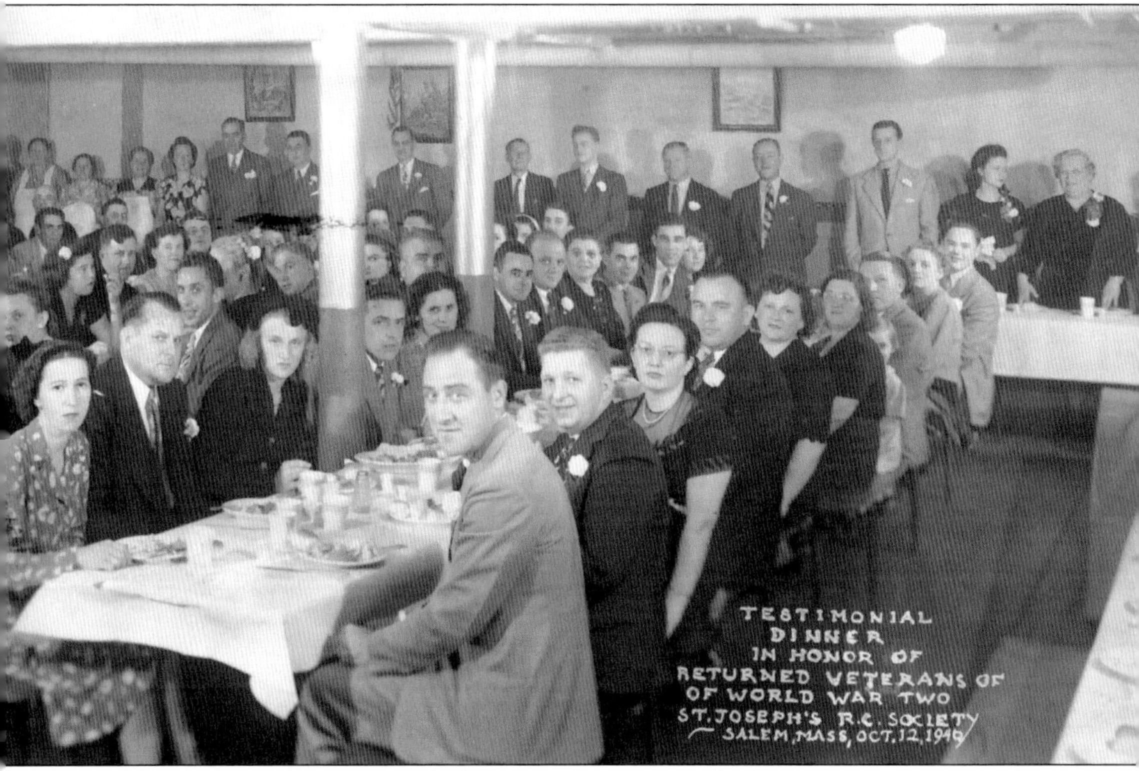

The Polish American community has always been proud of its US military service starting with Gens. Tadeusz Kosciuszko and Kazimierz Pulaski, both heroes in the American Revolutionary War. World War I was a complicated loyalty for Polish immigrants because of their split allegiances in continuing the fight to save their Polish homeland as well as fighting for their new United States homeland. However, by the time of World War II, the Poles were more firmly established as American citizens. Although still concerned about the freedom of the ancestral homeland, they had less ambivalence about their allegiances and much stronger ties to the United States' war effort. Many soldiers of Polish descent fought bravely in the US armed forces. Proud of its World War II veterans, the Polish community turned out to honor them at a banquet held at St. Joseph's Hall on October 12, 1946. (NPS.)

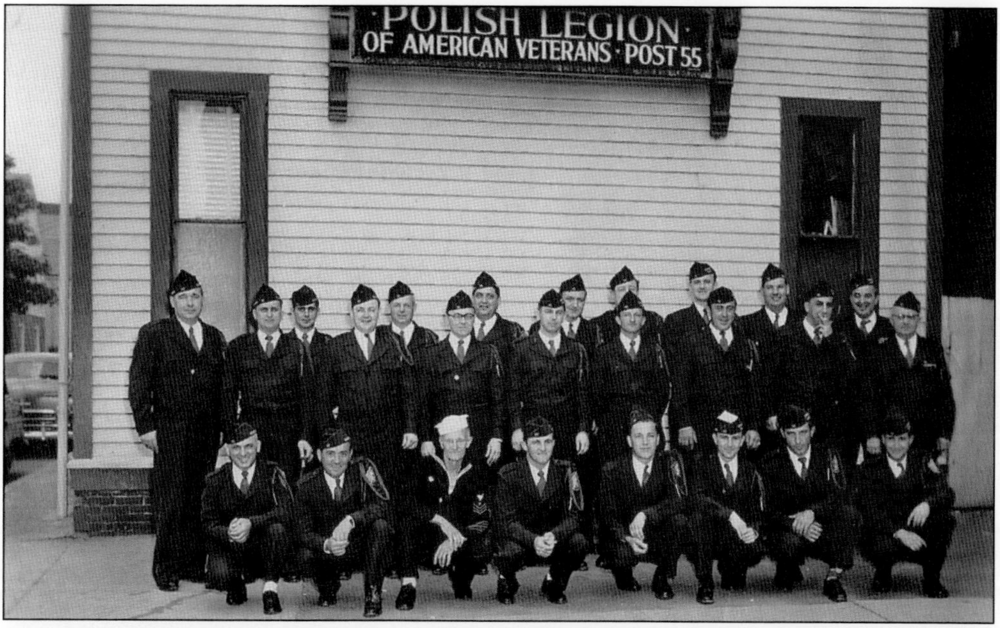

After World War I, groups of American veterans of Polish descent formed organizations to maintain and preserve patriotism and brotherhood. The Polish Legion of American Veterans (PLAV) Post No. 55 in Salem was established in 1930. PLAV members from various branches of the military are pictured shortly after they returned from World War II in front of their former clubhouse on Kosciuscko Street. The headquarters is now 9 Daniels Street. (PLAV.)

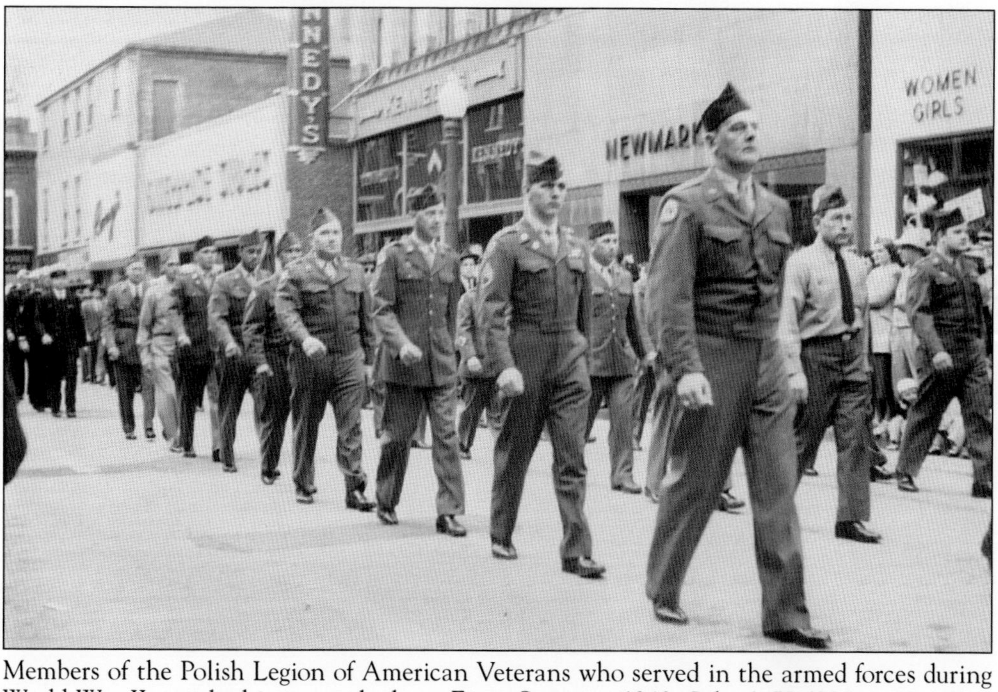

Members of the Polish Legion of American Veterans who served in the armed forces during World War II marched in a parade down Essex Street in 1948. Salem's PLAV Post No. 55 is named in honor of Stefan Starzynski, an inspirational leader and mayor of Warsaw, who died in a concentration camp fighting for freedom in Poland during World War II. (PLAV.)

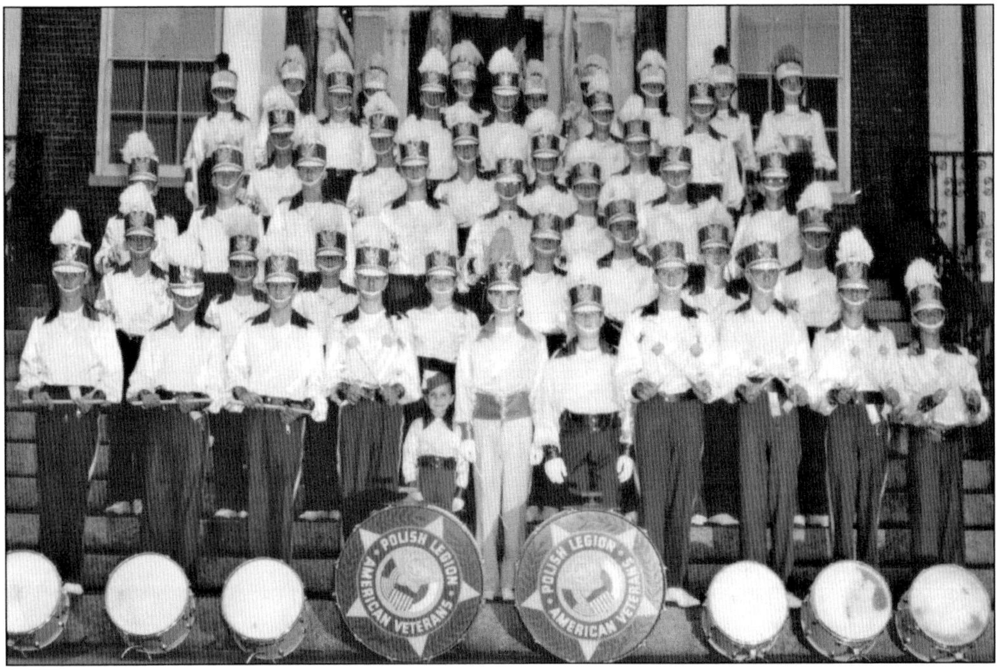

Here, the Polish Legion of American Veterans junior band, winner of the Eastern Massachusetts Junior Championships, assembled for a picture in the early 1950s on the steps of the US customhouse, Salem Maritime National Historic Site, on Derby Street. The PLAV's White Eagle Drum and Bugle Corps was often featured in parades. Local residents recalled that the windows would rattle when they played. (PLAV.)

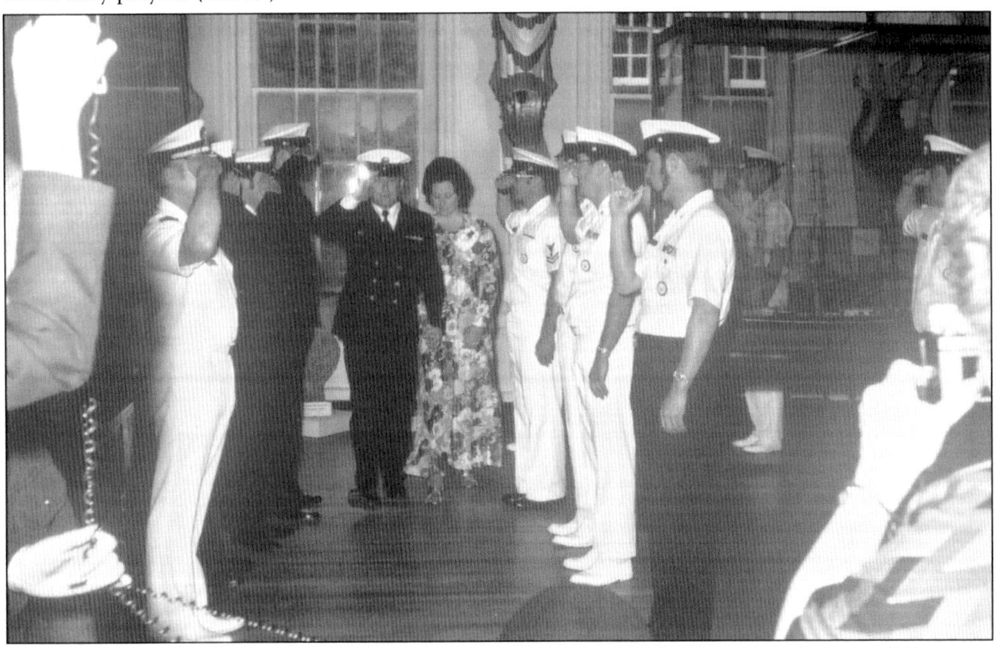

Richard F. Hincman Sr. was mustered out of the Navy in 1975 after 20 years of service. His group was sworn into service at the Peabody Essex Museum in Salem in 1955 and his mustering out ceremony took place in the same hall. (DHS.)

Brig. Gen. Albin Irzyk (right) with Polish Legion of American Veterans' Post No. 55 commander Ted Goclawski honored deceased veterans at St. Mary's cemetery on Memorial Day in 2000. A Salem native, Irzyk served under General Patton during the Battle of the Bulge and was awarded several medals for bravery in World War II. Irzyk Park on Fort Avenue in Salem is dedicated in his memory. (PLAV.)

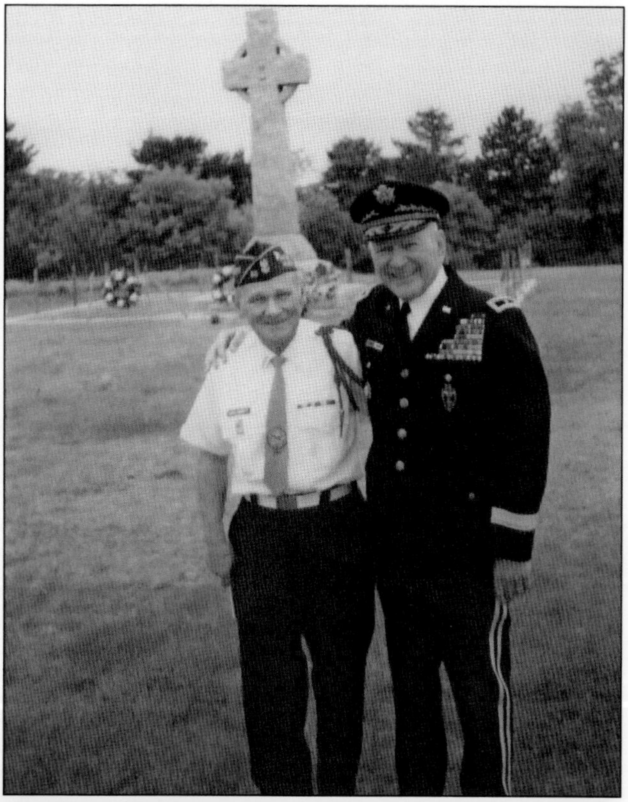

The Ladies' Auxiliary continues to be an important adjunct of the Polish Legion of American Veterans. They provide aid to veterans and their families through welfare work and fundraising, such as the famous Poppy Day solicitations. Members of Salem's PLAV Auxiliary are pictured in this 2002 photograph. (PLAV.)

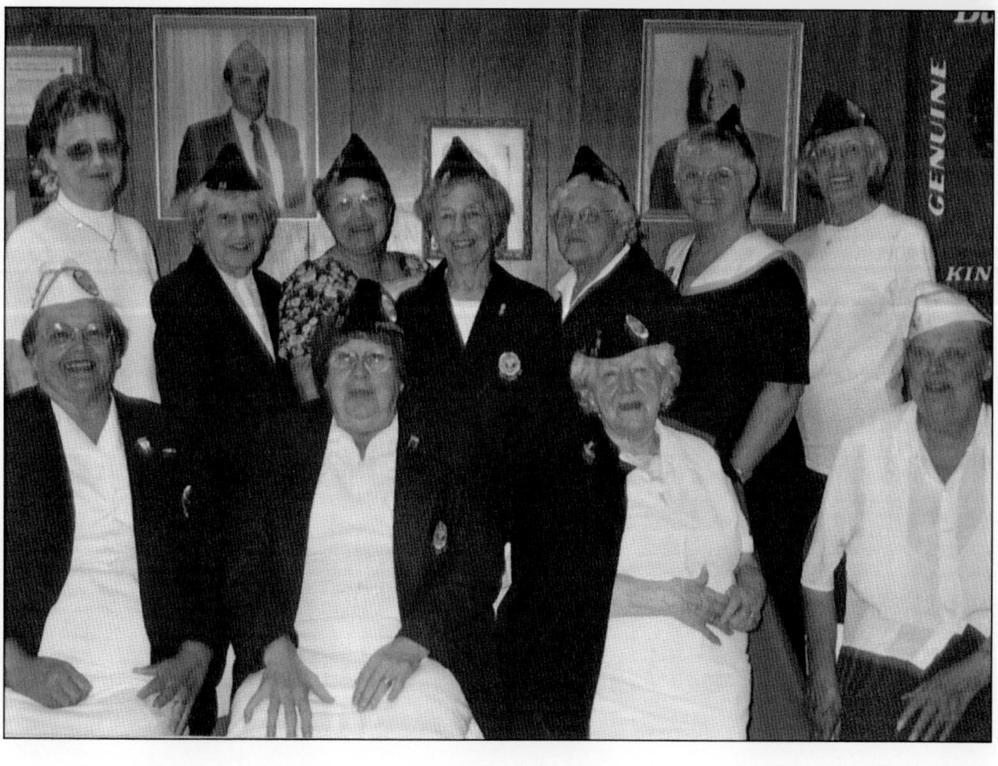

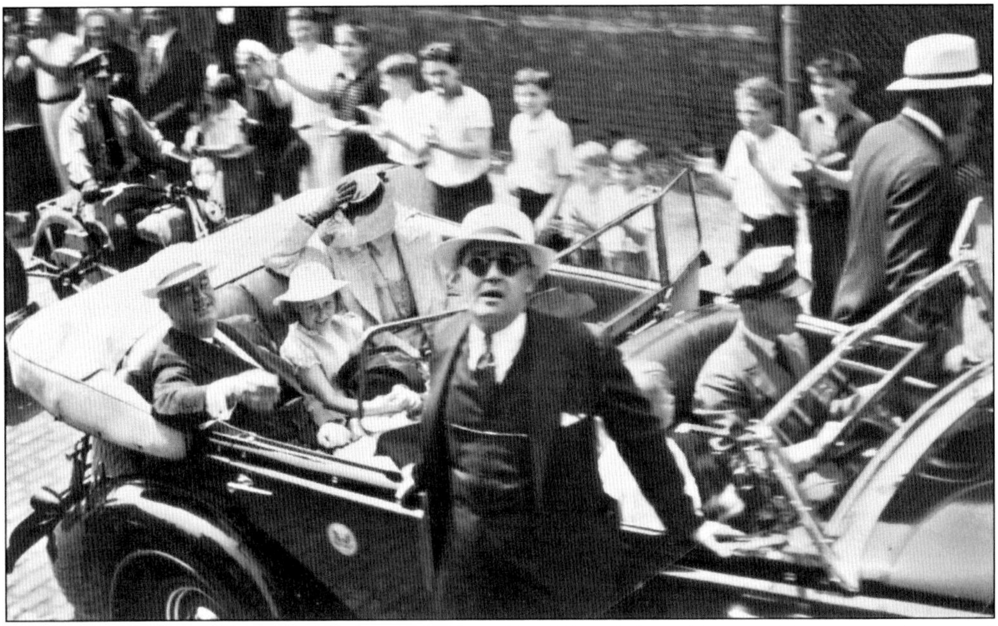

On a summer vacation, probably in 1940, Pres. Franklin Delano Roosevelt's motorcade passed through the Polish community of Ward One en route to Salem Harbor for a boat cruise. In the early 20th century, the North Shore, roughly defined as the coastal area from Boston to the New Hampshire border, was considered "Massachusetts's gold coast" with seaside summer estates for wealthy Bostonians. (LBM.)

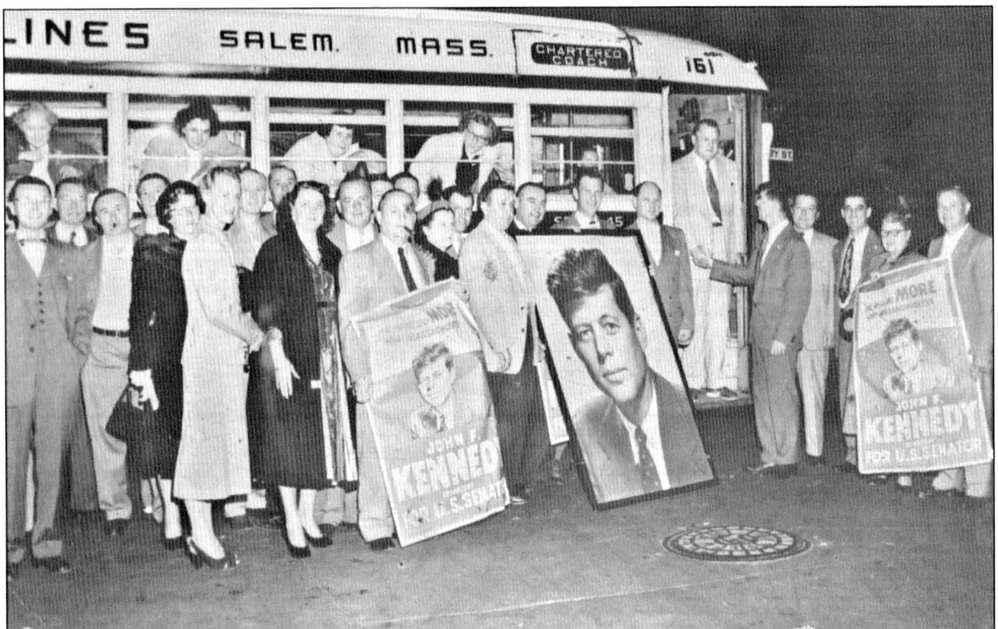

Salem's Ward One was a politically active, staunchly democratic, working-class, and predominantly Catholic district. Democratic candidates for office could always count on winning that ward. Here, members of the Polish community boarded buses to attend a rally in Boston to reelect Sen. John F. Kennedy. (NPS.)

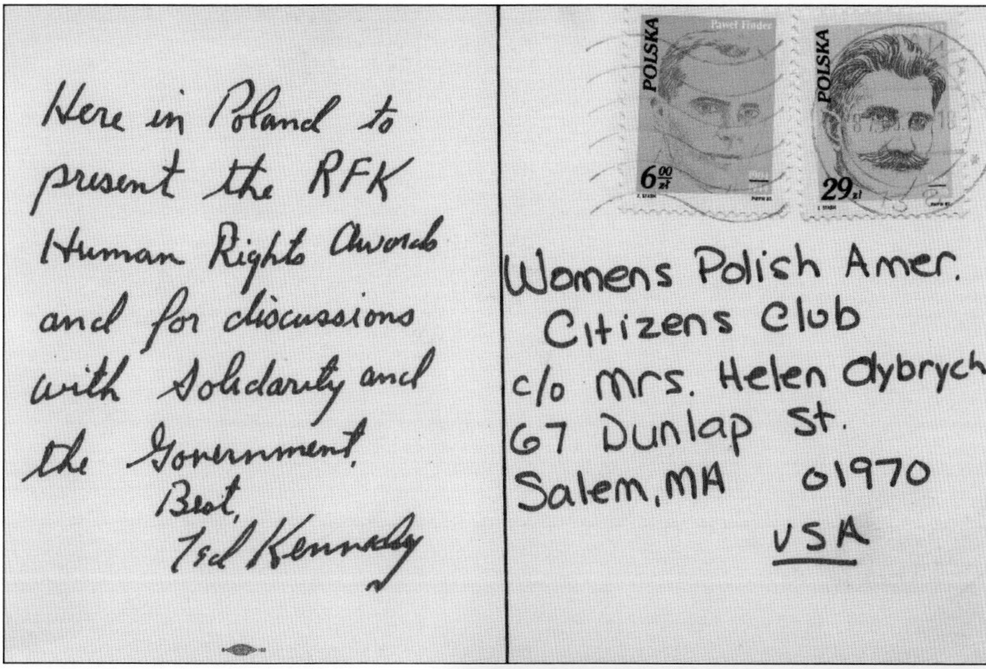

Sen. Ted Kennedy wrote a postcard to inform Helen Olybrych, president of the Salem Women's Polish American Citizens Club, of his work in Poland on behalf of solidarity. In 1986, the senator presented his brother's Robert F. Kennedy Human Rights Award to Zbigniew Bujak and Adam Michnik for opposing communist rule and promoting a democratic society in Poland. (LBM.)

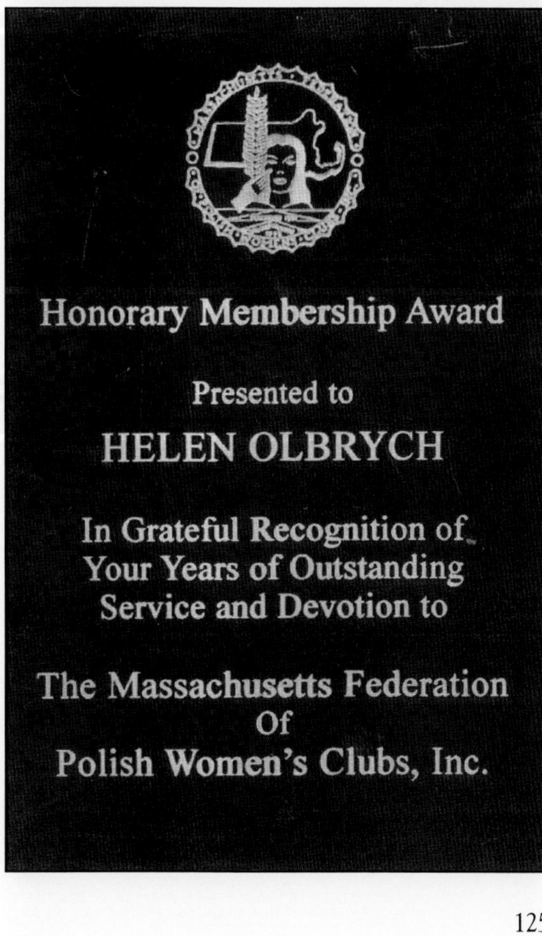

Women were very politically engaged in Salem's Polonia and were effective advocates for Polish causes. At the age of 90 in 1999, Helen Olbrych was honored by the Massachusetts Federation of Polish Women's Clubs at a reception at the Hawthorne Hotel. She served as president of the Salem Polish Women Citizens' Group for many years. Helen also volunteered her time to promote other local Polish organizations. (LBM.)

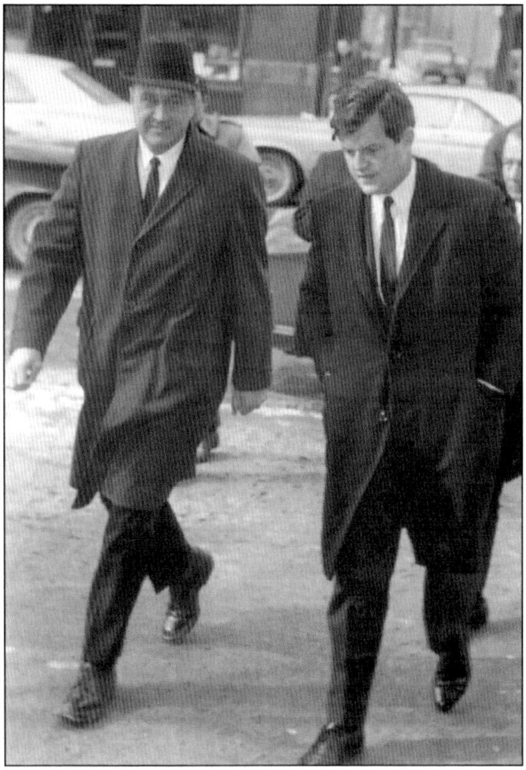

Thaddeus Buczko (left) was a democratic Salem politician who served as a city councilor, Massachusetts state representative for the Tenth Essex District, state auditor, and, until his retirement, a justice in the Essex County Probate and Family Court. Here, he is pictured accompanying US Senate candidate Ted Kennedy on a campaign swing through the North Shore during the 1960s. (TB.)

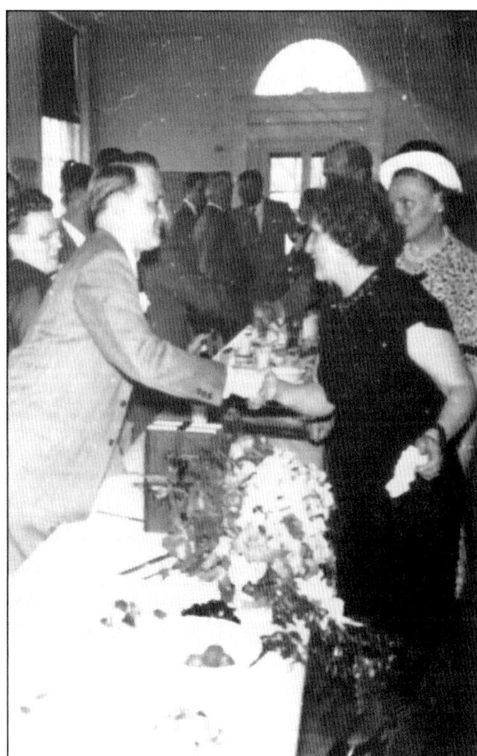

A party was held at the Polish Falcons Social Club in 1957 to celebrate Alfred Dobrosielski's "Dobbs" appointment as Salem's city solicitor. Al Dobb's shook hands with a well-wisher, while his mother, Constance, standing behind him, greeted supporters in the receiving line. (PD.)

George Nowak, with help from his family, ran a successful campaign for city councilor in 1970 from the Polish Ward One neighborhood. George wore out shoe leather personally contacting every family in the neighborhood. He climbed the steps to knock on the doors of second- and third-floor apartments where no other politicians had ever visited! (GNC.)

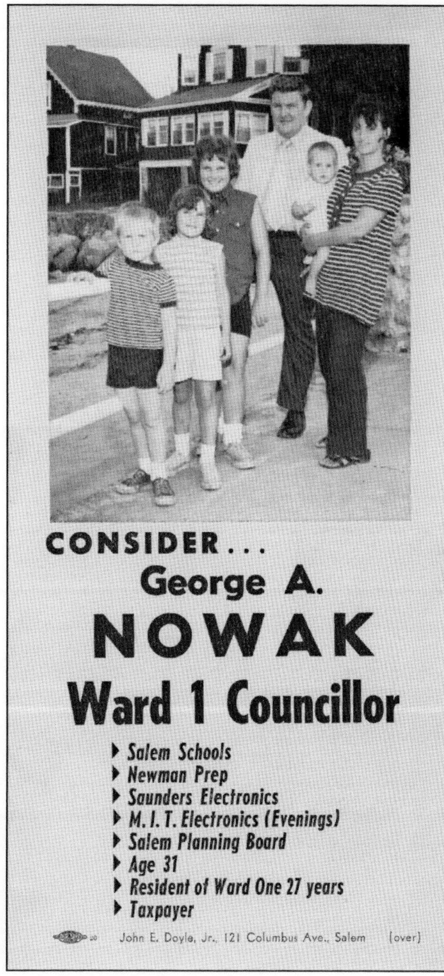

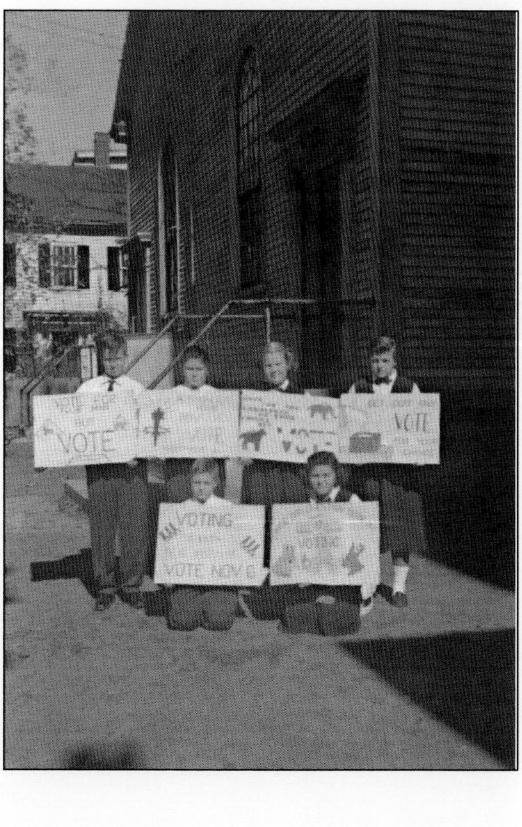

US citizenship and participation in democracy were important to members of the Polish community who did not enjoy those rights in Poland. Civic engagement was even encouraged among young children. St. John the Baptist School students had a civics lesson in democratic action in the mid-1950s by helping to get out the vote on November 6. (SJB.)